Finance in Organisations

Finance in Organisations – Tutor's Manual

Humphrey Shaw

Accompanying set of tested exercises, notes and other materials
(including overhead projection transparencies)
to support and extend the textbook.

isbn 1 85450 031 7   A4 Looseleaf binder with copying rights £49.00

Published July, 1991

Finance
in
Organisations

Humphrey Shaw

This first edition is published by ELM Publications of Seaton House, Kings Ripton, Huntingdon PE17 2NJ (Tel. 04873-238 or 254), printed by Tabro Litho Ltd of Ramsey Forty Foot and bound by Woolnough Bookbinding of Irthlingborough.

British Library Cataloguing in Publication Data

Shaw, Humphrey
    Finance in organisations.
    1. Business enterprise. Finance
    I. Title
    658.15

ISBN 1-85450-019-8

To My Family and Friends

CONTENTS

LIST OF FIGURES

Introduction

Every year more and more books are written about accountancy and finance to add to the ever growing volume of literature. If another book is going to be useful to students and managers, it must provide either new information or seek to contribute to a better understanding of the subject matter to a particular readership. This book seeks to explain all of the main theoretical concepts of financial management to students who are studying the subject for the first time. My aim in writing this book has been to write a descriptive account, combined with examples and diagrams, which explains the main concepts to the reader who does not have a financial background.

It's hard to define what financial management is, even though it is as old as money itself. Until recently it was left to the domain of accountants, but the Rolls Royce collapse in the 1970s demonstrated the need for the non financial manager to have an understanding of the need to control the firm's financial resources. As a result, finance has been included as part of the syllabus on many business and non business courses, such as engineering, estate management and a range of other vocational courses. It is not just these students who generally lack the financial background and find the subject difficult. Many accountancy students similarly seek an explanation of the main principles before they are able to be completely conversant with the concepts and principles. Unfortunately, many of the books on financial management are either too technical or over simplistic for many students and it may explain why so many of them find this such a difficult subject area.

This book has been divided into three sections. The first part explains the information contained in financial statements, the second concentrates on how accounting information can be used for decision making and the last section concentrates on financial control techniques. Each chapter assumes no prior knowledge and the reader is advised to work through the examples contained in the PEG Financial Management Book of Case Studies (isbn 1 85450 013 9) so that they increase their understanding of each topic area.

I hope that this book will be useful to both students, financial managers and entrepreneurs who seek to gain a greater understanding of this subject.

Finally I would like to thank the people and organisations who offered advice and gave permission to reproduce information. The following people all read sections of the book and made invaluable comments, Denise Donovan, Stephanie Fancett, Mark Inman, Frank Thompson, Tony Skone, Phil Wilson, Tony Head, Derek Hyde, Dr. Alan Booth, Sally Messenger and Dr Helena Shaw. I am also grateful to Boots plc for permission to reprint part of their annual accounts, the Chartered Institute of Management Accountants for permission to quote their definitions, Lloyds Bank for permission to use their tables showing how inflation has affected monetary values, and the Association of Corporate Treasurers for permission to reproduce extracts from their Treasurer's Handbook. Special thanks also to Sue Badger for all her hard work in typesetting the manuscript and to the students at the Polytechnic of North London who commented on many of the draft chapters. Finally I would like to thank Sheila Ritchie and all of the staff at Elm Publications for their help and guidance in the writing and production of this book.

Humphrey Shaw

Chapter 1
Financial Management

Introduction

Financial management is the study of money as it applies to business. All firms have their current objectives and plans for the future but these can only be realised if they can be financed. The business must be able to generate its own cash resources from profits to finance its long term investment programme. If this is not sufficient, other sources of finance must be found. It is the financial manager's role to ensure that the firm always has sufficient funds to meet its current and forecast liabilities.

How Financial Management Differs From Accounting

Financial management is concerned with interpreting accounting information and using it to make financial decisions. The information will be provided by the financial accountant and the cost accountant. Financial accounting is concerned with the recording and preparation of financial data. It provides information about what has been sold, what the firm's expenses have been and how profit has been used. It really performs a stewardship role, for it shows the owners how their money has been invested and what returns have been made.

All companies must keep accurate financial records in order to comply with the requirements of the 1985 Companies' Act. Many firms also employ cost accountants whose task is to ascertain the firm's costs and predict future profits at different levels of output. There is no legal duty to do this and the benefits of producing this information must outweigh its cost. Both accounting systems will provide financial data but it is management who must decide how best to use the firm's resources. Money is a very important resource and it is the financial manager's role to advise the firm on how different courses of action will affect cash flow and profitability.

1

Corporate Objectives

Corporate objectives give a sense of direction to the business. Once set, staff know whether or not they are achieving their goals and the objectives provide a reference point for managers engaged in planning the company's long term future goals. Until the objectives have been determined, management cannot formulate plans, for it is impossible to plan if one does not know what should be achieved.

If a corporate objective is going to be effective it must be capable of being translated into specific targets. These targets should follow what is often referred to as the SMART principle. They must be specific, measurable, agreed, realistic and timely. Many objectives will have a strong financial bias, such as to increase sales by ten per cent. These objectives can only be achieved through team work, but it is the financial manager's task to ensure that the business has sufficient cash resources to meet its current objectives.

Corporate Plans And The Financial Manager

Management courses continually stress the need for planning. Markets are in a constant state of change. New products, new technology and changing consumer tastes and preferences have meant that firms must continually adapt and change their products to meet current demands or face extinction. This means that management must always be planning for the future. Decisions must be made as to where the business should be, in so many years' time, compared with its current position. This is often referred to as its planning gap and is shown in the diagram below.

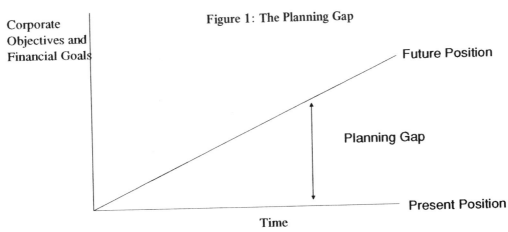

Figure 1: The Planning Gap

Figure 1 shows where the business currently is and where it wants to be in the future. The greater the distance between the lines, the more objectives must be accomplished to achieve the desired goals. These new aims will have to be financed, either by generating sufficient cash from sales, or by raising it from new sources. Any new investment must be appraised to ensure that optimum returns are made. Money once invested cannot usually be recovered, and so the ultimate cost is not just the financial cost but the cost of the other alternative foregone. Economists call this the opportunity cost and, while it is not shown by traditional accounting records, it must be considered by the financial manager when making decisions.

Stages In The Planning Process

Corporate plans should take account of the firm's current strengths and opportunities while seeking to maximise its weaknesses and threats. This process is called the S.W.O.T test. During any review of business activity the financial manager must critically appraise the business' current financial position and how it will be affected by proposed developments. Large expansion policies can carry particularly high risks, if large amounts of borrowed capital are needed to bring them to fruition. The financial manager must decide what is a safe level of borrowing, by assessing forecast earnings and profits. If it is too risky to borrow additional finance, the firm must consider approaching the owners for more share capital.

A firm's cash and profits are dependent on the goods and services it produces. Marketing textbooks refer to this as the product life cycle. The model charts the different stages of most products from the introductory stages, through to maturity and eventual decline and termination. At any time there will be certain key products which are responsible for generating the firm's sales, profits and cash. As these reach the decline stage the business's profits and cash will dwindle, unless new products can be launched which will generate future earnings. The diagram below shows the stages in a product life cycle and how a firm's financial fortunes are linked to it.

There is always a danger that, unless new products are launched, the firm will also follow the product life cycle. For many businesses, 80% of sales and profits come from 20% of the products. While the other products are needed to provide a comprehensive product range, their contribution to profits and cash flow is minimal.

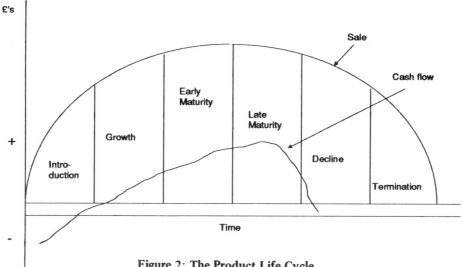

Figure 2: The Product Life Cycle

If the firm is to survive, new products must be developed and marketed to take the place of those currently producing the company's profits. The aim is to invest the current earnings wisely so that there will always be a stream of new products replacing those coming to the end of their life cycle. Unfortunately increased competition and changes in consumer tastes are making most product life cycles shorter. This inevitably increases the risks of investing, for even the successful ones must quickly make a return before they too become obsolete.

While market research will suggest the likely demand for a new product, it is the accountants and financial managers who must decide whether or not the new investment can meet the desired returns from the capital invested in it. The product must not just cover its own costs, but also a proportion of the unsuccessful one's losses. There is always a danger that the business may make a drop error or a go error. A drop error occurs whenever a decision is taken not to proceed with a product which would have been successful. A go error occurs when a product is launched unsuccessfully. In both cases large amounts of money will be lost and it is important not just to consider the financial implications of the proposed development, in isolation from the marketing opportunities. The aim is to achieve the correct balance between financial prudence and marketing innovation. If this is not achieved, the business' long term survival will be in jeopardy.

4

The Need For Financial Control

If the business is to survive, it must constantly monitor its resources and costs. Money tied up in unproductive assets will deplete cash reserves and cost overruns will make the firm uncompetitive. Corporate plans must be translated into financial objectives. Budgets must be set for all areas of the firm's activity and actual costs must be compared with budgeted costs. This is an ongoing task for the firm's financial position will change with different operating levels.

If the business is to have an efficient financial control system, management must be immediately aware of any difference between planned and current activity. This change will immediately affect cash flow forecasts and, if these are not revised, the business could experience cash flow problems. It is not cash flow problems alone which bring about financial collapse but managements' inability to recognise them and take corrective action.

The language of business is money. Firms can only continue by having sufficient cash resources to meet their current liabilities. If cash cannot be generated internally, the financial manager must seek outside sources. This will generally involve additional borrowing and the business must be able to show that it is a good lending proposition.

Sources of Finance

If additional finance is needed, it must be acquired at the minimum cost and on the most advantageous terms. No one would ever consider buying goods from just one supplier and, yet, many firms just use bank overdraft finance as their only source of loan capital. This can be a dangerous strategy, for theoretically the money is repayable on demand. If the overdraft facility is withdrawn, the firm will inevitably face liquidation, unless additional finance can be found (and this is unlikely to be available).

The financial manager must ensure that the business has a secure financial base and that there is a balanced mix of equity and debt capital. Borrowed funds have their advantages, but the amount borrrowed must never be excessive in relation to the firm's capital mix and earnings. If the economy enters a period of recession and sales and profits fall, it is the companies with high levels of borrowing which are most at risk. The temptation to pursue a fast growth strategy by acquiring assets with borrowed finance should be resisted, even when interest rates appear low. A sudden rise in rates can cause sales and profits to fall. When this happens, many businesses find that their cash resources are being drained because of their high interest rate payments.

If the business is to survive and prosper, it must have sufficient financial resources to withstand the prevailing economic climate. During economic booms firms experience a growth in sales and profits as the economy is stimulated by cheap and plentiful bank credit. This inevitably leads to an increase in corporate debt as managers seek to expand their companies to take advantage of the current trading conditions. When the boom ends and credit becomes less plentiful and more expensive, those firms which have high levels of borrowing may well face financial difficulties. If sales volumes fall and interest payments rise, positive cash flow balances can soon become negative ones. Management's attention then becomes dominated by the firm's current cash flow position. Long term planning is forgotten and management concentrate instead on short term decision making and survival.

In such conditions it is generally the smaller businesses which are forced into liquidation. Unable to borrow additional finance, they are wound up by their creditors. This fate may also happen to large companies who are unable to dispose of their assets quickly enough to meet their debt commitments. Those that do manage to survive will be smaller and often unable to compete effectively in the market place. Many will be taken over by firms who were more financially prudent and who controlled their borrowing and cash flows more effectively.

The key to corporate survival lies in having sound financial management, coupled with a good product range and a committed work force. Financial management control techniques cannot on their own guarantee the continued survival of any business, but the lack of them will certainly hasten its departure from the market place.

Chapter 2
Recording Financial Information

Introduction

We know from historical records that the early civilisations of the Babylonians and the Egyptians operated a system of recording financial information. While these early systems were important to the merchants of that time, they were not sufficiently advanced to become the foundations of our modern accounting system. Today's methods of recording business transactions are based on the system devised by the Italian merchants. An Italian monk, Pacioli, wrote the first exposition of the double entry method of recording financial information in 1494 and the system has remained unchanged since then.

Although financial management is the study of interpreting and analysing financial data, it is important to understand how financial information is recorded. The main financial statements — the profit and loss account and balance sheet - are prepared from information recorded, using the double entry method of book-keeping.

The Need for Financial Information

The purpose of book-keeping and accounting is to provide financial information about a business. Managers and owners need a wide range of financial information and the accounting system must be such that it shows:

1. whether the business is making a profit or a loss, and whether or not that profit is adequate when one considers the amount of money invested in the business;

2. how much money is currently financing the business has been provided by the owners or shareholders and how much from outside lenders;

3. whether the business has the ability to repay its short term and long-term debts (and to pay the necessary interest charges), as and when they fall due for payment;

4. who owes money to the business (debtors) and whether or not the debts are being collected on time;

5. to whom the business owes money for stock which has beeen bought on credit and how much is owed to each supplier. Mangement also need to know how long the firm is taking to pay its short term liabilities (creditors);

6. what the day-to-day running expenses of the business are. Management must know how much money is being spent on electricity, gas, telephone, insurance, wages, rent and whether or not the firm's profit margin is sufficient for the business to be able to meet these costs; and

7. how much money the business has at the bank, where the money has come from and how it has been spent.

The stages of recording financial information are shown in the diagram below.

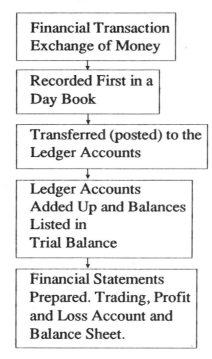

Figure 3: Recording Financial Information by the Double Entry Bookkeeping System

Recording Financial Information

Before explaining the mechanics of the double entry book-keeping system, you need to know what financial records must be kept and the information they contain.

The Day Books

These are sometimes referred to as the Journals, Subsidiary Books of Account, Books of Original Entry or Books of Prime Entry. The Day Books are used to record daily financial transactions of a business each day. Once this has been done, the transaction is recorded in the firm's ledger accounts.

Cash Book	Petty Cash Book	Sales Day Book	Purchases Day Book	Sales Returns Book	Purchase Returns	Journal (Proper)

Figure 4: The Day Books

Sales Day Book: Records goods sold on credit. The book shows in date order the invoices sent to customers.

Sales Returns Book: Sometimes called the Returns Inwards Book. It records the return of goods which had previously been sold to a customer. The goods may be returned because they were faulty or because the goods were sent in error.

Purchases Day Book: Sometimes called the Bought or Day Book. It records goods bought on credit to be resold in the normal course of business.

Purchases Returns Book: Sometimes called the Returns Outwards Book; records the return of goods bought from a supplier to be resold by the business.

Cash Book: Records all cash received and paid out by the business and all payments. The Cash Book will also show money paid into and out of the bank account.

Petty Cash Book: This book records small cash payments such as bus fares or payments for tea and coffee.

The Journal: The Day Book used for recording any transactions which will not fit appropriately into one of the other Day Books, such as correcting errors in the ledger accounts, recording the introduction of new capital and the purchase of assets.

Once the information has been recorded in the Day Books, it must be posted to the ledger accounts.

The Ledger Accounts

In a manual system, the ledger will either be a large book or a series of loose leaf cards. Today it is far more likely that the information will be stored on a computer disk using one of the many accounting packages which are currently on the market.

Each ledger account only records the financial details of one particular type of transaction. The more financial transactions there are, the more ledger accounts which must be opened Each ledger account will be given the name of what is being recorded and so the rent will be shown in the rent ledger. Each ledger will show.

1. the date the transaction happened

2. the amount of the transaction in money terms

3. a reference number which can be used to trace the transaction back to the Day Books and, hence, the documentation relating to the transaction.

4. the necessary debit and credit entries

Example of A Ledger Account

Figure 5: A Ledger Account

(Debit)   Rent A/c   (Credit)
   Dr   Cr

Date	Narrative (details)	Folio (reference)	£ p	Date	Narrative (details)	Folio (reference)	£ p

Ledger Accounts are often called "T" accounts because they are abreviated, as in the example below:

Debit   Rent A/c   Credit
Dr   Cr

In our examples we will use the simpler T account.

Accountants classify the firm's ledger accounts into different categories. The ledger accounts are split into three sections and these are shown in the diagram

Figure 6: 3 Sections of a Ledger Account

Real Accounts	Nominal Accounts	Personal Accounts
Records tangible assets, such as land buildings, motor vehicles and, intangible assets such as goodwill. The final balances on these accounts. will be shown in the balance sheet.	Records expenses, such as electricity wages, rent, rates telephone, travelling expenses. The total balances on these accounts will be shown in the profit and loss account after they have been adjusted for prepayments and accruals	Records sums of money owed by customers and owing to different suppliers as a result of sales an d purchases made on credit. Money owing to the firm is shown as debtors, and money owed as creditors. The total debtor and creditor balances will be shown in the balance sheet.

The Mechanics of Double Entry

The double entry method requires two accounts for each financial transaction. This is why the ledger is divided into two halves. The left hand side of the page is called the debit side and the right hand side the credit side. Double entry involves recording the two parts of every transaction - the giving of a benefit by one party and its receipt by another.

The accounting system should be thought of as a camera which takes a picture recording all financial transactions coming into or going out of the business, regardless of whether or not any money is actually exchanged.

There are only two ways that a business can acquire or sell goods and services and these need to be explained before the transactions, can be recorded. Firstly, the goods or services can be bought for cash or they can be acquired on credit.

12

When cash is used to finance the transaction, the firm will gain the benefit of the goods or services bought but will decrease its holding of cash. If they are bought or sold on credit, no money will have changed hands at this point and so the ledger accounts must show either the sum owed to the firm or what is owed to creditors.

The double entry system must record each of these transactions in a way which makes them immediately identifiable, while still only using two sides of the ledger paper. Let us now consider the recording of each of these two transactions in the ledger accounts.

Example

A firm purchases a van for £1,000 cash from Mr Nawaz on the third of May.

What has happened?
The business has received a van by giving up some of its cash. The van account has increased while the cash account has decreased.

How Is This Recorded?
Whenever the transaction involves an exchange of goods or services for money, the account which receives value is debited and the one which gives value is credited.

Which Account Has Received Value?
The Van A/c has received value because the firm has a van after the purchase and so this account must be debited.

Which Account Has Given Value?
The Cash A/c has given value because money has been taken from it to pay for the van. The firm's cash deposits have been reduced and this is shown by crediting the Cash A/c

The ledger accounts will now look like this. There must be two accounts to record the two parts of the one transaction.

Van Account and Cash Account

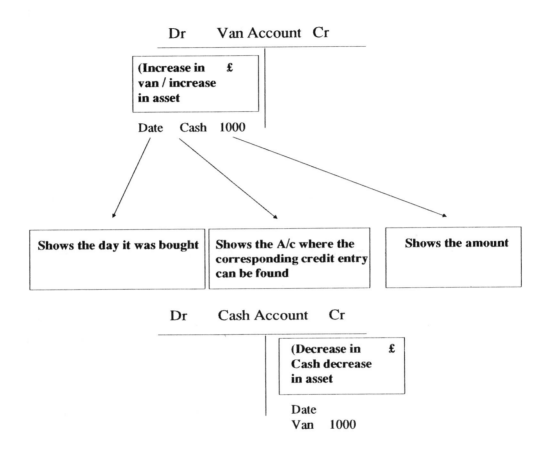

We will now consider the purchase of the van on credit. Let us assume that instead of paying for the asset we are allowed to have them on credit from Mr Nawaz.

How Is This Recorded?

Whenever the transaction involves an exchange of goods or services on credit, the business which has provided the goods or service is credited and the appropriate goods or service ledger account is debited. In this case Mr Nawaz's account will be credited and the Van A/c will be debited.

14

Which Account Has Received Value?

The Van A/c has received value because the firm has a van after the purchase. This account must now be debited, even though the goods have not yet been paid for.

Which Account Has Given Value?

The seller, Mr Nawaz, has given value by allowing the firm to have the asset on credit.

The ledger accounts will now look like this. Once again we must open two accounts to record the one transaction.

Purchases Account and Mr Nawaz

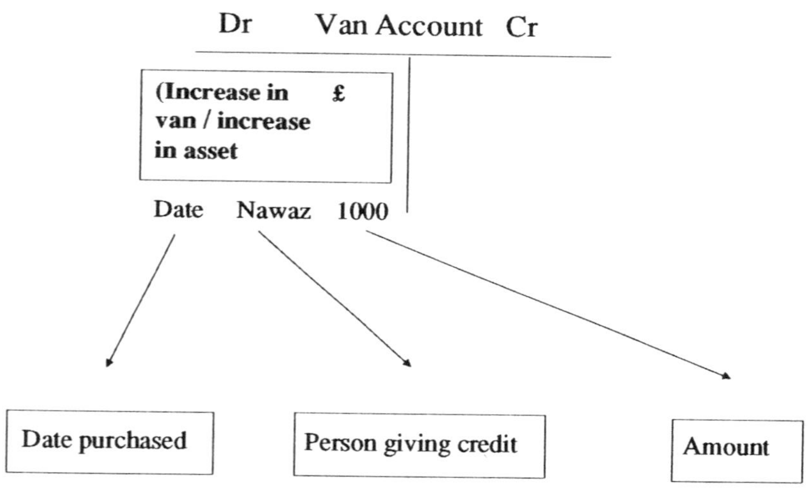

Dr Van Account Cr
(Increase in van / increase in asset £
Date Nawaz 1000
Date purchased
Person giving credit
Amount

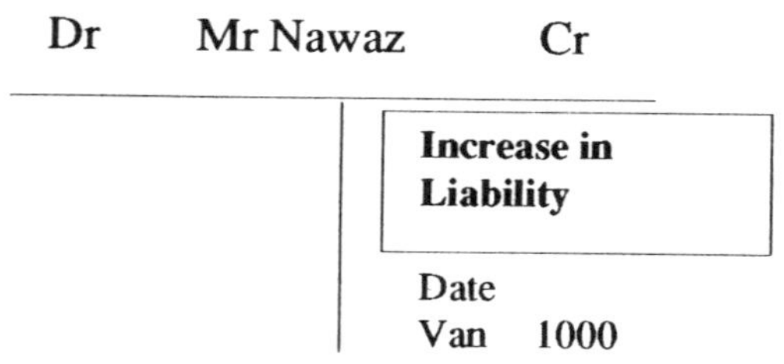

Dr Mr Nawaz Cr
Increase in Liability
Date
Van 1000

Summary of the Rules of Double Entry

If the transaction refers to an:

a) increase in an asset expense or loss — Debit the asset expense or loss account

b) a decrease in an asset expense or loss — Credit the asset expense or loss account

Rules (a) and (b) apply for all transactions involving the purchasing of goods or paying for expenses, either cash or by cheque. Similarly, when goods are sold for cash or a cheque is received, debit the bank or cash account and credit the sales account.

c) an increase in a liability — Credit the liability account.

d) a decrease in a liability — Debit the liability account

Rules (c) and (d) apply whenever a firm purchases goods on credit, takes out a loan or increases the capital of the business. In such cases the asset or expense gained by the firm will be debited and the account providing the money will be credited.

A Comprehensive Example
Julie Ellis started a floristry business. During the first week of trading the business entered into the following financial transactions:

Day	Transaction
1	Started the business with £5,000 in cash
2	Bought goods for £100 paid cash
3	Sold goods on credit to AB Ltd for £150
3	Bought motor van for £2,000 paid cash
3	Bought petrol paid cash £15
4	Bought goods for £50 on credit from JHL Supplies
5	Paid wages in cash £600
5	Paid electricity bill £50 cash
6	Sold goods for £150 received cash
6	Paid the rent on the shop £500 in cash

Before posting each transaction to the correct side of the ledger account, it is often best to consider the effect of the financial transaction and which account must be debited and credited

Date	Effect of The Financial Transaction	Account to be Debited	Account to be Credited
1	Increase in a Asset Increase in Liability	Debit to Cash Account	Credit Capital Account
2	Increase in Expense Decrease in Asset	Debit Purchases Account	Credit Cash Account
3	Increase in Asset Increase Income (sales)	Debit A B Ltd A/c Account	Credit Sales Account
3	Increase in Assets Decrease in Asset	Debit Motor Van Account	Credit Cash Account
4	Increase in Expense Decrease in Assets	Debit Petrol A/c	Credit Cash A/c
4	Increase in Assets Increase in Liabilities	Debit Purchases A/c	Credit JHL Supplies A/c
5	Increase in Expense Decrease in Asset	Debit Wages A/c	Credit Cash A/c
5	Increase in Expenses Decrease in Asset	Debit Electricity A/c	Credit Cash A/c

While the rules are relatively simple, it takes a while to master the technique of the double entry system. A checklist is provided later on in the chapter to act as an aide memoire.

```
              Dr        Cash Account      Cr

                          £                                    £
Day 1      Capital       5000    Day 2   Purchases      100
Day 6      Sales          150    Day 3   Van           2000
                                 Day 3   Petrol          15
                                 Day 5   Wages          600
                                 Day 5   Electricity      50
                                 Day 6   Rent           500


              Dr       Capital Account        Cr

                                                         £
                                 Day 1   Cash           5000


              Dr       Purchases Account      Cr

                          £
Day 2      Cash          100
Day 3      AB Ltd        150
Day 4      JHL            50
```

18

```
                Dr      A B Ltd Account        Cr
                    _____
                              £
Day 3           Sales        150
```

```
                Dr      Van Account    Cr
                    _____
                              £
Day 3           Cash        2000
```

```
                Dr      Petrol Account         Cr
                    _____
                              £
Day 3           Cash         15
```

```
        Dr        Wages Account          Cr
        ─────────────────────────────
                        £
Day 5   Cash            600
                               │
                               │
                               │
```

```
        Dr     JHL Supplies Account        Cr
        ───────────────────────────────
                        │                        £
                        │  Day 4   Purchases     50
                        │
                        │
```

```
        Dr       Electricity Account      Cr
        ───────────────────────────────
                        £        │
Day 5   Cash            50       │
                                 │
                                 │
```

```
          Dr      Sales Account    Cr
     _____|_____
                       |                      £
                       |   Day 3    AB       150
                       |      6     Cash     150
                       |
                       |


          Dr      Rent Account     Cr
     _____|_____
                £      |
Day 6    Cash   500    |
                       |
                       |
                       |
```

Balancing the Accounts

As the information is posted to the ledger account, no attempt is made to calculate a final or closing balance on each account. With a manual system this is often done at the end of each month, because of all the work involved. Computerised systems enable the accountant to balance the ledgers quickly and often because computers are excelent at storing and processing large amounts of data.

The Mechanics of Balancing the Ledgers

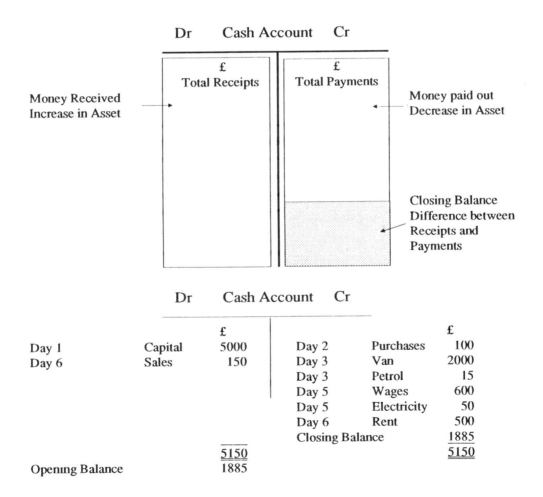

Dr   Cash Account   Cr

		£			£
Day 1	Capital	5000	Day 2	Purchases	100
Day 6	Sales	150	Day 3	Van	2000
			Day 3	Petrol	15
			Day 5	Wages	600
			Day 5	Electricity	50
			Day 6	Rent	500
			Closing Balance		1885
		5150			5150
Opening Balance		1885			

22

Explanation of Balancing the Cash Account

1. Add up both sides to find the total of each column. One side will have more entries than the other. Do not yet write down the total.

2. Leave a line below the longer column of figures

3. Insert the larger total at the bottom of both columns

4. Subtract the smaller number from the larger number and insert the balance in the space which you have left (note: Accountants do not show any working and this may be why the non-financial person finds it hard to ascertain where all the figures have come from)

5. Both columns will now be the same. (These end figures are double underlined, which shows that they will not be used any more). It is the closing balance which will become tomorrow's opening balance and must be brought down on the opposite side to the closing balance, so that the double entry rules are observed.

Once the accounts have been written up and balanced, a trial balance can be prepared. This is a list of all the debit and credit balances and it is prepared to test the accuracy of the book-keeping system.

We have already seen that the double entry system records each transaction twice. One part will be shown in the ledger accounts as a debit entry while the other will be shown as a credit. There can never be two debits or two credits for one transaction. It therefore follows that the total of the debit balances in the ledger accounts should be equal to the total of the credit balances. If the totals of the debit and credit balances do not agree, the cause must be found. The main reasons for a discrepancy between the debits and credits are shown below.

1. incorrect addition of the debit and credit columns of the trial balance.

2. a debit balance on one account being entered in error on the credit side of the trial balance and vice versa.

3. incorrectly recording the amount of a balance in the trial balance.

4. incorrectly calculating the balance on a ledger account.

5. not completing the double entry for a transaction.

6. Accidently recording two debit (or two credit) entries for a transaction.

7. putting two debits or two credits for one transaction in the ledger accounts

Trial Balance For Julie Ellis for the week ending

	Dr £	Cr £
Capital		5,000
Cash	1,885	
Purchases	150	
Petrol	15	
Creditors		50
Debtors	150	
Motor Van	2,000	
Sales		300
Electricity	50	
Wages	600	
Rent	500	
	5,350	5,350

Only now can accounting statements be prepared which will show the firm's assets and liabilities and whether or not a profit or loss has been made during the trading period. Before either of these statements can be prepared, it is necessary to understand the distinction which accountants make between two different types of income and expenditure. These are now explained.

Capital Income

This is income which a business receives on an irregular basis and which is not earned from its normal trading operations. Examples of capital income are funds invested in the business by the owners, or funds it receives in the form of loans. It is also derived from the proceeds of selling fixed assets, such as buildings or plant and machinery.

Revenue Income

Income which is earned by the business on a daily basis, such as income from sales, or income from property (rents received), or income from bank deposits (interest received).

Capital Expenditure

Capital expenditure arises from the acquisition of new fixed assets or from improving the earning capacity of an existing fixed asset. An example would be an extension to a factory. The term also applies to the reduction or repayment of loans.

Revenue Expenditure

Revenue expenditure arises from the costs a business incurs when it goes about its normal trading activity, e.g. purchases, rent, electricity, telephone and the maintenance of fixed assets.

Revenue income and expenditure will be recorded in the profit and loss account and capital expenditure will be shown in the balance sheet. In order to calculate whether a business has made a profit or a loss for a particular period, it is necessary to determine the revenue income of the business for that period and to deduct from it the revenue expenditure. Capital expenditure must be separated and will be shown in the balance sheet. Only by keeping records showing the income earned and the costs incurred, is it possible to ascertain whether the business has made a profit or a loss and what assets or liabilities it has. The profit and loss account and the balance sheet are explained in Chapter 3.

Ledger Checklist

Recording Liabilities	Debit	Credit
Opening Capital	Bank or Cash A/c	Capital A/c
Additional Capital	Bank or Cash A/c	Capital A/c
Loan	Bank or Cash A/c	Loan A/c
Repayment of Loan	Loan A/c	Bank or Cash A/c
Owner's Drawings	Drawings A/c	Bank or Cash A/c
Goods Bought on Credit	Purchases A/c	Supplier's A/c
Recording Income		
Cash or Cheque Sales	Cash A/c or Bank A/c	Sales A/c
Credit Sales	Name of Buyer A/c	Sales A/c
Discount Received	Name of Supplier A/c	Discount Renewal A/c
Rent Received	Bank or Cash A/c	Rent Received A/c
Commission Received	Bank or Cash A/c	Commission Received A/c
Recording Assets		
Premises	Premises A/c	Bank or Cash A/c
Fixtures & Fittings	Fixtures & Fittings A/c	Bank or Cash A/c
Plant & Machinery	Plant & Machinery A/c	Bank or Cash A/c
Motor Vehicles	Motor Vehicles A/c	Bank or Cash A/c
Recording Expenses		
Discount Allowed	Discount Allowed A/c	Cash A/c
Carriage Inwards	Carriage Inwards A/c	Cash A/c
Wages	Wages A/c	Bank or Cash A/c
Light & Heating	Light & Heating A/c	Bank & Cash A/c
Postage	Postage A/c	Bank & Cash A/c
Other Business Expenses	Business Expenses A/c	Bank or Cash A/c
Carriage Outwards	Carriage Outwards A/c	Bank or Cash A/c

Chapter 3
Understanding Financial Statements

Introduction

Once a year all businesses must produce a set of accounts which show the profit or loss from trading activities together with a statement of assets and liabilities. These two financial statements are often referred to as a set of annual accounts. The profit and loss account will show the profit or loss made during the last financial year and the balance sheet will show the firm's assets and liabilities at the year end.

These two financial statements seek to summarise the day to day business transactions, thereby showing the overall financial position at a particular date. In this way the financial data describes the business in the same way as an ordnance survey map portrays a picture of the countryside, by using a variety of symbols. The key to mastering finance is first to understand the meaning of these two accounting statements.

The Profit and Loss Account

People start businesses for a variety of reasons. They all believe that they can sell their product or service at a profit, but they need to know how much profit they are making. During the year stock is purchased and sold and expenses are paid without the owner being certain how much profit is being made. The profit and loss account summarises all these transactions into a single statement. It shows the gross profit made before expenses are paid and the net profit after they are paid.

What Is Profit ?

Profit is the money surplus made from selling a product or service for more than it originally cost. The profit will be used to pay the business costs, pay a return to the people who have financed the firm and provide funds which can be re-invested to provide the future profits. Profits are therefore the life blood of any business, but they should not be thought of as being a cash surplus at the end of a year because the profit and loss account is not prepared on a cash basis. This means that a sale and an expense is recorded as soon as it has been made or incurred, and not when the cash is received or paid. Also in many firms the cash will have been spent either in paying expenses or in acquiring additional assets such as stock. It is for this reason that sometimes profitable firms are forced to cease trading because they have been unable to keep sufficient profits in cash to meet their day to day expenses.

How are Profits Calculated

One way of calculating the profit made each year would be to keep a record of all items sold together with the profit margin put on each article or service. At the end of the year the total profit could be added up and the expenses subtracted to yield the annual profit.

While this method would work in theory, it would be impracticable in many businesses. Imagine a modern supermarket checkout person having to record the margin on every item as well as the selling price. It would just take too long and so a simpler method is needed. Provided a record is kept of all stock purchased and all sales, it is possible to calculate the profit made by subtracting the cost of goods bought from the sales figure.

| Sales | £10,000 |

Less

| Purchases | £5,000 |

Equals

| Gross Profit | £5,000 |

Figure 7: The Calculation of Profit

In a Profit and Loss Account this would be recorded as:

Profit and Loss for the year ended 5 April Year One

	£
Sales	10,000
Less Purchases	5,000
Gross Profit	5,000

This is a very simple example for it assumes that all purchases are sold during the year. This is unlikely to happen for the end of a financial year must not affect trading. Some stock is likely to remain unsold and must be accounted for.

Cost of goods Sold

Imagine a sweet shop selling a range of confectionery. The shop's customers always want to be able to buy sweets and so the shop must always carry sufficient stock.

The profit and loss account is drawn up at the end of the shop's financial year. If the owner could so arrange things that on that date all stock had been sold, it would be simple to calculate the cost of the goods sold as it would just be the invoice value of goods purchased. If the owner subtracted this figure from the sales figure, the gross profit or loss could be calculated.

This situation does not often happen, because the owner knows that, regardless of the end of the financial year, the shop must be fully stocked so that customers can always buy their sweets. For this reason, there will always be some stock unsold at the end of the year which must be valued and which will be called closing stock. The next day, on the start of the new financial year, it will become the business's opening stock. If this closing stock were not included, the profit would be understated for, once this stock is sold, profit will be earned. The stock which has not been sold at the end of the financial year must be valued at the lower of cost or its net realisable value. This means that all firms will apply the same policy when valuing stock. If this were not done, profits could be distorted by applying different valuations to the final stock figure.

In most businesses there will always be some unsold stock at the end of the year which is still of merchantable quality and which can be sold during the following financial year. An adjustment to the year's purchases figure must be made in the accounts, by adding opening stock to purchases and then subtracting

29

closing stock. This will show how much the goods sold during the accounting period actually cost the firm and are referred to in accounts as the cost of goods sold. This information is shown in a trading account which precedes the profit and loss account.

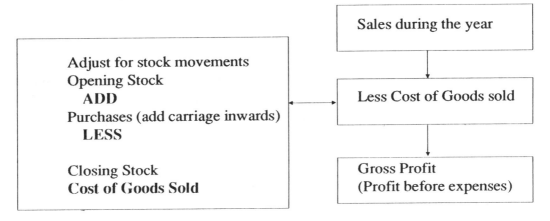

Figure 8: Calculating Gross Profit with unsold stock remaining

In a Trading Account this would be recorded as:

Trading Account for the Year Ended Year Two

	£	£
Sales		12,000
Add Opening Stock	1,000	
Purchases	5,000	
	6,000	
Less Closing Stock	2,000	
Cost of Goods Sold		4,000
Gross Profit		8,000

Note

Arithmetic signs are not shown in the accounts. Instead lines are drawn underneath the figures to be added or subtracted and the total is then displayed to the right. The numbers at the extreme right hand page are always the final figures while the ones to the left show the calculation. Final figures are always double underlined.

So far we have only considered how to calculate the gross profit. If all expenses incurred in operating the business such as wages, rent, electricity and rates are subtracted from the gross profit, the net profit can be calculated.

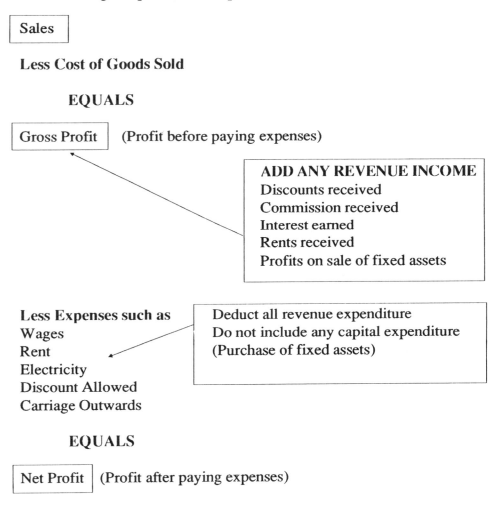

Figure 9: Calculating Gross & Net Profit

Explanation of Terms

Carriage Inwards

When goods are bought for resale someone must pay for having the goods delivered; if the firm pays which is buying the goods, the amount is added to the cost of the purchases and increases the cost of the stock. If the firm pays to have its finished goods transported to customers, the amount is called carriage outwards and is shown as an expense in the profit and loss account.

Discount Received

When a bill is paid early, a sum of money may be offered off the invoice price by the seller as an inducement to pay the bill promptly. Accountants treat this as money earned and call it discount received. It is shown in the profit and loss account as additional income.

Commision Received

Income earned from selling goods on someone else's behalf.

Rents Received

Rental income earned.

Interest Earned

Interest earned on monetary deposits.

Example of A Profit and Loss Account for the year ended Year Two

	£	£
Sales		25,000
Opening Stock	3,000	
Add Purchases	10,000	
	13,000	
Less Closing Stock	5,000	
Cost of Goods Sold		8,000
Gross Profit		17,000
LESS EXPENSES		
Wages	3,000	
Rent	1,000	
Heating	2,000	
Postage and Stationery	1,000	
Rates	500	
Travelling Expenses	500	
Total Expenses		8,000
Net Profit		9,000

If taxation and dividends payments are ignored, the net profit of £9,000 would enable the business to grow because the profit would be kept within the firm. In order to calculate the profit a time period must be chosen which takes into account the seasonal fluctuations of the trading cycle. For most businesses this is twelve months, although a profit and loss account can be drawn up more frequently to see how the business is performing

Sales

The sales figure in the profit and loss account shows the total sales value of goods delivered to customers. It is the total sum of all invoices during the financial year. Unless the firm is a retailer selling goods only on a cash basis, the sales figure does not represent the amount of cash actually received. Most sales are on credit and so the sales figure simply shows the figure for invoiced goods irrespective of whether the cash has actually been paid.

The profit and loss account therefore shows that the amount of goods sold is not the same thing as the purchases during the year. Similarly, the cash outflow and expenses in the profit and loss account are not the same thing. Some of the purchases are likely to have been made on credit and, at the end of the financial year, they may not have been paid. Any money owed to the business will be shown as a debtor in the balance sheet and any money owed by the business as a creditor.

Expenses Owing and Prepaid

At the financial year end some bills will have been paid in advance while others will still be owing. An adjustment must be made so that the profit and loss account shows the income earned, less the expenses incurred during that financial period. Expenses owing are included in the profit and loss account by adding them to the sum already paid. The amount owing is then shown in the balance sheet as a liability under the heading current liabilities. Accountants call this sum an accrual.

Similarly, any money paid in advance must be deducted from the total payments and will be shown in the balance sheet, usually by adding the prepayments amount to the debtors figure.

The Balance Sheet

If we consider our example of the sweet shop, the owner has to have premises, fixtures and fittings, a van, stock and some money for paying the day to day expenses. We would expect a sweet shop to possess all of these assets. The balance sheet is simply a statement showing the assets which a business has at a particular time and how they have been financed. It records all capital income (shares and loans) and capital expenditure (fixed assets) and this is why these financial transactions are excluded from the trading and profit and loss account

The balance sheet gets it name because the total assets must equal the total liabilities and hence the two sides always equal each other, or balance. This is so because the liabilities show where the finance has come from to pay for the assets which have been acquired by the firm.

<table>
<tr>
<td>

Liabilities

Money financing
the business

</td>
<td>

Assets

Possessions
which the
business needs
for trading

</td>
</tr>
</table>

Figure 10: The Balance Sheet – Liabilities equal Assets

Balance Sheet (a Business as at Year One)

CAPITAL	FIXED ASSETS
Long term money used to finance the business. Shown as Share Capital Past Profits Long term Loans	Assets acquired for long term use such as buildings, machines and motor vehicles. They are shown in order of permanence and are not primarily for resale The assets must be shown at their cost price or valuation less depreciation

Assets and liabilities which will have a life longer than 12 months

Assets and liabilities which will have a life less than 12 months

CURRENT LIABILITIES	CURRENT ASSETS
Short term liabilities which must be repaid within 12 months Examples Creditors Bank Overdraft Taxation Owing Dividends	Short term assets which the business uses to trade and from which it derives its profit. Current Assets are always shown in order of liquidity (how quickly the asset can be turned into cash) with the most illiquid being shown first. The order is stock, debtors, bank and cash balances
Total Liabilities =	**Total Assets**

Figure 11: Horizontal Format of a Balance Sheet

CAPITAL			FIXED ASSETS		
	£	£		£	£
Capital	10,000		Premises	5,000	
Add Profit	9,000		Fixtures	4,000	
	19,000		Motor Car	2,000	11,000
Less Drawings	4,000				
Owner's Equity		15,000			
CURRENT LIABILITIES			CURRENT ASSETS		
Creditors		3,000	Stock	4,000	
			Debtors	2,000	
			Bank	1,000	7,000
		18,000			18,000

Figure 12: Example of Balance Sheet in Horizontal Format as at Year One

When a balance sheet is prepared in horizontal format it shows the total assets and liabilities. Some time balance sheets are prepared in what is called vertical format. While they still show the assets and liabilities, a different final figure will result because instead of showing total assets and liabilities the vertical balance sheet shows the net assets of the business which will equal the capital. Net assets are calculated by adding together the fixed and the current assets and subtracting the current liabilities, thereby showing the net assets owned by the firm.

We have already seen that assets equal liabilities and so the net assets must equal the capital which is financing the firm.

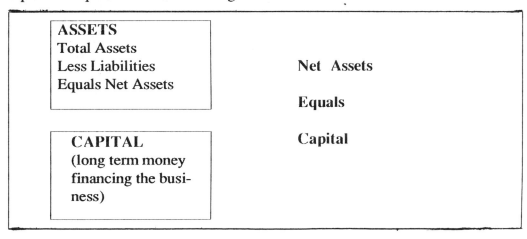

Figure 13: Balance Sheet in Vertical Format as at Year One

36

A balance sheet can be prepared in either horizontal or vertical format. Both are correct but as a general rule the horizontal format is used for sole traders and partnerships while most companies prefer the vertical format. This is mainly for presentation reasons as it fits neatly on an A4 page. Some people also believe that the information in this format is easier to understand.

Fixed Assets

	£	£	£
Premises	5,000		
Fixtures	4,000		
Motor Car	2,000		
			11,000
Current Assets			
Stock	4,000		
Debtors	2,000		
Bank	1,000		7,000
			18,000
Less Current Liabilities			
Creditors			3,000
Net Assets			15,000
Capital			
Capital	10,000		
Add Profit	9,000		
		19,000	
Less Drawings		4,000	
Capital Employed			15,000

Figure 14: Example of Balance Sheet in Vertical Format as at Year One

Balance Sheet Explanation

Fixed Assets

These are the long term assets of the business. They are deemed to have a life longer than twelve months and they will be shown in the balance sheet in order of permanence. Land and buildings are the most permanent assets and so they are shown first. All assets have a limited life and, as they are used, they will gradually wear out. In recent years buildings have proved to be an exception to this rule for property prices have tended to rise, thereby increasing the asset value of property. Nevertheless the fact remains that old property needs more repairing and so a cost of using the asset should be charged as an expense in operating the business. This cost is called depreciation and will be shown in both the profit and loss account and balance sheet. In the profit and loss account it will be shown as an expense against profit and in the balance sheet it will be shown as a reduction in the assets value to reflect the cost of its use. Depreciation, therefore, reduces the initial cost of the asset. The cost price of the assets less the total depreciation is refered to as the assets' net book value.

Cost of fixed asset purchased 3 years ago for **£10000**	Accumulated depreciation 10% on cost **£3000**	Assets Net Book Value **£7000**

Figure 15: Depreciation Shown in a Balance Sheet

Valuation of Fixed Assets

The balance sheet shows what fixed assets the firm has. Although they will be shown at their cost price, or valuation less depreciation, a balance sheet should not be taken as a guide to the assets' market value. This is because the business is viewed as a going concern, which means that the owners have no intention of ceasing trading and so there is no need to sell the assets and to seek a current market valuation of them.

Current Assets

These are the short term trading assets of the business. They are shown in order of liquidity. The word liquidity refers to the ease with which the asset can be turned into cash. Stock is the most illiquid asset and so it is shown first.

The word debtor is used to describe someone who owes money to the firm. Most of this money will be owed by individuals and companies who have bought goods on credit. We saw that the profit and loss account shows the total sales from invoices and not the amount of cash received. The balance sheet makes this position clearer by recording, under debtors, the amount of money still owed. This money is expected during the next twelve months, unless a provision for bad debts has been declared, which would reduce the debtors figure in the balance sheet.

Bank and cash balances show the firm's liquid assets at a particular date. They are shown last because they are the most liquid assets.

These then are the assets owned by the firm. How they have been financed will be seen from the other side of the balance sheet. Basically the money will have been provided on a long term or short term basis, either by the owners or by lenders to the business. The important thing to remember is that the two sides will always balance because assets must equal liabilities. This is so because the balance sheet shows how the assets have been financed and so the money financing the asset will be the same as the asset.

Capital
In accounts the word capital is used to describe the money which is financing the business. It is money which has been subscribed by the owners or by lenders who do not seek repayment within the coming twelve months. Profits retained in the business will increase the firm's capital just as losses will reduce it.

Drawings
During the year the owner has to pay bills and so s/he takes money out of the business. The amount of money taken out is called drawings and reduces the amount of profit which the business has made. This is why it is not shown in the profit and loss account as an expense, for it is a use of profit. It is shown in the balance sheet because drawings reduce the amount of capital in the business. It is a use of profit which could otherwise be re-invested in the firm.

Current Liabilities

These are short term debts which the business owes. The money must be repaid within one year from the balance sheet date. If purchases have been made on credit and they have not yet been paid for, then the amount owing will be listed under the heading creditors. Any other money owing because bills have not yet been paid will similarly be shown under this heading as creditors.

A Comprehensive Example

Trading and Profit and Loss Account and Balance Sheet for A Traders for the Year Ending Year Two

Trading Account

	£	£
Sales		50000
Less Returns Inwards		2000
Net Sales		48000
Opening Stock	3000	
Add Purchases	20000	
	23000	
Add Carriage Inwards	1000	
	24000	
Less Returns Outwards	5000	
Net Purchases	19000	
	22000	
Less Closing Stock	4000	
Cost of Goods Sold		18000
Gross Profit		30000

Profit and Loss Account

	£	£
Gross Profit		30000
Add Discount Received	500	
Commission Received	1000	
Rents Received	2000	
Interest Earned	<u>500</u>	
		<u>4000</u>
		34000
Less Expenses		
Wages	3000	
Rent	1000	
Rates	800	
Bank Interest	400	
Heating	100	
Motor Expenses	400	
Depreciation	1000	
Bad Debts	100	
Stationery	300	
Postage	600	
Carriage Outwards	100	
Telephone	<u>200</u>	
Total Expenses		<u>8000</u>
Net Profit		<u>26000</u>

Note.

Firms will have different revenue and expenditure. This example shows how each item is treated in the Trading and Profit and Loss Account.

Balance Sheet as at Year Two

Fixed Assets	Cost/Valuation	Depreciation to Date	Net Books Value
	£	£	£
Premises	60000	-	60000
Fixtures & Fittings	10000	2000	8000
Plant & Machinery	20000	4000	16000
	9000	6000	84000

Current Assets

Stock	25000	
Debtors	15000	
Bank	8000	
Cash	2000	
	50000	

Less Current Liabilities

Creditors	20000	

If applicable Bank Overdraft and Long Term Loans

Working Capital		30000
Net Assets		114000
Financed By		
Capital	100000	
Add Profit	26000	
	126000	
Less Drawings	12000	
Capital Employed		114000

42

Chapter 4
Accounting Concepts and Conventions

Introduction

If every business was allowed to prepare its final accounts based upon its own assumptions it would not be possible to compare one firm's accounts with another for both profits and assets employed could be over or understated. Worse still, firms could change their accounting methods each financial year making it impossible to monitor past performance.

In order to remedy this situation a number of accounting conventions have evolved to ensure consistent treatment of financial information. The underlying objective of financial statements is to provide information about a business. This information should be relevant, comprehensible, reliable, complete, timely, comparable and objective. It is therefore important that financial statements are prepared in such a way that they can be compared on an equitable basis with those of previous years.

The Need For Accounting Concepts

This is best illustrated by an example.

The Furniture Company and Wooden Furniture Limited are two hypothetical businesses engaged in manufacturing tables. During the last financial year they each bought the same quantity of wood from the same supplier at a cost of £20,000. Both companies made the same number of tables and sold them for £50,000.

At the end of the financial year neither company had paid their supplier in full and both owed £6,000. Both companies had also made credit sales and were owed £2,000.

The managers of both companies prepared their companies' accounts prior to having them audited but both managed to declare a different profit. This is shown below.

Profit and Loss Accounts for the year ended Year Two for the Furniture Company and Wooden Furniture.

Furniture Company		Wooden Furniture	
	£		£
Cash received from sales	48,000	Actual sales made	50,000
Less Cash paid to suppliers	14,000	Less cost of materials used	20,000
Profit	<u>34,000</u>		<u>30,000</u>

If every business were allowed to prepare its accounts in whichever way they wished, financial statements would be meaningless. With firms using different methods to calculate their profits, inter-firm comparisons would be impossible. The accounting conventions seek to limit this type of situation so that all users of financial information can be assured as to its accuracy and that financial matters have been treated consistently. The rules which ensure that these standards are adhered to are known as the accounting concepts, principles, postulates, standards or conventions. This chapter seeks to explain the main concepts as they apply to the study of financial management.

The Entity Concept

In accounting a business is always treated as a separate entity from its owners. This is most clearly illustrated in the case of a limited company where the owners (the shareholders) enjoy limited liability status for the debts of the business. If a limited company is forced into liquidation because it has insufficient funds to pay its creditors, the maximum loss which the shareholders can sustain is the value of their shares.

This concept also holds true for sole traders and partnerships. Although in law the business is not treated as a separate legal entity, in accounts the business and the owner are still treated as separate entities. Consider, for example, a small family-owned hairdressing salon called Hair Style. The two owners have subscribed all of the capital and the business has no other shareholders. Nevertheless, the owners' private financial transactions must be kept separate from the business.

The Going Concern Concept

It is a convention that a business will continue unless there is information to the contrary. The owners might be getting close to retirement and may consider ceasing trading, in which case this fact must be shown as a note in the accounts. Otherwise it will be assumed that the business will continue indefinitely. It is this concept which governs the treatment of fixed assets in the final accounts.

An understanding of this concept helps to explain why a business shows fixed assets in a balance sheet at their cost price rather than their current market value. Firms purchase fixed assets with the intention of using them for a number of years. They are not bought with the intention of selling them quickly for a profit and so it is logical to show them at their cost price instead of their market value.

The Money Measurement Concept

The accounts only record items which have a monetary value and so place no value on the non monetary assets of the business such as a loyal workforce or an excellent management team. The money measurement concept also ignores the effects of inflation for assets are shown in the accounts at their cost price. Similarly, liabilities are shown as the amount borrowed or owed and fail to show current purchasing power. This is considered in more detail in chapter eight which looks at the problems of accounting for inflation.

The Prudence Concept

This concept dictates that when accounts are prepared, which could contain either an optimistic or prudent approach to the presentation of the information, that the prudent concept should prevail. As a result, revenue and profits may only be included in a firm's accounts either when the cash is actually received or the firm is reasonably certain of receiving payment from the person or business owing the money (referred to in accounts as a debtor). It would be imprudent to treat an anticipated order as revenue, for the customer might withdraw the order and it is only once the goods have been despatched with an invoice that the debt is legally enforceable. Prudence therefore dictates that it is only at this stage that the accounts can show the revenue and profit from this sale.

This is why stock is always valued in the accounts at the lower of cost or its net realizable value. Similarly, any anticipated losses must be included in the profit and loss account. Lastly, a provision must be made if it is considered likely that any debtors will not pay their debts and will in fact become bad debts for the firm. A provision must be declared if the management believe that any of these debts will never be paid.

The Realisation Concept

As a general rule, a business is said to earn its income, and hence, its profit when a sale is made and the goods are passed to the customer (who then incurs a liability to pay for them). In accounting income is not considered earned just because a customer has placed an order, signed a contract or actually paid for the goods.

As a result of this concept the profit and loss account shows how much the business has earned from its sales in a particular period and therefore, supports the accruals concept which states that the firm's expenses must be matched with the income which has arisen from that expenditure.

One disadvantage of the realisation concept is that the profit and loss account may not take account of returned goods for which an allowance has been made in a different accounting period. Although this type of situation may arise, it is unlikely that the amounts involved will be so significant as to materially affect the profit figure which could mislead users of financial information.

The Accruals Concept

This is a very important accounting concept for it governs the way in which a profit and loss account is prepared. In accounts sales and expenses are shown when the sale is made or the expense incurred and not when the money is received or paid. If a business incurs an expense at the end of its financial year, it will be shown as an expense in the profit and loss account, even though the bill has not yet been paid. The amount owing will then be shown as an accrual or lumped together with creditors and shown as a current liability in the balance sheet. Likewise, any sale made before the receipt of cash will be shown as a sale in the profit and loss account. The amount owed must then be shown as a prepayment or included with the debtors and shown in the balance sheet.

46

Lastly, any sum of money paid in advance must be deducted from the amount shown in the profit and loss account, for it does not relate to this financial year and must be shown as a prepayment or debtor in the balance sheet.

The Consistency Concept

Once a particular accounting method has been adopted, it should not be changed from one accounting period to another, unless there is a very good reason. For instance the firm may decide to calculate an asset's depreciation on its cost price. If this is done, it is said to be using the straight line method, and so should not alter to another method because it would increase or decrease profits. If a change is made, a note must be made in the accounts stating that a change has been made and the reason for it. Only by applying this concept, can a firm's accounts be compared with previous years' figures.

The Materiality Concept

This refers to the relative importance of an item or an event. Accountants are primarily concerned with significant information and not with those items which have little effect on the financial statements. If a firm decides to purchase some new calculators for £50, a decision must be made as to whether this should be shown as an asset in the balance sheet or just written off as an expense against profit. There is no hard and fast rule. It really depends upon the size of the firm and the amount of the purchase. The materialitly concept allows a firm to treat such expenditure as seems most appropriate. Generally an asset will not be treated as capital expenditure if it would be too costly to depreciate it each year and the expenditure would not materially alter the final accounts.

Separate Valuation Principle

This is a new principle introduced by the 1985 Companies' Act which states that when calculating assets or liabilities, which are made up of more than one asset or liability, each must be separately valued or determined before being shown in aggregate in the annual accounts.

By applying these concepts or principles when preparing financial statements, the users can be assured that the accounts have been prepared in a consistent manner. The accounts can then be used for comparative purposes. This information is useful for managers and outside bodies such as investors, trade creditors and bankers who need to assess the firm's financial stability.

While this chapter has covered the main accounting concepts and conventions, it is not possible to explain in detail all of the regulatory framework governing the preparation of annual accounts. The Accounting Standards Committee issues Standard Statements of Accounting Practice (SSAPs) in order to regulate the information contained in annual accounts. These seek to review and redress matters not currently covered by any concept or convention, and are referred to in the following chapters where appropriate.

Chapter 5
Company Accounts

Introduction

Anyone who has ever looked at a set of company accounts could be forgiven for saying that they can be split into two halves. The first, containing the chair's statement, photographs of directors and buildings, together with graphs showing sales and other financial data, is reasonably comprehensible. The second half, showing the accounts together with the relevant accounting notes, is a complete mystery made even more baffling by the fact that so many numbers seem to balance with each other. Unfortunately it is the second half of the report which contains the relevant information but, before it can be understood, certain facts relating to companies and their accounts must be explained.

Before studying company accounts, one needs to understand how companies are formed and the legal terminology which applies to them. This chapter seeks to introduce you to the main legal requirements and explains the technical terms relating to company accounts.

Every year companies are required by law to maintain administrative and accounting records, to publish their annual accounts and to send a copy to every shareholder and debenture holder. A copy must also be filed with the Registrar of Companies at Companies' House. The 1985 Companies' Act consolidates the previous acts and lays down what information must be disclosed, how it must be presented and when it must be published.

Many people who decide to start their own business form a company. As a result they range in size from the small family firm, employing a few people, to the large multi-national companies such as Marks and Spencers, I.C.I and British Petroleum. Although companies differ in size, they all have two things in common. Firstly, they owe their origin to an act of Parliament and, secondly, they must comply with the legal requirements of the 1985 Companies' Act.

What is a Company?

Companies are an invention of Acts of Parliament. During the 19th Century entrepreneurs were forming businesses at a very fast rate but it was felt that their growth could be further increased if two obstacles could be removed. The first problem was raising sufficient funds to start (for Sole Traders and Partnerships) often lacked sufficient capital and found it difficult to raise further capital from outside sources. The second main problem was that the owners were responsible for their business's debts. A business failure could therefore lead to bankruptcy, making many people reluctant to invest in commercial ventures.

In 1855 Parliament sought to remove these two obstacles by creating a new business organisation called the limited company. This meant that the members' liability for company debts would not extend beyond the amount of their shareholdings. This made company shares an attractive form of investment for, although there was risk involved, a shareholder could only lose the monetary value of the shares. Companies could now raise funds from investors who were prepared to accept a limited risk in return for what they considered to be an acceptable return.

Another advantage for the shareholders is that they can delegate the management function to directors who will manage the company on their behalf. The directors are appointed by the shareholders at the firm's annual general meeting and companies are required by law to hold such a meeting of shareholders.

The privilege of limited liability is subject to strict rules and regulations, as laid down in the Companies' Acts. These are designed to protect investors and lenders of money who are not allowed to sue the owners in the case of a company defaulting on its debts.

Different Types of Company

The 1985 Companies' Act states that any two persons, associated for a lawful purpose, may form an incorporated company with or without limited liabilty. The word incorporation means that a company has most of the benefits, rights and responsibilities of an individual in law and is often referred to as being a legal entity. This means that it has an identity of its own apart from the people who own it. This allows the company to make contracts in its own name, employ people and own property. There are two types of company as defined by the Companies' Act 1985. These are private companies and public companies.

A Private Company Limited By Shares

This is the most common type of company and is favoured by many small businesses as it has no minimum requirement for issued share capital and needs only two shareholders (one of whom must be a director). The owners' liability is limited to the amount of share capital its members have agreed to pay, but the company is not allowed to advertise the sale of its shares to the general public.

A Public Company

In order to be a public company, it must be incorporated with a share capital of at least the authorised minimum £50,000 and at least a quarter of this must be paid up when the company is formed. Such companies may raise capital by selling their shares on a recognised stock exchange and have the letters plc in their title.

Before either of these companies can be formed, certain documents must be filed with the Registrar of Companies. The two main documents are the Memorandum of Association and the Articles of Association.

Memorandum Of Association

This is a document drawn up by a solicitor which governs the company's dealings with the outside world. It must contain the following information:

a) the name of the company

b) its registered office

c) the objectives of the company

d) the amount of share capital

e) a statement that the liability of its members is limited

f) the maximum limit of the company's borrowing powers.

Articles of Association

This document covers the internal constitution of the company and must contain the following information:

a) the rights of different types of shareholders

b) how shares can be issued and transferred

c) when company meetings must be held

d) the powers of the directors

Once these documents have been submitted, together with the other necessary information, the Registrar will issue a Certificate of Incorporation which gives the company its legal identity. The certificate will show the date of incorporation and the company name. Once a private company has received its certificate of incorporation, it can commence trading, but a public company wishing to raise funds must first issue a prospectus outlining its assets, past profitability and its future prospects so that subscribers can decide whether or not to invest. As soon as the prospectus has been registered and approved, a Certificate of trading will be issued by the Registrar of Companies and the firm can commence trading.

The Published Accounts of Companies

Every private and public company must keep accounting records which will give a true and fair view of the company's financial position. Once a year it must have its accounts audited and it must send a copy to every shareholder and debenture holder before the company's annual meeting. A copy must also be kept at its registered office.

The 1985 Companies' Act states what information must be included and which accounting statements must be prepared. All companies must publish a profit and loss account, a balance sheet and a director's report. This is the minimum information which must be published, but many public companies use this opportunity as a public relations exercise and publish relevant information about their company, its products and staff. By doing this they seek to make their shareholders, employees and other interested parties more aware about the company and its future developments.

Private companies rarely produce more than the statutory minimum information and are of little interest to outside parties because of the small scale of the business. Larger private companies employing more than five hundred people may attract more attention if it is thought likely that they will consider a stock market listing. If this is the case, the accounts will often be more akin to those of a public company for the directors will wish to gain as much valuable publicity as possible before bringing their company to the Stock Market.

Consolidated Accounts

Companies often expand by purchasing other companies. Sometimes they will purchase all of the shares, in which case the other company becomes a wholly-owned subsidiary. In other cases, a controlling interest, (over 50% of the voting shares) or a percentage of the shares, will be acquired.

In such cases the accounts must reflect the profits earned by the subsidiaries, and the assets and liabilities which they have. There are two ways that this accounting information could be shown. The first is called the Entity Concept, which treats the minority interests as co-owners and the latter is called the Parent Company Concept, which regards the holding company as the main shareholder.

In Britain the accounts are always prepared under the Parent Company Concept, and the Standard Statement of Accounting Practice 14, (SSAP14) states that, when preparing Consolidated Company accounts they must be prepared to show a true and fair view from the viewpoint of the shareholders of the holding company.

Most large PLC's own subsidiaries, and so their accounts always reflect the fact that their profits and assets derive from the holding and subsidiary companies.

The Profit and Loss Account

Companies are not required to publish details of all of their expenses against profit but must summarise the main items. In this way, the owners and outside interested parties have access to useful information, whilst not forcing the company to publish material which could be useful to competitors or costly to produce. The following information must be disclosed and the 1985 Companies Act allows two different formats to be used. Whichever one is adopted, it is helpful to classify the information under four different headings as this makes it easier to remember.

1) Income

The company must provide details about its:

a) Turnover (sales)

b) Income from investments

c) Rental income received (rents received)

d) Profit or loss on the sale of fixed assets

2) Expenses Against Profit

a) Staff costs

b) Directors' emoluments (income)

c) Employees' emoluments

d) Interest payments

e) Hire of plant

f) Auditing fees

g) Depreciation

h) Reduction in the value of investments (write-downs)

3) Appropriation of Profit (How Profit is Used)

a) Taxation (Corporation Tax)

b) Reduction in goodwill

c) Transfer to reserves

d) Dividends paid

4) Notes to The Accounts

a) Extraordinary items and abnormal items

b) Changes in accounting procedures

This information will now be considered in greater detail by studying the two formats prescribed by the 1985 Companies' Act. Format One is the most commonly used and shows cost to sales, whereas Format Two shows changes in stock.

Format One

1. Turnover
2. Cost of Sales
3. Gross Profit or Loss
4. Distribution Costs
5. Administration expenses
6. Other operating income
7. Income from shares in group companies
8. Income from shares in related companies
9. Income from other fixed asset investments
10. Other interest receivable and similar income
11. Amounts written off investments
12. Interest payable and similar charges
13. Tax on profit or loss on ordinary activities
14. Profit or loss on ordinary activities after taxation
15. Extraordinary income
16. Extraordinary charges
17. Extraordinary profit or loss
18. Tax on extraordinary profit or loss
19. Other taxes not shown under the above items
20. Profit or loss for the financial year

Format Two

1. Turnover
2. Change in stocks of finished goods and in work in progress
3. Own work capitalised
4. Other operating income
5. (a) Raw materials and consumables
   (b) Other external charges
6. Staff costs:
   (a) wages and salaries
   (b) social security costs
   (c) other pension costs
7. (a) Depreciation and other amounts written off tangible and intangible fixed assets
   (b) Exceptional amounts written off current assets
8. Other operating charges
9. Income from shares in group companies
10. Income from shares in related companies
11. Income from other fixed asset investments
12. Other interest receivable and similar charges
13. Amounts written off investments
14. Interest payable and similar charges
15. Tax on profit or loss on ordinary activities
16. Profit or loss on ordinary activities after taxation
17. Extraordinary income
18. Extraordinary charges
19. Extraordinary profit or loss
20. Tax on extraordinary profit or loss
21. Other taxes not shown under the above items
22. Profit or loss for the financial year

Example of the Boots Company plc Group Profit and Loss Account for the year ended 31 March 1990.
Explanation of the Information Contained in the Profit and Loss Account.

	Notes	1990 £m	1989 £m
Turnover	2	**3381·4**	2704·4
Trading profit	3	**386·5**	283·0
Net interest	4	**(26·9)**	23·7
Servicing cost of convertible capital bonds	22	**(1·6)**	—
Profit on ordinary activities before taxation	2	**358·0**	306·7
Taxation on profit on ordinary activities	5	**(112·6)**	(96·8)
Profit on ordinary activities after taxation		**245·4**	209·9
Minority interests		**(·6)**	(·8)
		244·8	209·1
Extraordinary items after taxation	6	**(·9)**	(5·7)
Profit for the financial year attributable to shareholders	7	**243·9**	203·4
Dividends	8	**(107·8)**	(92·6)
Profit retained		**136·1**	110·8
Earnings per share	9	**25·5p**	22·6p

1. Turnover:

The total sales (net of returns & taxation including UK VAT) made during the year must be shown, together with information about the source of the sales and the geographical markets where they were made. This latter information may be omitted if the directors believe that it would be against the company's interest, in which case a note must be made in the accounts stating the reason for non-disclosure.

Example From Boots plc Annual Accounts 1990

	1990		1989	
	Turnover £m	Profit £m	Turnover £m	Profit £m
Pharmaceuticals Division				
UK (including exports)	324·6	35·5	315·4	37·3
Overseas	293·8	75·6	244·5	58·0
Intra-divisional	(34·6)	—	(35·3)	—
	583·8	111·1	524·6	95·3
Boots The Chemists Division	2268·9	190·0	2084·0	151·0
Retail Division				
Halfords	170·6	12·0	—	—
Payless	139·9	11·8	—	—
A G Stanley	70·2	4·7	—	—
Boots Opticians	57·1	2·2	49·3	3·6
Childrens World	42·3	(6·4)	26·6	(6·5)
Overseas	59·2	(·3)	145·2	1·5
	539·3	24·0	221·1	(1·4)
Property Division				
Net rents	—	39·2	—	34·4
Profit from property sales	—	15·2	—	11·7
	—	54·4	—	46·1
Inter-divisional	(130·4)	—	(125·3)	—
Net interest and unallocated items	—	(29·8)	—	15·7
	3261·6	349·7	2704·4	306·7
Discontinued operations	119·8	8·3	—	—
	3381·4	358·0	2704·4	306·7

The results of the former Ward White businesses have been included from 22nd August 1989 and amount to £39·0m before interest. The Property Division was established with effect from 1st April 1989 to manage and develop the group's UK property portfolio. Accordingly, the 1989 results have been restated on a comparable basis. Results from discontinued operations relate to the former US Ward White businesses now sold, or in the process of sale.

Turnover by geographical destination and related profits are as follows:

	1990		1989	
	Turnover £m	Profit £m	Turnover £m	Profit £m
UK	2846·6	289·7	2254·4	221·2
Europe	187·8	13·5	157·3	12·1
US	258·4	74·9	111·9	46·1
Other Americas	4·9	·5	100·4	2·9
Rest of World	83·7	7·8	80·4	7·5
	3381·4	386·4	2704·4	289·8
Share of results of related companies	—	1·4	—	1·2
Net interest and unallocated items	—	(29·8)	—	15·7
	3381·4	358·0	2704·4	306·7

Turnover comprises sales to external customers excluding sales taxes.

2. Investment Income

If a company has surplus funds, it may choose to invest them in other companies' shares and fixed interest loan stocks or in Government Securities. If the shares are quoted on a recognised stock exchange, they are referred to as listed investments and, if not, they are called unlisted investments. Short term deposits refers to cash held in interest-bearing deposits where the money can be withdrawn relatively quickly.

NET INTEREST

Interest receivable:		
Listed investments	4·1	7·0
Short term deposits	21·2	24·3
	25·3	31·3

3. Rental Income

If the company owns any property which it has let during the year, the amount received in rent must be shown as a separate category in the profit and loss account.

4. Profit or Loss on the Sale of a Fixed Asset

During the financial year, the company may decide to sell certain fixed assets which are surplus to requirements. The profit and loss account must show any profit or loss recorded on the sale of the asset.

Example from Boots plc Annual Accounts 1990

Property Division				
Net rents	—	39·2	—	34·4
Profit from property sales	—	15·2	—	11·7
	—	54·4	—	46·1

5. Staff Costs, Directors' Emoluments and Employee Emoluments.

Staff Costs

The amount paid in wages and salaries to staff, together with social security payments (National Insurance and State Pensions) and any contributions to company pension schemes, must be disclosed.

The average number of persons employed by the group during the year was as follows:

	1990	1989
Pharmaceuticals Division	9,491	9,666
Boots The Chemists Division	55,168	53,873
Retail Division	13,077	5,206
Property Division	46	42
Central	866	1,180
Total employees	78,648	69,967

Total number of persons employed by the group at 31st March 1990 was 84,165 (1989 68,828).

The aggregate payroll cost was as follows:

	£m	£m
Wages and salaries (including profit earning bonus of £28·0m) (1989 £22·3m)	539·1	449·7
Social security costs	45·4	39·9
Other pension costs	13·8	17·1
	598·3	506·7

Directors' Emoluments

The accounts must show the total amount paid to directors inclusive of expenses, pension contributions and benefits, such as company cars. The amount of money paid as pension income to former directors from company pension schemes, together with any amount paid to a director for "loss of office", must also be shown.

If the amount paid to directors exceeds £60,000 the following information must be shown:

a) the number of directors whose emoluments fall within the range £0-£5,000, £5,001-£10,000, £10,001-£15,000 and so on in bands of £5,000.

b) the chair's emoluments

c) the emoluments of the highest paid director, if they are not the chair, their name does not have to be disclosed.

d) the number of directors who asked not to be paid any emoluments during the year.

The following remuneration of directors and senior employees is included in the aggregate payroll cost.

	1990 £000	1989 £000
i Remuneration of directors:		
Fees	54	44
Other remuneration	2373	2105
Payment to former director	200	6
	2627	2155

ii The remuneration of the chairman excluding pension contributions was £162,000 (1989 £203,000)

iii The remuneration of the highest paid director excluding pension contributions was £383,000 (1989 £307,000)

iv An analysis of remuneration of directors (except where duties were discharged mainly outside the UK) and UK employees earning over £30,000 in the year, is shown overleaf, excluding pension contributions:

Employee Emoluments

The number of employees employed mainly in UK earning over £30,000 a year in bands of £5,000.

	Numbers Directors		Numbers Employees			Numbers Directors		Numbers Employees	
	1990	1989	1990	1989		1990	1989	1990	1989
£380,001 — 385,000	1	—			£95,001 — 100,000	—	—	5	—
£305,001 — 310,000	—	1			£90,001 — 95,000	—	—	4	1
£215,001 — 220,000	1	—			£85,001 — 90,000	—	—	7	3
£200,001 — 205,000	—	1			£80,001 — 85,000	—	—	8	4
£190,001 — 195,000	1	—			£75,001 — 80,000	—	—	7	5
£170,001 — 175,000	1	—			£70,001 — 75,000	—	—	9	8
£160,001 — 165,000	1	—			£65,001 — 70,000	—	—	5	8
£155,001 — 160,000	—	1			£60,001 — 65,000	—	—	7	6
£150,001 — 155,000	—	1			£55,001 — 60,000	—	—	19	2
£145,001 — 150,000	1	—			£50,001 — 55,000	—	—	29	11
£140,001 — 145,000	1	—			£45,001 — 50,000	1	—	30	25
£135,001 — 140,000	2	1			£40,001 — 45,000	—	—	67	38
£130,001 — 135,000	—	1			£35,001 — 40,000	—	—	144	83
£115,001 — 120,000	—	2			£30,001 — 35,000	1	1	367	174
£110,001 — 115,000	—	1	1	—	£15,001 — 20,000	1	1		
£105,001 — 110,000	—	1	—	1	£10,001 — 15,000	4	3		

6. Interest Payments

If money is borrowed, interest will have to be paid on the amount borrowed and the total interest payments made must be shown.

Interest payable:

Repayable within five years:		
Bank and other loans	**(49·0)**	(7·4)
Interest capitalised	**2·6**	—
Loans repayable after five years	**(5·8)**	(·2)
	(52·2)	(7·6)
	(26·9)	23·7

7. Hire of Plant

If any machinery has been hired during the year, the amount paid must be disclosed. During the last year the Boots Company plc did not hire any plant.

8. Auditors' Fees

All companies must have their accounts audited. This means that their books of accounts must, with a few exceptions, be checked by either a Chartered or Certified Accountant. The accounts must then be signed by the auditors, subject to any qualification, that the accounts show a true and fair view of the company's financial position.

AUDITORS' REPORT

to the members of The Boots Company PLC.

We have audited the accounts on pages 28 to 50 in accordance with Auditing Standards. In our opinion the accounts give a true and fair view of the state of affairs of the company and of the group at 31st March 1990 and of the profit and source and application of funds of the group for the year then ended and have been properly prepared in accordance with the Companies Act 1985.

KPMG Peat Marwick McLintock
Chartered Accountants, Birmingham
7th June 1990

THE BOOTS COMPANY PLC

9. Taxation

Companies pay Corporation Tax on their profits and are also liable for Capital Gains tax arising out of any monetary gain from the sale of a fixed asset. Firms may mitigate their tax liability by claiming capital allowances from their investment in fixed assets. Deferred taxation reconciles the notional tax in the accounting profit with the actual tax assessment on the taxable profit because not all expenses are tax deductible. The firm may also be able to affect its tax payments by using tax allowances, such as capital allowance relief from investing in fixed assets.

	1990 £m	1989 £m
The charge on the profit of the year consists of:		
UK corporation tax at 35%	**96·6**	93·9
Deferred taxation	**3·4**	(3·4)
Relief for overseas taxation	**(4·4)**	(5·2)
Total UK taxation	**95·6**	85·3
Overseas taxation	**15·0**	9·3
Overseas deferred taxation	**1·5**	1·6
Share of taxation of related companies	**·5**	·6
	112·6	96·8
Unprovided deferred taxation in respect of the year:		
Capital allowances	**3·6**	6·2
Capital gains taxation	**2·0**	2·5
Other items	**2·5**	(2·4)
	8·1	6·3

10. Goodwill

Goodwill arises when assets are bought for more than their market value. The difference between the purchase price and the asset value is called goodwill. Although goodwill is shown as an asset in the balance sheet, firms often seek to reduce the value of this intangible asset by writing it off against profit. The profit and loss account must show any amount written off for goodwill.

11. Reserves

A reserve is created whenever profit is kept within the company and is not distributed as dividends to the shareholders. The amount transferred to the reserves must be shown in the profit and loss account and will be discussed further when we look at company balance sheets.

12. Dividends

Dividends represent a share of the company's profits and are paid to the shareholders. There are two types of dividend which may be paid by companies. Preference Dividends are paid to the holders of preference shares and these are fixed in advance as a certain percentage, so the holder always knows the amount of money which will be received. Ordinary dividends, on the other hand, vary. If profits are good, the dividend may be increased and, if poor, they may be reduced. The amount paid will either be shown in pence per ordinary share, or as a percentage of the company's issued ordinary share capital.

Today preference shares are less common than they once were. The main reason being that, as they carry a fixed rate of dividend, they are really more akin to a loan stock and so their value fluctuates according to market interest rates. Most preference shares were issued a long time ago and now pay a small return compared with current interest rates.This has led to their owners seeing a fall in the capital value of the shares, which has made them unpopular with investors. Boots plc has no prefence shares and so only pays a dividend to its ordinary shareholders.

Large companies, such as Boots plc, often pay an interim dividend before they know their final year's profit and then a final payment once the total profit has been ascertained. This means that a shareholder will receive two payments during the year. If this was not done, a shareholder would have to wait until after the company's year end before receiving a dividend payment.

In the financial year ending 31 March 1990, Boots plc paid an interim dividend of 3.85p per ordinary share and a final dividend of 7.15p, making a total payment to shareholders during the year of 11p per ordinary share held.

13. Extraordinary and Exceptional Items

An item is classified as extraordinary when it does not relate to the ordinary activities of the business. In order to be classified as extraordinary, it must derive from events or transactions outside the ordinary activities of the business, be material and must not be expected to reoccur frequently. A good example of an extraordinary item is the profit or loss arising from the sale of a fixed asset.

An exceptional item arises out of the ordinary trading activities of the business. The sum involved must be material and so its non-disclosure would mean that the accounts did not give a true and fair view of the business's financial position. An example of an exceptional item would be reorganisation costs.

EXTRAORDINARY ITEMS AFTER TAXATION

Loss on closure and disposal of businesses	(·9)	(9·7)
Profit on disposal of businesses	—	3·0
	(·9)	(6·7)
Taxation	—	1·0
	(·9)	(5·7)

14. Changes in Accounting Procedures

A note must be made to the accounts if a change has been made to the accounting procedures in previous years, such as a change in the method of calculating depreciation or valuing closing stocks, and the effect of the change.

Company Balance Sheet

A company balance sheet follows the same principles as any balance sheet in that it shows company assets and liabilities. Companies however, have to show their assets and liabilities in greater detail and the 1985 Companies' Act specifies what must be shown and in what order.

Companies may chose either the vertical or horizontal method of presentation. Today most companies produce their annual accounts in A4 format and therefore choose the vertical format. The horizontal format is now considered old fashioned and in our example we will use Boots plc which has chosen the vertical method of presentation. If the other method is chosen, the information will be the same, although the final figures will differ. This is because the vertical balance sheet will show the net assets equalling capital, whereas the horizontal balance sheet will show total assets and total liabilities. Both answers are correct and the difference in final figures is due solely to the method of presentation adopted.

Balance Sheet Format as defined by the Companies' Act 1985

Balance sheet - format 1

A.   **Called up share capital not paid**

B.   **Fixed assets**
I   **Intangible assets**
    1.   Development costs
    2.   Concessions, patents, licences, trade marks and similar rights and assets.
    3.   Goodwill
    4.   Payments on account
II   **Tangible assets**
    1.   Land and buildings
    2.   Plant and machinery
    3.   Fixtures, fittings, tools and equipment
    4.   Payments on account and assets in course of construction
III   **Investments**
    1.   Shares in group companies
    2.   Loans to group companies
    3.   Shares in related companies
    4.   Loans to related companies
    5.   Other investments other than loans
    6.   Other loans
    7.   Own shares

C.   **Current assets**
I   **Stocks**
    1.   Raw materials and consumables
    2.   Work in progress
    3.   Finished goods and goods for resale
    4.   Payments on account
II   **Debtors**
    1.   Trade debtors
    2.   Amounts owned by group companies
    3.   Amounts owned by related companies
    4.   Other debtors
    5.   Called up share capital not paid
    6.   Prepayments and accrued income
III   **Investments**
    1.   Shares in group companies
    2.   Own shares
    3.   Other investments
IV   **Cash at bank and in hand**

D   **Prepayments and Accrued income**

E   **Creditors: amounts falling due within one year**
1. Debenture loans
2. Bank loans and overdrafts
3. Payments received on account
4. Trade creditors
5. Bills of exchange payable
6. Amounts owed to group companies
7. Amounts owed to related companies
8. Other creditors including taxation and social security
9. Accruals and deferred income

F   **Net current assets (liabilities)**

G   **Total assets less current liabilities**

H   **Creditors: amounts falling due after more than one year**
1. Debenture loans
2. Bank loans and overdrafts
3. Payments received on account
4. Trade creditors
6. Amounts owed to group companies
7. Amounts owed to related companies
8. Other creditors including taxation and social security
9. Accruals and deferred income

I   **Provisions for liabilities and charges**
1. Pensions and similar obligations
2. Taxation, including deferred taxation
3. Other provisions

J   **Accruals and deferred income**

K   **Capital and reserves**
I   **Called up share capital**
II   **Share premium account**
III   **Revaluation reserve**
IV   **Other reserves**
1. Capital redemption reserve
2. Reserve for own shares
3. Reserves provided for by the articles of association
4. Other reserves
V   **Profit and loss account**

Example of the Boots Balance Sheet as at 31 March 1990

	Notes	Group 1990 £m	Group 1989 £m	Parent 1990 £m	Parent 1989 £m
Fixed assets					
Intangible assets	10	**37·3**	5·6	**10·3**	5·2
Tangible assets	11	**1513·9**	1277·0	**163·0**	214·0
Investments	12	**3·5**	3·3	**1122·6**	290·3
		1554·7	1285·9	**1295·9**	509·5
Current assets					
Stocks	13	**532·8**	405·9	**157·0**	161·3
Debtors	14	**319·1**	212·2	**422·1**	385·0
Investments	15	**28·9**	324·6	**1·9**	266·6
Cash at bank and in hand		**5·2**	4·2	**·1**	·1
		886·0	946·9	**581·1**	813·0
Creditors: amounts falling due within one year	16	**(952·4)**	(553·4)	**(672·9)**	(430·6)
Net current (liabilities)/assets		**(66·4)**	393·5	**(91·8)**	382·4
Total assets less current liabilities		**1488·3**	1679·4	**1204·1**	891·9
Creditors: amounts falling due after more than one year	17	**(165·0)**	(24·3)	**(324·2)**	(41·4)
Provisions for liabilities and charges	18	**(36·1)**	(16·4)	**(8·3)**	(14·4)
		1287·2	1638·7	**871·6**	836·1
Capital and reserves					
Called up share capital	19	**245·0**	231·7	**245·0**	231·7
Share premium	20	**22·0**	14·0	**22·0**	14·0
Revaluation reserve	20	**561·6**	571·0	—	32·7
Profit and loss account	20	**302·0**	820·6	**604·6**	557·7
		1130·6	1637·3	**871·6**	836·1
Convertible capital bonds	22	**155·0**	—	—	—
Minority interests		**1·6**	1·4	—	—
		1287·2	1638·7	**871·6**	836·1

Approved by the board

Robert N Gunn
James Blyth } Directors
7th June 1990

Explanation of the Boots Balance Sheet

Fixed Assets

The Companies' Act distinguishes between three different types of fixed assets- intangible assets, fixed assets and investments. An asset is classified as a fixed asset, if the company intends to keep it for trading purposes for a time period greater than one year.

Intangible Assets

These are assets which represent money spent by the company to acquire a long term benefit. They are called intangible assets because they lack a physical identity. Goodwill, development costs, patents and trademarks are all good examples of intangible assets. These assets must be shown in the balance sheet at cost less depreciation. If any fixed asset has been revalued during the year, a note must be made to the accounts and the name and qualification of the valuer, together with the method used to value the asset.

Example of Boot s Intangible Assets
Note a

INTANGIBLE FIXED ASSETS

Patents, trade marks and other product rights acquired.

	Group £m	Parent £m
Cost		
At 31st March 1989	7·3	6·8
Additions	33·1	5·9
At 31st March 1990	40·4	12·7
Depreciation		
At 31st March 1989	1·7	1·6
Depreciation for year	1·4	·8
At 31st March 1990	3·1	2·4
Net book value at 31st March 1990	37·3	10·3

Non depreciable trade marks and associated rights held by a subsidiary amounted to £12·2n (1989 £—m).

Tangible Assets

These are the long term assets of the business which have not been purchased primarily for resale and which are needed for carrying out the company's business. In a balance sheet they are shown in order of permanence. These assets must be shown at their cost price or valuation, less any amount charged for depreciation. The accounts will then show the asset's net book value, which is unlikely to be its market value because, as we have already seen, the accounts are prepared under the going concern concept. Examples of fixed assets are land and buildings, plant and machinery and motor vehicles.

Example of Boots' Fixed Assets
Note b

	Land and buildings £m	Plant and machinery £m	Fixtures, fittings, tools and equipment £m	Payments on account and assets in course of construction £m	Total £m
Parent					
Cost or valuation					
At 31st March 1989	94·9	133·6	105·0	6·8	340·3
Additions	·7	12·7	14·6	1·1	29·1
Disposals	(·3)	(9·3)	(3·3)	—	(12·9)
Transfer to Property Division	(44·3)	(·4)	(6·3)	—	(51·0)
Reclassifications and transfers	(4·5)	(5·7)	1·6	(4·0)	(12·6)
At 31st March 1990	46·5	130·9	111·6	3·9	292·9
Depreciation					
At 31st March 1989	14·2	60·6	51·5	—	126·3
Depreciation for year	1·2	8·6	10·7	—	20·5
Disposals	—	(6·5)	(2·4)	—	(8·9)
Transfer to Property Division	—	(·1)	(2·8)	—	(2·9)
Transfers	(1·4)	(3·3)	(·4)	—	(5·1)
At 31st March 1990	14·0	59·3	56·6	—	129·9
Net book value at 31st March 1990	32·5	71·6	55·0	3·9	163·0

	Group		Parent	
	1990 £m	1989 £m	1990 £m	1989 £m
Net book value of land and buildings comprises:				
Freehold	771·1	728·8	32·5	78·9
Long leasehold (more than 50 years unexpired)	143·1	128·3	—	·5
Short leasehold	51·4	54·6	—	1·3
	965·6	911·7	32·5	80·7
Analysis of cost or valuation:				
Cost	1102·2	752·5	285·1	284·2
Independent valuation 1989	803·5	818·5	—	48·3
1965	·9	1·1	—	—
1959	·1	·1	—	—
1958	7·8	7·8	7·8	7·8
	1914·5	1580·0	292·9	340·3
Net book value of tangible fixed assets under the historical cost convention	947·5	701·0	162·3	180·2

On 1st April 1989 the Property Division was formed and ownership of certain freehold, long leasehold and short leasehold properties of the parent company was transferred to Boots Properties PLC.

73

FIXED ASSETS—INVESTMENTS

	Related companies £m
Group	
Share of net tangible assets at 31st March 1989	3·3
Share of results for the year	·9
Dividends paid	(·3)
Disposals	(·2)
Currency adjustments	(·2)
Share of net tangible assets at 31st March 1990	3·5

The cost of investments in related companies is £·5m (1989 £·5m).

	Shares in subsidiaries £m	Loans to subsidiaries £m	Shares in related companies £m	Total £m
Parent				
Cost				
At 31st March 1989	247·6	296·6	·5	544·7
Additions	836·4	85·6	—	922·0
Repayments	—	(75·7)	—	(75·7)
Currency adjustments	—	8·9	—	8·9
At 31st March 1990	1084·0	315·4	·5	1399·9
Provision				
At 31st March 1989	127·2	127·1	·1	254·4
Movement	102·9	(79·9)	(·1)	22·9
At 31st March 1990	230·1	47·2	—	277·3
Net book value at 31st March 1990	853·9	268·2	·5	1122·6

Investments

Investments refers to paper assets such as shares, loan stocks or other fiduciary issues. It is the length of time which the company intends to hold these investments which determine whether or not they are fixed assets. If the intention is to keep them longer than twelve months, they are classified as fixed assets and, if they are to be held for a shorter period, they are classified as current assets.

Note c

Listed investments	·8	64·8	—	64·7
Short term deposits	28·1	259·8	1·9	201·9
	28·9	324·6	1·9	266·6
Market value of investments listed on The International Stock Exchange	·8	65·1	—	65·0

Current Assets

These are the short term trading assets of the company. They are shown in reverse order of liquidity with the most illiquid shown first.

Stock

If the company is a manufacturing business, the accounts must show the amount of raw materials, work in progress and the stock of finished goods. A retailing business will just show its stock of goods for resale. The stocks must be valued according to the prudence concept, which means that they will be valued at the lower of cost or net realizable value (market price).

Example

Note d

	Group		Parent	
	1990	1989	**1990**	1989
	£m	£m	**£m**	£m
Manufacturing:				
Raw materials	**29·0**	31·4	**17·3**	19·1
Work in progress	**17·3**	19·9	**11·2**	14·7
Finished goods	**34·8**	33·8	**10·8**	9.7
	81·1	85·1	**39·3**	43·5
Retailing	**443·7**	320·8	**117·7**	117·8
Properties under development	**8·0**	—	**—**	—
	532·8	405·9	**157·0**	161·3

Debtors

The amount of money owed to the company within the next twelve months by its trade debtors must be shown, together with any money owed by related companies. This could be net of provision for doubtful debts and discounts allowable, but we do not know as there is no need to disclose this. If the money is to be repaid later than one year from the balance sheet date, the amount must be shown under a separate heading. Examples of such debtors would be money owed by related companies or loans made to directors.

Example
Note e

Falling due within one year:				
Trade debtors	**141·6**	128·1	**85·9**	82·2
Owed by subsidiaries	**—**	—	**225·0**	252·6
Owed by related companies	**·1**	—	**·1**	—
Other debtors	**102·8**	26·0	**18·0**	8·9
Prepayments and accrued income	**40·5**	30·2	**12·3**	16·3
	285·0	184·3	**341·3**	360·0
Falling due after more than one year:				
Owed by subsidiaries	**—**	—	**53·2**	—
Advance corporation tax	**23·4**	20·1	**23·4**	20·1
Other debtors	**10·7**	7·8	**4·2**	4·9
	319·1	212·2	**422·1**	385·0

Investments

Any money held short term which will be used by the company during the coming twelve months is classified as an investment and shown under the current assets section in the balance sheet.

Example
Note f

Listed investments	**·8**	64·8	**—**	64·7
Short term deposits	**28·1**	259·8	**1·9**	201·9
	28·9	324·6	**1·9**	266·6
Market value of investments listed on The International Stock Exchange	**·8**	65·1	**—**	65·0

Liabilities

The balance sheet must show liabilities due within twelve months and those due after twelve months.

Creditors Requiring Repayment Within 12 Months

Any money which must be repaid during the next twelve months must be shown in the balance sheet. Examples are trade creditors, bank overdraft, bills of exchange payable, dividends, taxation and any other liability which must be repaid within the coming twelve months.

Example

Note g

	Group		Parent	
	1990 £m	1989 £m	1990 £m	1989 £m
Bank loans and overdrafts	91·3	96·1	71·5	75·8
Bills of exchange—bank acceptances	65·8	—	65·8	—
—trade	5·6	4·3	·1	·4
Commercial paper	107·6	—	107·6	—
Trade creditors	294·5	148·7	203·9	122·8
Due to subsidiaries	—	—	34·0	46·3
Corporation tax	78·2	72·4	14·3	27·4
Advance corporation tax	34·9	30·1	34·9	30·1
Taxation and social security (including value added and other sales taxes)	31·6	23·4	18·9	20·6
Other creditors	94·6	81·7	37·4	36·2
Accruals	78·2	36·5	14·4	10·8
Proposed dividend	70·1	60·2	70·1	60·2
	952·4	553·4	672·9	430·6

Overdrafts of certain subsidiaries amounting to £·6m at 31st March 1990 (1989 £1·0m) were secured on the assets of those subsidiaries.

Creditors' Falling Due After 1 Year

This section will generally show the long term loans which the company owes, as well as payments for taxation and creditors where the amount paid will be settled after one year from the balance sheet date.

Companies can raise additional funds by selling long term fixed debt securities to investors. The investor is paid a given rate of interest during the life of the bond and, on redemption, will receive repayment of the loan. These loans may be secured on the company's assets, or they may be unsecured, in which case an investor cannot sell company assets in the event of the firm defaulting on its debts. Examples of such loans are debentures and secured or unsecured loan stock. The balance sheet must show the amount of the loan, the interest rate payable and the date the loan must be repaid, the interest rate and the date of redemption.

Example
Note h

Unsecured loans.				
Variable rate notes 1999	**36·7**	12·3	**36·7**	12·3
US$ 175m 9% bonds 1997	**107·4**	—	**107·4**	—
7¾% stock 1988/93	**5·7**	5·7	**5·7**	5·7
Variable rate notes 1993	**1·7**	—	**—**	—
Variable rate notes 1992	**3·2**	—	**—**	—
Foreign currency bank loans	**1·0**	·8	**—**	—
Due to subsidiaries	**—**	—	**172·6**	21·6
Other creditors	**4·5**	3·0	**1·8**	1·8
Accruals	**4·8**	2·5	**—**	—
	165·0	24·3	**324·2**	41·4

The 9% bonds are redeemable at their principal amount in 1997. The 7¾% stock is repayable on or before 30th September 1993 at the option of the company. The variable rate notes 1999 are repayable at the option of the holder on or before 1st August 1999. Interest on these notes is payable at the prevailing London Inter Bank Offered Rate. Other creditors are repayable within 5 years.

79

Provisions for Liabilities and Charges

Any amounts of money (provisions) set aside for pension or tax must be disclosed in the balance sheet.

Example
Note i

	Deferred taxation £m	Group Acquisition provisions £m	Total £m	Parent Deferred taxation £m
At 31st March 1989	16·4	—	16·4	14·4
Reclassification	—	5·6	5·6	—
Currency adjustments	(·2)	—	(·2)	—
Acquisitions	(11·5)	44·2	32·7	—
Expenditure	—	(22·3)	(22·3)	—
Profit and loss account	4·9	—	4·9	(6·1)
Revaluation reserve	(1·0)	—	(1·0)	—
At 31st March 1990	8·6	27·5	36·1	8·3

In view of the disclosure of the movements in acquisition provisions now required by SSAP 22 and dealt with in note 21, provisions amounting to £5·6m included within creditors last year have been reclassified as acquisition provisions.

	1990 £m	1989 £m	1990 £m	1989 £m
Analysis of deferred taxation provision:				
Capital allowances	23·6	18·5	7·4	10·4
Capital gains taxation	3·0	4·0	—	—
Other items:				
UK	(12·1)	1·1	·9	4·0
Overseas	(5·9)	(7·2)	—	—
	8·6	16·4	8·3	14·4
Unprovided deferred taxation:				
Capital allowances	60·1	56·5	28·5	26·8
Capital gains rolled over	42·9	35·0	·4	·4
Other items	(·2)	(2·7)	—	—
	102·8	88·8	28·9	27·2

It is not anticipated that any significant taxation will become payable on the revaluation surplus, as taxation on gains on properties sold in the normal course of business is expected to be deferred indefinitely.

Share Capital

The shareholders are the owners of the business and the amount of share capital which they have subscribed must be stated in the balance sheet. There are a number of terms which relate to share capital and these are now explained.

Ordinary Shares

The owners of these shares are entitled to receive a share of the profits after all expenses have been paid. The amount of dividend will vary according to the profits of the firm. Ordinary shareholders are usually entitled to voting rights, although some companies do issue non-voting ordinary shares. If this is done, the shares are generally distinguished by calling one the A shares and the others the B shares. The voting shares are normally more expensive because they allow the holder to vote on issues affecting the company.

Preference Shares

Preference shares also form part of the company's capital. The holders of these shares receive a fixed rate of dividend, once all the expenses have been paid, and often enjoy preferential rights over the ordinary shareholders with respect to dividend payments and when the company is wound up. If the shares are cumulative preference shares, the holders have the right to have any unpaid dividend paid to them as soon as the firm has remade sufficient profits. In such cases, the preference shareholders will receive their dividend, even if other shareholders receive nothing.

Lastly, a firm may have issued participating preference shares. These entitle the holder to receive an extra dividend, once the ordinary share holders have received more than a stated return on the capital and the preference dividend has been paid.

Authorised Capital

This is the amount of share capital a company is authorised to raise when it is first incorporated. The company's memorandum of association must state the number, value and type of shares which the company intends to issue. Once the company is registered, this becomes its authorised share capital, and the amount must be shown in the balance sheet or in the notes to the accounts.

Issued Capital

This is the amount of share capital which the company has issued to shareholders. The amount of issued capital may be less than the authorised capital if the directors believe that they do not yet need to raise the amount of share capital they were authorised to issue.

Called Up Capital

When shares are issued, the purchase price is often not payable in one amount. By allowing the shareholder to pay by instalments, it allows the investor time to either earn extra income or liquidate other investments. When a company asks for the next instalment, it is said to be making a call. The amount of called up and fully paid up capital is the same as a company's issued capital.

Issued and Partly Paid

This term is used to describe shares which have been sold to shareholders but which have not yet been fully paid for. The amount owing will be shown as a current asset in the firm's balance sheet.

Reserves

There are two types of reserves and they both belong to the shareholders for they represent either past undistributed profits, or surpluses made and kept within the business.

Revenue Reserve

A revenue reserve arises when an amount of profit is retained within the company. It may be kept for a particular purpose, such as a Foreign Exchange Reserve, or it may be kept for a general purpose, such as a General Reserve. These revenue reserves can be used to pay dividends to the shareholders and are mainly called upon to maintain the dividend payments when company profits fall. With the exception of the Profit and Loss Account, all other revenue reserves have the word reserve in their title. The retained profit is treated as a reserve because it represents small amounts of profits which have not been distributed as dividends to the shareholders, but which have been kept within the company. The main reason for this is that there are insufficient profits to pay a reasonable dividend to each shareholder, and so the balance is kept for possible later distribution.

Capital Reserves

A capital reserve cannot be used to make dividend payments to shareholders, but the proceeds may be distributed by way of bonus shares and will then rank as equal with the other ordinary share capital. A good example of a capital reserve is the share premium account which arises when shares are sold for more than their nominal value. The surplus is shown as a capital reserve under the heading share premium. These reserves are sometimes called statutory reserves.

The Directors' Report

This is the last legal requirement to be complied with and the report must contain the following information. Some companies choose to mention other relevant information which will be of interest to shareholders and other outside bodies, but they are under no legal duty to do so. The directors' report must diclose:

1. **Review of the Business** - the principal activities of the company and any changes which have taken place during the year. The report must give a fair review of the company's development during the year and its position at the year end

2. **Results and Dividends** - the after tax profit, amount of money transferred to reserves and the recommended dividend.

3. **Share Capital** - details of the number of transactions in the firm's shares, their nominal value, aggregate consideration and the percentage of the called up capital represented by the shares purchased.

4. **Market Value of Land and Buildings** - the difference between market value and book value should be shown if it is significant and the directors believe it is of significance to members (shareholders).

5. **Political and Charitable Contributions** - if the company has donated £200 to charities or political parties it must disclose separate totals for each, together with the name of the recipient of each political contribution over £200.

6. **Fixed Assets** - details of any significant changes in the company's or subsidiaries' fixed assets during the last financial year.

7. **Disabled Persons** - this information does not have to be given unless the firm employs more than 250 staff. If it does, the company must state its policy with regard to recruitment, employment and training of disabled persons.

8. **Directors** - the names of directors during the last financial year, together with a statement showing their interests in shares and debentures of the company and other group companies at the start of the year or, if later, their appointment date.

9. **Events Since The Year End** - the report must supply details of any important event affecting the company which has occurred since the end of the financial year.

10. **Future Developments** - an indication of the future developments for the company.

11. **Research and Development** - information about the company's research and development programme.

12. **Employee Information** - the report must state what action has been taken to introduce, maintain or develop employee information, consultation, involvement and company performance during the year.

13. **Health and Safety** - the directors' report must state arrangements for securing the health, safety and welfare at work of employees and other persons connected with the work activities of their employees.

The Corporate Report

In August 1975 the Accounting Standards Committee issued a discussion paper entitled the "Corporate Report". The report addressed itself to the main issues of corporate reports and the information which they should contain.

The main users were defined as investors, lenders, employees, financial advisors, government, the public and interested corporate bodies such as suppliers.

The Committee's main recommendations were that the report should be relevant, understandable, reliable, completely objective, timely and comparable, and that an additional financial statement should be included called a "Statement of Added Value". Such a statement shows the wealth which has been created by the owners (capital) employees and government. It is a broad based measure of wealth creation and therefore differs from the profit and loss account because this only shows the wealth created by the owners of capital.

What is Added Value?
It is the difference between what a company is paid for its products, and the cost of material and services. It represents, therefore, the value of the conversion process.

```
Sales                              £300
Less Materials and Bought
     in Parts & Services            130
leaving Added Value                 170
```

The wealth credited from this process has to be used to reward the providers of this wealth. They are:

1. Employees who require wages, salaries, pensions and other benefits

2. Providers of capital who require dividends and interest

3. Government who requires taxation for the benefit of the nation

4. The company which requires re-investment for the replacement of existing assets and for growth.

Example of a Value Added Statement for the Year Ending Year Six

```
                                          £
Sales                                   350000
Less: Bought in goods & services        190000
Value added by the company              160000


To employees:
Wages and Benefits                       45000


To providers of Capital:
Interest                      15000
Dividends                     20000      35000


To Government
Taxation                                 20000


To Finance & Maintain Fixed Assets:
Depreciation                             20000
Retained Profits                         40000
Value Added                             160000
```

How Can Value Be Increased?

1. By increasing the selling prices, providing it exceeds any increases in costs and does not affect the volume

2. By buying in raw materials and services at more competititive rates

3. By reducing wastage and encouraging greater efficiency

4. By increasing productivity through capital expenditure and by having a motivated and loyal workforce.

The 1985 and 1989 Companies' Acts have not incorporated any of the Committee's proposals although some companies do show Value Added Statements.

Most public limited companies try to make their annual accounts as attractive and informative as possible by using statistical techniques, such as pie charts and bar charts, to show key performance indicators, as well as photographs of staff, factories or shops and other key areas relating to the firm's work. The recent number of large corporate failures, such as Polly Peck, have intensified the debate about what information must be shown. In the meantime all of these factors help to promote a greater understanding of the company's work to a wider audience than would be possible by simply publishing a set of annual accounts, but do little to avert the fears of investors, lenders and other interested parties.

Chapter 6
Source and Application of Funds

Introduction

The Chartered Institute of Cost and Management Accountants defines a source and application of funds statement as "a statement showing the sources and values of funds flowing into an entity, the way in which they have been used and how any net surplus or deficiency in short and long term funds has been applied." In order to be able to draw up this statement, the opening and closing balance sheets and the profit and loss account for the period under review will be needed. From this the statement can be prepared to show how the business acquired its funds and how they were used.

Figure 16: Financial Statements needed for Source & Application of Funds

Balance Sheet   Profit and Loss Account   Balance Sheet
At Beginning   ◄─────────────────────────────►   At The End

Source and Application
of Funds Statement

The Difference Between Profits and Cash

We have already seen that profits are not the same as cash. The profit and loss account and balance sheet do not show a firm's inflows and outflows of cash, but simply record the assets and liabilities of a business and whether or not a profit or loss has been made, after deducting expenses from sales. While these two financial statements are useful, they fail to show the changes in a firm's liquidity during a financial year. No business can continue once it has insufficient cash to pay its day to day expenses and so the source and application of funds statement is very useful in showing what has happened to the firm's cash resources during the past financial year.

This information cannot be readily arrived at by just looking at the profit and loss account and balance sheet, for the accounts are not prepared on a cash basis but on what accountants call the accruals concept. This means that a sale and expense is simply recorded as soon as it has been made or incurred and not when the cash is received or paid. Any money owing is then shown in the balance sheet as a current liability and any money owed is recorded as a current asset. The debtor amounts, therefore, show the amount of sales for which cash has not yet been received and, similarly, the creditors account shows the amount of money owing at the financial year end.

The final accounts also will not show the cash outflow when fixed assets are purchased, whether they have been paid for by reducing the firm's cash resources, or by raising additional funds from the owners (by issuing more share capital) or by borrowing extra funds from outside sources. Whichever method is used to finance their purchase, the initial cost is not shown in the profit and loss account. Instead a charge against profit is made in the accounts, called depreciation, which will usually reflect the loss of value of the asset being matched with the benefit derived.

The cost of stock is also not shown as an expense in the profit and loss account until it has been sold, and so any unsold stock is shown as a current asset in the balance sheet at the year's end. The accounts, therefore, do not show the amount of cash which has been used to purchase stock.

Lastly, any taxation owed and dividend payments are shown in the final accounts, but the cash payments will not be made until the following year.

The source and application of funds statement must take all these factors into consideration so that the movement of funds into and out of the business can be shown in one single statement.

The Information Contained In A Source and Application of Funds Statement

By analysing two sets of final accounts, it is possible to list all the receipts and applications of funds. An application occurs whenever an asset is purchased or liability repaid. This can only be done by acquiring funds from any one of three sources. These are by making profits, selling fixed assets or by gaining additional funds by borrowing or selling more shares. It is very unlikely that receipts of funds will balance with payments, and so the firm will show either a surplus or a deficit during the year. If a distinction is made between long term sources and long term applications, then the difference, be it a surplus or deficit, will be reflected by an increase or a decrease in its working capital position. This is best illustrated by a diagram.

Long Term Sources

Profits/Losses
Issue of Shares
Sale of Assets
Additional Loans

Long Term Application

Purchase of Fixed Assets
Tax Payments
Dividend Payments
Loan Repayments
Shares Redeemed

The surplus or deficit will then correspond to the change in working capital by similarly recording short term sources and short term applications of funds.

Short Term Sources

Decrease in stock
Decrease in debtors
Decrease in bank and cash deposits
Increase in bank overdraft
Increase in creditors

Short Term Applications

Increase in Stock
Increase in debtors
Increase in bank and cash deposits
Decrease in bank overdraft
Decrease in creditors

Figure 17: Source & Application of Funds

The statement will then show how the firm has sourced its funds and how they have been used, together with changes in the composition of working capital. There is no set format for preparing these statements and an example is shown overleaf followed by an explanation of how to prepare such a statement.

Figure 18: Example of Source & Application of Funds

SOURCE OF FUNDS

Profit before taxation

Adjustment for items not
involving the movement of
funds (Usually depreciation)

Total generated from operations

Funds from other sources
Sale of Fixed Assets
Issue of New Shares/Loans

APPLICATION OF FUNDS

Dividends paid (or drawings)
Tax paid
Purchase of fixed assets
Loans repaid or debentures redeemed

MOVEMENT IN WORKING CAPITAL

Movement in debtors
Movement of stocks
Movement in creditors

NET MOVEMENT OF FUNDS

How to Prepare a Source and Application of Funds Statement

Next Day Printers are a newly established firm. They have been trading for two years during which sales and profits have increased. Unfortunately the business has been hampered by a lack of cash and the owners cannot understand why a successful and profitable business can be so short of cash. In an attempt to overcome the problem, they have even invested more share capital in the business. Their last two balance sheets are shown on page 91.

90

Next Day Printers' Balance Sheet as at 5 April Year Two

	Year 1		Year 2	
	£'000	£'000	£'000	£'000
Fixed Assets				
Premises		100		150
Fixtures and Fittings		30		50
Motor Vehicles		10		20
		140		220
Current Assets				
Stock	40		60	
Debtors	10		30	
Bank	7		–	
	57			90
Current Liabilities				
Creditors	8		15	
Bank Overdraft	–		10	
				25
		49		65
Net Assets		189		285
Capital				
Share Capital		150		200
Profit and Loss A/C		39		85
Shareholder's Funds		189		285

First Steps in Preparing the Source and Application of Funds Statement

The first task is to consider the changes which have occurred during the two years and which can be detected by looking at the two sets of accounts. A good way of preparing this information is to list any changes under two columns, entitled source and application.

	Source	Application
	£'000	£'000
Premises		50
Fixtures		20
Motor Vehicles		10
Stock		20
Debtors		20
Bank	7	
Overdraft	10	
Creditors	7	
Share Capital	50	
Profit	46	
	120	120

The statement cannot be prepared until sources equal applications. Often the reason why the two sides will not balance is because additional information has been given relating to the depreciation or sale of assets, repayment of loans and the payments of dividends and taxation. In these situations further calculations will be required, and they are now explained.

Calculation of Profit

Not all of the expenses charged to the profit and loss account will be represented by a cash outflow of funds. For instance, any amount charged for depreciation or reduction in goodwill will not have involved the business in reducing its cash resources. These payments are really a use or appropriation of profit and so the amount set aside must be added back to the profit before tax.

Similarly, certain items credited to the profit and loss account, such as an overprovision for bad debts or a reduction in depreciation, will not have been represented by a cash inflow into the business. If this has been the case, the amount credited to the profit and loss account must be deducted from the retained profit figure because it does not represent a cash inflow.

Issue and Redemption of Loans

Sometimes when fixed term debt is sold or redeemed, the amount of cash received or parted with may be more (premium) or less (discount) than the loan stock's nominal value. In either case the amount paid or received should be shown in the source and application of funds statement and a check should then be made, by referring to the nominal value of the loan stock in the balance sheet, to see whether a premium or discount has been incurred on its issue or redemption.

Sale of Assets

The business may have sold surplus fixed assets during the year. The sale price is unlikely to be the same as the assets' net book value as shown in the balance sheet, so the firm will have made either a profit or loss on the sale. These profits or losses will have then been transferred to the firm's profit and loss account. When preparing a source and application of funds statement, the profit from the sale should be deducted from the retained profit figure and any loss should be added to it. The amount of money received from the sale must then be shown as a source of funds. By doing this the statement will show the cash received from the sale and the profit made from trading.

Dividends and Taxation Payable

Dividend and tax payments are always made in the following financial year (except for interim dividends). Any opening balance for dividends or taxation in the opening balance sheet will be shown as an application in the source and application of funds statement, for it will have been paid during the last financial year, thereby reducing the firm's cash resources. Similarly, any proposed dividend or tax owing in the closing balance sheet will not yet have been paid and so the amount will be added back to the before tax profit figure.

When these adjustments have been made, the sources and applications of funds should be equal. The next step is to distinguish between long and short term sources of funds. A source and application of funds statement follows the same principles as a balance sheet, and so anything which is not part of the current assets and current liabilities must be regarded as either a long term source or application of funds.

Source and Application of Funds Statement for Next Day Printers for the year ending 5 April Year 2

SOURCE OF FUNDS	£'000	£ '000	
Profit		46	
Adjustments for items not involving the movement of funds (Usually depreciation)			(No details given)
Total generated from operations		46	
Funds from other sources			
Additional share capital		50	
Total funds generated		96	
APPLICATION OF FUNDS			
Dividends paid (or drawings)	-		
Tax paid	-		
Purchase of fixed assets			
Premises	(50)		
Fixtures	(20)		
Motor Vehicles	(10)		
Loans repaid	-		
Total application of funds		(80)	
Net Sources and Applications		16	
MOVEMENT IN WORKING CAPITAL			
Movement in debtors	(20)		
Movement of stocks	(20)		
Movement in creditors	7	(33)	
Net movement of cash		£(17)	

What the Statement Shows

The statement shows that during the year the firm's long term sources of funds were £96,000, of which £46,000 was generated by the firm, and the balance was received by an increase in share capital. These funds were used to purchase additional fixed assets which, in total, cost £80,000, leaving a surplus of £16,000.

During the year the business has seen a deterioration in its liquidity position. At the year end more money has been invested in stock and the firm is owed more money from its debtors. In order to be able to finance trading the bank account has become overdrawn and there has been an increase in creditors. The increase in stocks and debtors has led to the deterioration in liquidity and, in the coming year, stocks and debtors must be more effectively managed, releasing cash which can be used to repay the bank overdraft and the creditors.

It is possible to prove that the answer is correct by constructing a cash flow statement. This is done by subtracting the opening cash figures from the closing figure on the two balance sheets.

Closing cash figure	Overdraft	£(10,000)
Opening cash figure	Cash	7,000
Difference = movement		£17,000

Unlike the source and application of funds which begins with the firm's profit, the cash flow statement starts with its opening cash position and then works backwards to arrive at its present cash position. Using the same figures as in the previous example, a cash flow statement can be prepared.

Cash Flow Statement for Next Day Printers as at 5 Year Two

	£'000	£'000
Opening Bank Balance		7

Inflows

Profit	46	
New Share Capital	50	
Increase in creditors	7	
		103
		110

Outflows

Increase in Stocks	20	
Increase in Debtors	20	
Purchase of Fixed Assets	80	
		120
Bank Overdraft		(10)

What the statement Shows

At the start of the year Next Day Printers had a £7,000 deposit at the bank. During the year they received cash inflows of £103,000 but spent £120,000, which has left the business with an overdraft of £10,000.

While this example may at first appear complex, it is relatively straightforward as the profit figure is made up of only one figure. In practice this is unlikely to be the case, as the profit figure will have to be adjusted for items not involving the movement of cash. The following example explains how this is done.

Example
The Wine Shop

The Wine Shop is a successful high street business selling quality wines from around the world. The owner knows that her business is profitable but cannot understand why the business has an overdraft and is constantly short of cash. The firm's last two balance sheets are shown on page 97.

The Wine Shop's Balance sheet as at 31 December Year Two

	Year 1 £		Year 2 £	
Fixed Assets at Cost				
Fixtures and Fittings	16,000		16,000	
Depreciation	3,600			3,900
Net Book Value		12,400		12,100
Motor Vehicle	3,000		17,340	
Depreciation	1,000		2,340	
Net Book Value		2,000		15,000
Total Fixed Assets		14,400		27,100
Current Assets				
Stocks	6,880			11,300
Debtors	2,340			5,320
Bank	6,400		-	
Cash in hand	280			500
	15,900			17,120
Current Liabilities				
Creditors	4,300		3,720	
Bank Overdraft	-		4,000	
Taxation	1,700		2,150	
Dividend	4,800		6,250	
		10,800		16,120
Net working capital		5,100		1,000
Net assets		19,500		28,100
Financed By				
Share capital	10,000		10,000	
Reserves	2,700		9,500	
Net retained Profit for the year	6,800		8,600	
Shareholders' Funds		19,500		28,100

During the year the owner decided to replace all of the shop's fixtures and fittings and received £4,000 for the old ones.

Preparation of the Wine Cellar's Source and Application of Funds Statement follows.

In this example the first task is to calculate the firm's profit by building it up from the information given. Although it may seem strange, this can only be done by adopting a bottom up approach. This is now shown:

	£
Net Profit for period retained	8,600
Add dividend provided	6,250
	14,850
Taxation provided for	2,150
Profit after tax	17,000
Deduct profit on disposal of	
fixtures and fittings	2,000
Trading profit	15,000

Only now can the statement be prepared.

Sources	£	£
Start with the profit (before tax as shown above)	17,000	
Add back items not involving movement of cash-the charge for depreciation	5,240	
Adjust for profits/losses on disposals. These are only book profits, that really represent whether you charged enough depreciation. Add back a loss (undercharge) and deduct a profit (overcharge)		
In this case it was a loss	8,400	
Funds generated by operations		30,640
Other Funds Generated		
Cash received from the disposal of assets (see note at end of question)	4,000	
Cash received from issue of shares, raising of loan stock or debentures, and share premium	-	
(Note bonus issues and revaluations do not generate cash)		
Total Sources of Funds Generated (A)		34,640

Applications

	£
(There are usually four items)	
Purchase of fixed assets	
New Fixtures	(16,000)
New Motor Vehicle	(14,340)
Payment of tax (last years)	(1,700)
Payment of dividend (last years)	(4,800)
Repayment of loans or debentures	-
Total Applications (B)	(36,840)
	£(2,200)

Working Capital	£	
Movements on:-		
Stock	(4,420)	
Debtors	(2,980)	
Creditors	(580)	
Net movement of working capital (C) excl. bank		(7,980)
(Cash and overdraft balances) = A - B +/-C		(10,180)

Once again this figure's accuracy can be proven by calculating:

Closing cash at bank and in hand	£(3,500)
Minus opening cash at bank and in hand	6,680
Movement	(10,180)

The statement shows that the business is profitable and that additional money has been invested in new fixtures. The owner has withdrawn £4,800 for her own use in the form of dividends. There has been a substantial increase in working capital, which has manifested itself in a large increase in stocks and debtors. This would cause cash flow problems in itself, but they are being compounded by the owner who is paying the creditors quicker than previously, thereby reducing the firm's cash operating cycle. This fact is made all the more clear by preparing a cashflow statement for the business.

Cash Flow Statement for the Wine Cellar

		£
Opening cash balances		6,680
(these have been combined Bank & Cash)		

	£	
Add incomings:		
Profit per accounts	17,000	
Adjust for		
Book loss on disposal	8,400	
Depreciation	5,240	
	30,640	
Cash received from disposals	4,000	34,640
		41,320
Deduct outgoings:		
Increase in stocks	(4,420)	
Increase in debtors	(2,980)	
Decrease in creditors	(580)	
Purchase of fixtures	(16,000)	
Taxation paid	(1,700)	
Dividend paid	(4,800)	
Purchase of motor vehicle	(14,340)	44,820
Net balances per balance sheet		£(3,500)

Both these examples highlight the changes in liquidity during a financial year and are useful to management, investors and lenders. Ideally a firm should aim for a steady and stable cash flow, but there may be times when it is still prudent to reduce liquidity levels if good profit-generating assets can be acquired. The problem arises when these assets cannot generate the necessary sales and profits, leaving the firm badly exposed to its current financial commitments.

Chapter 7
Interpreting Financial Statements

Introduction

When a company has drawn up its annual accounts, they should be analysed so that the financial strengths and weaknesses can be assessed, together with any trends which may have led to its current position. The amount of information which can be gained by looking at a set of accounts is limited because companies are only required by law to publish certain details and the directors may decide not to show any additional information which could assist competitors. In order to gain a better insight, it is prudent to compare present performance with past and to compare one company's performance with another operating in the same business. Accounting ratios provide further information about the firm's liquidity, profitability, use of assets, financial structure and the returns paid to investors.

What is an Accounting Ratio?

An accounting ratio is the same as any arithmetic ratio in that it seeks to measure the relationship between two numbers. This information can be presented in several ways and these are now explained.

Example
If a company has £5,000 invested in debtors and owes £1,000 to creditors, the relationship between these two figures can be shown as follows:

a) The ratio of Debtors to Creditors is 5:1

b) The ratio of Creditors to Debtors is 1:5

c) Debtors represent five times (5 x) Creditors

d) Creditors represent ⅕ of Debtors

e) Creditors represent 20% of Debtors

It is an accounting convention that ratios are expressed in different ways. While the arithmetical calculation is relatively straightforward, it is the interpretation which is difficult, for it us unlikely that one set of accounts will contain all the information one needs.

When interpreting accounts, the ratios used should follow a logical sequence. If a company is having liquidity problems, its future existence may well be in jeopardy, even if it is profitable. It is therefore a good idea to assess its liquidity first, then its profitability and, finally, to see if there is a link between these two factors, and how effectively it uses its assets. Lastly the accounts should be analysed so that the firm's capital structure is assessed, together with the risks involved in its chosen method of long term finance, as this will affect the returns which investors expect.

1 Ratios Which Measure Liquidity

The word liquidity refers to the firm's ability to meet its short term liabilities by having sufficient cash or near cash resources. All companies buy and sell on credit. In a competitive market, credit terms have to be offered in order to win contracts and to keep existing customers. At the same time the firm's own liabilities can only be paid in cash. If a firm is unable to pay its liabilities in cash, it may be wound up by its creditors and so management, investors, lenders and employees are all concerned that the firm should have sufficient current assets to meet its current liabilities. There are two ratios which measure a business's liquidity.

The Current Ratio   =   Current Assets
                                Current Liabilities

Current assets are assets of a circulating nature which generate the firm's profit. They are stock, debtors, and cash and bank deposits. Current liabilities are short term debts which must be repaid within one year of the balance sheet date. The main components of current liabilities are creditors, bank overdraft, taxation due and proposed dividends.

Caution dictates that current assets should exceed current liabilities, for not all of the current assets will be in cash or near cash, such as debtors. The speed with which the firm can turn its stock and debtors into cash will determine the amount of money which must be invested in current assets relative to current liabilities. A building company operating in a recession may find it prudent to have a ratio of say 2:1, whereas a fast food chain may operate at 1:1. It is not just the ratio for one year which is important, but the trend for this will show whether the business is maintaining its liquidity ratio or whether it is rising or falling. If the ratio is rising, further investigation may show that stocks are increasing because they cannot be sold. If this is the case, it is a bad sign for it suggests liquidity problems in the future, as most of the firm's cash resources are tied up in stock. If, on the other hand, the ratio is decreasing, the firm may be improving its efficiency by converting its stock and debtors into cash in a shorter time.

The Acid Test or Quick Ratio	$\dfrac{\text{Current Assets Less Stock}}{\text{Current Liabilities}}$

This is a stricter measurement of a firm's liquidity for it measures a firm's ability to meet its current liabilities out of its cash or near cash current assets. If the managers are totally risk averse, they must have a minimum ratio of 1:1 and would probably prefer a higher one. In this way all liabilities can be met without worry.

Once again the ratio will depend upon the type of business in which the firm is engaged and the ease with which it can convert its stock and debtors into cash. The quicker this can be done, the less liquid it needs to be and the more it can finance its current assets by borrowing short term from its creditors. Generally the higher the ratio of current liabilities to current assets, the more profitable the firm as it is able to use its creditors to finance its current assets (usually interest free). Part of the cost of this increased profitability is the increased risk, but ratios of 0.4 :1 are not uncommon for the large supermarket chains. These businesses can operate at this level because they can extract advantageous credit terms from their suppliers and can sell the goods quickly to customers for cash. If these same techniques were applied by many manufacturing companies or retailing firms which have a slow stock turnover, they would be in great danger of insolvency and would probably be described as overtrading.

Overtrading is an accounting term which describes a business which is trying to finance too high a level of trading with too little working capital. Once again, in order to assess whether or not a firm is overtrading, it is necessary to look at the liquidity ratios for several years to see whether its liquidity ratios are relatively stable or deteriorating. Firms which are overtrading normally have increasing stock and debtors balances, coupled with decreasing cash balances and a rapid rise in creditors. If this situation occurs, and cannot be abated by acquiring additional finance, the firm is in danger of imminent collapse as creditors and lenders ask for immediate repayment of their loans.

2 Profitability

In the long run companies must be profitable if they are to survive. There are a number of measures of profitability which calculate the percentage profit made when goods are sold and after all expenses have been made.

It is not possible to say what percentage profit a firm should make for it will depend upon its stock turnover. As a general rule, the higher the stock turnover the smaller the profit margin, and the slower the turnover, the higher the profit margin. In either case sufficient gross profit must be earned so that the business can meet its expenses, pay a reasonable return to its owners and still leave sufficient funds for reinvestment in the business.

The gross profit percentage should remain reasonably stable but, if a change does occur, this should be investigated. It may have been brought about by heavy discounting, increased production costs caused by price increases in raw materials, excessive wage claims or by changing the firm's product range (usually referred to as its product mix). The published accounts do not usually contain sufficient information to analyse why costs and net profits have increased or decreased. Nevertheless, one should look for large increases in overheads or debt repayments which could cause financial problems if the firm found its sales and profits fall because of a recession.

The two main ratios for calculating the firm's profits from sales are the gross profit and net profit to sales ratio. They are calculated by the following formulae:

$$\text{Profitability Ratios} = \frac{\text{Gross Profit} \times 100}{\text{Sales}} \quad \text{and} \quad \frac{\text{Net Profit} \times 100}{\text{Sales}}$$

Once the profit percentages earned from each sale have been calculated, managers, investors and lenders need to know the return which the company can make on its capital employed. Capital is a scarce resource and the owners want to earn the maximum return relative to the risk involved. The firm needs to make as high a return as possible so that it can attract investor's funds, which are always seeking a safe and secure investment.

A company cannot be judged financially successful just by the size of its profits for this takes no account of the profit made in relation to its size or capital base. The Return on Capital Employed ratio seeks to measure the business's earnings power and can be calculated by this ratio:

Return on Capital Employed =
or Primary Ratio

$$\frac{\text{Profit} \times 100}{\text{Capital Employed}}$$

While this ratio shows the return earned from the company's capital, it is not specific as to what capital or profit figure has been used to measure its earnings power. For instance should the profit be after tax, or before interest payments and preference dividends are paid? The answer really lies in how the firm has raised its long term capital, which can come from two main sources. Firstly, from the shareholders who are the owners of the business and, secondly, from lenders who are not owners, but creditors. If the company has any reserves, these will belong to the shareholders, giving rise to a third possible definition of capital. As a result, three different figures for the return on capital employed can be used, each of which will show a different percentage return.

The broadest definition includes all of the capital financing the business from trade creditors and also long term loans to shareholders' funds and reserves. If this interpretation is applied, the ratio should be called the Return on Long Term Capital Employed and is calculated as follows:

Return on Long Term Capital Employed

$$\frac{\text{Profit before interest and tax}}{\text{Loan Capital + Share Capital and Reserves}} \times 100$$

It is also possible to calculate the return earned from the shareholders' investment in the business, and so this ratio excludes any debt capital. When this ratio is used, the company's preference shareholders are treated as debt capital, because they receive a fixed rate of dividend, and so the earnings are the profit after tax and preference dividend. This ratio is called the Return on Equity Capital and is calculated by using the ratio:

Return on Equity Capital

$$\frac{\text{Profit after tax and preference dividend}}{\text{Ordinary Share Capital plus Reserves}} \times 100$$

Lastly, the return on capital employed may be taken as the shareholders' funds, which is made up of both ordinary and preference shares plus reserves. This ratio is called the Return on Shareholders' Capital and is calculated as follows:

Return on Shareholders' Capital

$$\frac{\text{Profit after tax}}{\text{Share Capital plus Reserves}} \times 100$$

It is important to know which figure has been used to calculate the return on capital employed, as each method will yield a different answer. Most companies seek to increase their return on capital over time and so, whichever method is used, one should look to see if the ratio is increasing. A mere increase on its own should not be immediately regarded as a good sign, for the increase, if adjusted for inflation, may in fact be negative. Similarly, there is also a danger that if the firm's assets have not been recently revalued to reflect the increase in asset values brought about by inflation, the ratio will have been based upon an unrealistic figure for capital and so the returns will be overstated.

Whilst the return and profits made are important, there is always a danger that too much profit may be distributed as dividend to the owners. If the company is to grow and have a secure financial base, it needs to reinvest past profits back into the business. The retained profit to sales and the net working assets to sales ratios show the amount of capital needed to finance extra sales. If the firm lacks the cash to finance these extra sales, it will have to fund it from outside sources, which will generally involve additional borrowing.

Retained Profit
Sales

This ratio shows how much new capital each extra sale will generate for the business, while the net working capital to sales ratio measures the amount of additional capital which will be needed to finance extra sales.

Net Working Capital   where net working capital =
———————————   stock + Debtors - Creditor
Sales

As a general rule, if the net working capital ratio is higher than the retained profit to sales, the business will need additional capital to finance any increase in sales. If this is not provided from a long term source, there is always a danger that the management will fund it by increasing their creditors, which could lead to financial problems in the future.

3 Use of Assets

Companies seek finance either from the owners or from lenders to purchase both fixed and current assets which will make profits for the business. It is by effectively managing the current assets that firms are able to generate profits. The quicker raw materials can be turned into finished goods, sold and the cash received, the greater the profits, for this process can then be undertaken more times each financial year. The use of assets ratio seeks to measure how effectively the firm uses its fixed and current assets.

A firm needs its fixed assets so that it can trade. For instance, a shop cannot exist without a building and fixtures where customers can come and browse before purchasing. All investments in fixed assets must yield returns and one measure of assessing the return is to look at the ratio of sales to fixed assets:

$$\frac{\text{Sales}}{\text{Fixed Assets}}$$

As a general rule the sales should always be higher than the investment in fixed assets for, otherwise, the investment has not been effective; it has failed to generate sales income. When assessing this ratio it is important to look at when the fixed assets were last revalued for, if the assets are shown at their original cost price, there is always a danger that the ratio has been distorted by inflation.

Lastly, any new investment takes time to generate returns and so, if the balance sheet shows a large investment in fixed assets, it may not be realistic to see a corresponding increase in sales. Nevertheless, if the ratio of sales to fixed assets is falling, it would suggest that the business is not using its assets effectively and should consider rationalising the scale of its operations.

Another useful ratio is the relationship between a company's fixed and current assets. A large shop with a small amount of stock would be likely to lack customers because most of the firm's capital has been invested in fixed assets which are not for sale. It may be difficult to assess this ratio because of seasonal factors or attempts by the management to destock before the final accounts are prepared, so that the company appears to have a higher liquidity ratio. Nevertheless, if a firm has a high ratio of current assets to fixed assets, coupled with a high stock turnover rate, it will be able to improve its profitability and return on capital employed.

The key to profitability lies in being able to sell the stock as many times as possible in any one financial year and to receive the cash quickly from the debtors so that it can be invested in more stock. The following ratios show how long it takes the business to sell stock or receive cash in days and is referred to as its cash operating cycle. Before the cash operating cycle can be calculated, the following ratios must be worked out:

Stock Turnover Ratio

$$\frac{\text{Average Stock} \times 365}{\text{Cost of Goods Sold}} = \text{Days to sell stock}$$

The average stock figure is calculated by adding the opening and closing stock together and dividing it by two to find the average. By dividing the number of days taken to sell the stock, it is possible to calculate the number of times the stock is sold during the year.

If the company is a manufacturing one, raw materials must be purchased, turned into finished goods (work in progress) and, finally, kept as finished stock until sold. The following ratios will show how long it takes in days for this to happen. Once again the average stock is found by adding together the opening and closing stock and calculating the mean.

a) Stock Turnover For Raw Materials

$$\frac{\text{Average Stock of Raw Materials} \times 365}{\text{Cost of Raw Materials Consumed}} = \text{Number of days the firm holds its stock of raw materials}$$

b) Stock Turnover For work in Progress

$$\frac{\text{Stock Turnover For Work in Progress} \times 365}{\text{Cost of goods Manufactured}} = \text{Number of days it takes to turn work in progress into finished stock}$$

c) Stock Turnover For Finished Goods

$$\frac{\text{Stocks of finished Goods}}{\text{Cost of Goods Sold}} \times 365 = \quad \text{Number of days it takes to sell finished goods}$$

If stock is bought on credit, the creditors are in fact financing its purchase. The longer the credit period, the greater the savings, for the firm is often able to use this money interest free. The time taken to pay creditors can again be expressed in days by using this ratio:

d) Time Taken To Pay Creditors

$$\frac{\text{Trade Creditors}}{\text{Purchases on Credit}} \times 365 = \quad \text{Number of days credit allowed by trade creditors before payment must be made}$$

Unfortunately this benefit is offset because most firms also sell on credit and so have to give credit to their customers. The length of time which the firm has to wait for payment is calculated by the Sales to Debtors ratio.

e) Time Taken To Receive Payment From Debtors

$$\frac{\text{Debtors} \times 365}{\text{Credit Sales}} = \quad \text{Days taken to receive payment from credit sales}$$

The shorter the time period the better, for then the money can be reinvested in more stock. Ideally the firm would like to receive payment before having to pay its creditors so that the money can be invested in interest bearing deposits which will earn the business additional profits.

Once these ratios have been calculated, the firm's cash operating cycle can be worked out. This is best explained by an example.

Example

The Iron and Steel Manufacturing Company has just calculated the following ratios:

Ratio	Days
Raw Materials Turnover	20
Work in Progress Turnover	30
Finished Goods Turnover	40
Credit Given To Customers	30
Total Days to receive Payment	120
Less Credit From Customers	25
Cash Operating Cycle	95 days

The cash operating cycle shows the number of days the firm's cash is needed to finance its stock and credit sales. Any extension which can be gained from creditors will help to conserve the firm's cash, as will any reduction in manufacturing time or reduction in the time taken to receive payment. These ratios are useful for they provide further insight as to the firm's liquidity and should be compared with previous years and other companies operating in the same industry.

4 Capital Ratios

Capital ratios show who has provided the long term capital which is financing the firm. The ratio of debt to equity capital is called gearing and is explained further in Chapter 18. The ratio is:

Gearing Ratio = $\dfrac{\text{Debt Capital}}{\text{Equity Capital}}$

The main problem is —what should be included as debt and equity capital? The simplest method is to divide the ordinary share capital into the long term debt capital, but stricter measures include all long term and short term debt as well as ordinary share capital plus reserves. Preference shares are normally treated as debt capital because they pay a fixed rate of dividend and so are more akin to debt than equity capital. Whichever method is used, the ratio shows who has provided the majority of the money which is fiancing the business.

This can also be calculated by another ratio which measures what percentage of the total assets have been financed by the shareholders.

Shareholders' Investments
Total Assets

Both these ratios provide some indication of the risks involved in investing in the company. The shareholders are the owners and should provide the majority of the money, for all the profits will accrue to them. A loan holder will want to see the majority of the money coming from the shareholders, otherwise the lenders will demand a higher interest rate to compensate for the extra risk involved.

The more money financed by long term debt, the greater the gearing ratio and the risk to the firm. Highly geared firms have a ratio of 1:1 or even higher. When the level of debt reaches these proportions, the level of risk is increased to both the owners and borrowers for there is always a danger that, if sales and profits fall, the firm will default on its loan and interest payments. If the debts cannot be rescheduled, the firm may be wound up by its creditors who will seek to sell the assets to recover their money. Rescheduling may be a way out for a firm having problems meeting its interest payments, provided it has sufficient assets. When a firm asks to reschedule its debts, it means that it wants its interest payments reduced in the short term and the difference added to the capital owing. Then, when profits and cash flow improve, it will be able to meet its liabilities. This option may suit both parties if it is felt that the business is only suffering from short term financial instability.

One way of assessing a firm's stability is to calculate the number of times its loan interest can be met out of profits. The ratio is:

Net Profit before Interest
Interest Charges

The higher the ratio, the less risk involved and this will be reflected in the company's credit rating and in its cost of borrowed capital.

5 Investment Ratios

These ratios are concerned with measuring the returns which a shareholder receives by purchasing shares in one company as opposed to another. Investment ratios show what the firm can earn with its share capital and the returns paid to shareholders.

An equity investor will want to know what return the company can earn with its share capital. If the return is 12 per cent, it shows that at the end of the financial year the business has earned an additional 12p on every pound invested in it. The ratio for calculating the earnings per share is:

Earnings Per Share = $\dfrac{\text{Profit after tax and Preference Dividend}}{\text{Issued Ordinary Shares}}$

Companies usually only distribute part of their profits as dividends and so a shareholder will not receive a share of the total earnings. Nevertheless, the higher the earnings, the more profit which can be distributed and so investors seek companies making high returns on their issued capital.

Dividend Yield

The dividend payments are always calculated on the nominal value of the share. This is the price as shown on the share certificate but which is likely to be different from its market value. If a compay has £1.00 shares and pays a dividend of 10p per share, the return to a shareholder would be 10% if the market price is the same as the nominal price. This is unlikely to be the case, for the share price will rise if the company is profitable and distributes part of its profits as dividends.

If the market price rose to £2.00, the return to the shareholder would be 5% because, in order to receive the dividend, they have had to pay £2.00 a share. This inevitably reduces their return (in this case by fifty per cent). The dividend payable as a percentage of the share's market price can be calculated:

Dividend Yield = $\dfrac{\text{Dividend Per Ordinary Share x 100}}{\text{Market Price Per Share}}$

This ratio is useful for making comparisons with other investments and is likely to influence investors' choice about which company's shares they should buy.

Dividend Cover

The dividend cover shows what proportion of the firm's profit is distributed as profit and how much is retained to finance future investment. It is a useful measure of a company's ability to pay its ordinary shareholders a dividend while, at the same time, witholding sufficient profit for reinvestment. The ratio is:

Dividend cover =   Profit after tax, less Preference Dividend
                   Gross Dividend on Ordinary Shares

Price to Earnings Ratio

This ratio is useful to potential investors, for it shows how many years it would take for the earnings per share to equal the ordinary share's market price. The ratio is:

Price to Earnings Ratio =   Market Price Per Share
                            Earnings Per Ordinary Share

Many people believe that a low price to earnings ratio is good because its earnings are a greater proportion of its market price. The price of a share is governed by the laws of supply and demand and, if a share is popular, its price will rise as more investors seek to purchase shares in the company's future earnings. Companies which are very profitable, and which pay good dividends, tend to have a high price to earnings ratio because of their expected future earnings potential. A low ratio suggests that, either the company is only making small profits and returns for its shareholders, or that stock market investors have not yet realised its future earnings potential.

Limitations of Accounting Ratios

Accounting ratios can only provide a guide to the present and the future. They do not on their own provide answers but they do allow managers, investors and lenders to focus on the financial strengths and weaknesses of the business. Unfortunately the outside investor does not have access to the same amount of information as the internal management and what information there is may not be representative of the company's normal financial position. For instance, stock levels may be unrealistically low and cash deposits artificially high because of the seasonal nature of the business. We must also be careful when appraising a firm's profitability and return on capital as there are also different definitions which make inter-company comparisons difficult, unless the ratios used are known. Despite these limitations, ratio analysis is an important management tool for it forces managers, investors, and lenders to focus on the future and it is a useful attitude development device.

Chapter 8
Accounting for the Effects of Inflation

Introduction

When a firm's annual accounts are prep ed under the historical cost accounting convention they make no allowance for inflation. Although the accounts comply with the requirements of the 1985 Companies' Acts and the Standard Statements of Accounting Practice, they will generally understate the firm's assets and overstate its profits. By failing to adjust the annual accounts for the affects of inflation, it can be argued that they do not give a true and fair view of the business's financial position. Inflation accounting seeks to mitigate this defect by amending the accounts, showing managers, investors and lenders how inflation has affected the company's financial performance.

What is Inflation?

Inflation can be defined as a persistent rise in the general price level of goods and services over a period of time. Alternatively it can be thought of as a decrease in the purchasing power of a unit of currency over a period of time. This is best illustrated by the following table which assumes that, if the purchasing power of the Pound was a Pound in 1900, by 1989 its purchasing value had declined to 2.3p.

Purchasing Power of the £ Taking Value as Equivalent to 100p in Various Years

1900	100p
1913	92.9
1929	56.5
1939	55.3
1949	29.5
1959	21.0
1969	14.9
1979	4.6
1989	2.3

Source: Lloyds Bank Economic Profile of Britain 1990.

The purchasing power of a Pound is calculated by using index numbers which compare the number of goods which a unit of currency can buy one year with another. An index number is a statistical technique which uses the figures for one year's set of data as a base and then calculates the following year's figures as a percentage of this base. Most indices take the base figure as being a hundred, and percentage changes are then shown upwards or downwards from this figure. If the price of a good last year was £100 and this year it is £120, the index would be calculated as follows by the formula:

$$\text{Price Index} \quad \frac{\text{Price in Year Two}}{\text{Price in Year One}} \quad \text{x } 100 = \frac{£120 \quad \text{x} \quad 100}{£100} = £120$$

The index would then show the information as follows:

Last Year	100
This Year	120

The Retail Price Index is calculated by using a Weighted Average Index which takes into account the movement in price of a number of household items between one year and the next. The Retail Price Index is commonly used as a measure of the rate of inflation and is useful for comparison purposes.

How Does Inflation Affect Financial Statements?

In Britain annual accounts are prepared under the historical cost accounting convention. The Chartered Institute of Management Accountants defines this as a system of accounting in which all values in revenue and capital are based on the costs actually incurred or as revalued from time to time. The final accounts therefore ignore the different purchasing power of money, making comparison of past profits, sales and shareholders' funds nearly impossible. Although the accounts may show the business to be profitable, if the profits were adjusted to show the affect of inflation, the profits and returns could turn out to be negative. This can be illustrated by three examples.

Examples of How Inflation Distorts Accounts Prepared Under the Historical Cost Accounting Convention

All of these examples consider the effects of inflation on three hypothetical businesses. They show how inflation affects a firm's fixed assets, stocks of goods and its capital structure.

Example One

Four years ago a farmer purchased a combine harvester and rented it out to other farmers. The machine cost £80,000 and was depreciated over the four years using the straight line basis. The farmer retained all profits in cash. The profits for each year were as follows

	Year One	Year Two	Year Three	Year Four
Retained Profit after Depreciation	£15,000	£25,000	£35,000	£40,000

At the end of the fourth year the combine harvester had been completely depreciated as it had no residual or resale value.. In spite of depreciating the full cost of the machine over four years' trading and accumulating profits of £115,000, the farmer was unable to purchase a new machine because its cost had risen to £150,000.

Although the annual accounts prepared under the historical cost accounting convention show profits of £115,000, these are not enough to purchase a new machine. If one takes the effects of inflation into account, it can be argued that the business has only made £45,000 profit over the four years and that the annual accounts should reflect this fact.

Example Two

At the beginning of the financial year a market trader started a business with £20,000 and bought 20,000 £1.00 plants. The business had no other assets and so its opening balance sheet was as follows:

Balance Sheet For Market Trader at Start of Year One

Capital		Assets	
Owner's equity	£20,000	Stock	£20,000
	£20,000		£20,000

During the year all of the stock was sold for £40,000 and £5,000 expenses were incurred. The trader decided to purchase a further 20,000 plants before the end of the financial year, but the cost of each plant had risen to £1.75. The trader's profit and loss account prepared under the historical cost accounting convention will look like this:

Profit and Loss Account for the Year Ending Year One

	£
Sales	40,000
Less Cost of Goods Sold	20,000
Gross Profit	20,000
Less Expenses	5,000
Net Profit	15,000

Balance Sheet for Market Trader at Year End

Capital		Assets	
	£		£
Owner's Equity	20,000	Stock	35.000
Retained profit	15,000		
	35,000		35,000

At the start of the year the firm had a stock of 20,000 plants and it had the same stock at the year end. If the stock had been bought before the price increase, the firm would have made a holding gain by having the stock which had increased in price. Unfortunately the firm placed its order after the price increase and so, although the firm has made profits of £15,000, the price increase has resulted in all the profits being reinvested in stock just to maintain the same level of trading as last year. In such a situation the £15,000 profit ceases to have any real meaning.

Example Three

The Cash Poor Company and the Cash Rich Company

These two companies make similar goods and operate in the same market where the rate of inflation is 10%. The Cash Poor Company has to give credit and is unable to purchase new stock until it has received payment from its debtors. The company is unable to purchase goods on credit because of its poor credit rating which has been brought about by its cash shortages. Unfortunately while it has been waiting to receive payment from its debtors, its raw materials have increased and so it has effectively lost money by not having the cash to purchase the stock before the price increase.

The Cash Rich Company, on the other hand, is able to give and accept credit. As soon as the stock is sold, more is ordered on credit ahead of the the price increase, giving the company a holding gain by the time the goods are ready to be sold. This holding gain will inflate the firm's profits.

The last three examples have all illustrated how inflation affects a firm's annual accounts. These gains will be made on fixed assets and on stocks. The problem is to whom do these gains belong? Let us consider two different companies called the Share Capital Trading Company and the Share and Loan Trading Company.

The shareholders are the owners of a company and they are entitled to any profits made after all other expenses and liabilities have been met. The loan holders, on the other hand, do not own the business but will receive interest on the money lent and must have their capital repaid at the end of the loan. If there is inflation, the amount repaid will have had its purchasing power reduced during the life of the loan and the lender must hope that the interest payments have compensated for this. This is the only return which the loan holder receives for, not being an owner, they are denied any holding gains which accrue from inflation. In the Share Trading Company all of the gains will accrue to the shareholders as they have provided all of the finance. This will also be the case in the Share and Loan Trading Company, because the loan holders receive none of the benefits as they are not owners. During times of inflation, the shareholders see their funds in the company increase through the creation of reserves which show the holding gains at the expense of the loan holders, who see the monetary value of their loan fall as inflation rises.

Limitations of Historical Cost Accounting

When accounts are prepared under the historical cost convention, the assets in the balance sheet are shown at their original cost or revalued amount. Many companies now regularly revalue their property assets, but this is rarely done to the other assets. During times of inflation, the accounts will fail to show the value of the assets employed by the business and, as a consequence, it become nearly impossible to measure the business's profitability.

Once fixed assets and stock are incorrectly valued, the profit and loss account will not show the correct profit for, it will have under-provided for depreciation and included stock-holding gains as part of its profits. When this is done, the firm is in danger of paying out too high dividends, leaving it short of retained profit which will be needed to finance new investment.

In an attempt to overcome these shortcomings, the accountancy bodies and academics have given much thought as to how accounting information can be presented to show the effects of inflation. Two main methods have been considered. These are the Current Purchasing Power and the Current Cost Accounting Methods.

Both methods seek to measure the affects of inflation by adjusting a unit of currency to show its real purchasing power. The problem is whether to adjust the accounts to show the effect on the shareholders' or the business's purchasing power. The current purchasing power method shows how inflation has affected purchasing goods in general, while current cost accounting will show its effect on the goods and services which the business needs to purchase in order to trade.

The C.P.P and C.C.A. methods seek to adjust accounts prepared under the historical cost accounting convention by using two different measurements of how inflation affects businesses. The Current Purchasing Power Method seeks to show the affects of inflation on the shareholders' capital base, while current cost accounting explains how it has affected the firm's operating capacity.

In the United Kingdom the current purchasing power method was first adopted to try to show how inflation affects accounts prepared under the historical cost convention. This method seeks to make adjustments to monetary values by using index numbers, making comparison of previous financial accounts possible. One of the main problems with this method is that, while it adjusts the value of money brought about by inflation, it does not show the correct value of the firm's assets or liabilities. This makes it difficult to assess the firm's profitability and there is still the danger that the firm will distribute too much of its profits as dividend, because it has underprovided for depreciation and included stock holding gains in its profit calculations.

In an attempt to overcome these limitations, the Accountancy bodies (following the Sandilands report) introduced a new system of accounting for inflation for a three year trial period, in 1980. The new method was called Current Cost Accounting and applied mainly to the large public limited companies. The method proved unpopular with industrialists and some members of the profession because of the costs involved in preparing the information and the subjectivity of placing correct market values on company fixed assets. Although the accounting standard Standard Statement of Accounting Practice 16 was finally withdrawn in 1985, the Accounting Standards Committee recommended that the final accounts should show the following when calculating the profit made during a financial year:

a) whether the firm's assets have been valued on a historical or current cost basis.

b) the effect of inflation on the firm's working capital and long term capital which is referred to as the capital maintenance concept.

c) whether the accounts show just the monetary value of the currency or whether some attempt has been made to calculate the current purchasing power of the currency.

The Principles of Current Cost Accounting

Current cost accounting techniques adjust final accounts prepared under the historical accounting convention to show the effects of inflation. Four adjustments are made and these are known as:

1) Depreciation Adjustment

2) Cost of Sales Adjustment (C.O.S.A.)

3) Monetary Working Capital Adjustment (M.W.C.A.)

4) Gearing Adjustment

Depreciation Adjustment

During times of high inflation the monetary value of assets increases. If the depreciation provision is not calculated on the replacement cost, the business will not set aside sufficient funds out of profit to be able to purchase new equipment. In order to remedy this situation, current cost accounting charges an additional provision (based on the replacement cost of the asset) and this amount is then deducted from the historical profit.

Cost of Sales Adjustment (C.O.S.A.)

Under the historic cost convention the profit and loss account does not distinguish between a stock operating and holding gain. An operating gain occurs when the stock is sold in the course of trading for a higher price, while a holding gain is made when stock increases in value because of inflation before the stock can be sold. Under the system of current cost accounting, this holding gain is calculated by using index numbers to calculate the opening and closing stock. This is done by applying the following formula:

Opening Stock   x $\dfrac{\text{Average Index During the Accounting Period}}{\text{Index at the Start of the Year}}$

Closing Stock   x $\dfrac{\text{Average Index for Financial Period}}{\text{Index at the End of the Year}}$

Monetary Working Capital Adjustment

When stock prices rise because of inflation a company needs more capital to purchase the same amount of stock. This cost can be offset if it is able to purchase the goods on credit, for then it is the creditor who is financing the extra cost. Unfortunately, when the firm sells goods, it will also have to give credit and so part of this gain will be lost to its debtors. As a result, a further adjustment is needed to the cost of sales adjustment, depending on whether debtors exceed creditors or vice versa. If debtors exceed creditors, then the firm is in effect giving away money to its debtors and this fact must be reflected by adding the cost to the cost of sales adjustment. If creditors exceed debtors, the firm is saving money and this saving should be deducted from the cost of sales adjustment, increasing the current cost profit. Once again the calculation is made using index numbers and the formula is:

$\dfrac{\text{Closing Monetary Working Capital}}{\text{Closing Index Number}}$ x $\dfrac{\text{Average Index Number}}{1}$

$\dfrac{\text{Opening Monetary Working Capital}}{\text{Opening Index Number}}$ x $\dfrac{\text{Average Index Number}}{1}$

Adjustments For Stock and Monetary Working Capital

Both of these adjustments will either reduce or increase the historical profit, depending upon whether or not trade has expanded or decreased. If trade has expanded, one would expect larger stocks and monetary working capital at the end of the year than at the beginning. In times of high inflation this would also be the case, even if the volume of trading remained at the same level - because inflation will increase its monetary value. Unless there is a fairly dramatic downturn in business activity, the end of year figure should be higher than that at the beginning and so the adjustment will be shown as a deduction from profits.

Gearing Adjustment

The gearing adjustment seeks to measure the gain to the business from being financed partly by long term debt capital instead of being financed entirely from share capital. This is because any unrealised holding gains, such as the revaluation of a fixed asset, or realised holding gain, such as the sale of stock, will be shown as a reserve in the current cost balance sheet.

While current cost accounting seeks to amend the historical accounts so as to show the effects of inflation, it has proved to be a most contentious subject. The Accounting Standards' Committee, on withdrawing their Statement of Accounting Practice 16, were only able to recommend that some attempt be made to consider how inflation can distort accounts prepared on a historical cost basis.

Unfortunately, since the end of the Second World War, Britain has suffered from persistent inflation at such high levels, that past monetary values have become meaningless. The real problem with any method which takes inflation into account, is that one is treating the symptoms rather than the disease.

Chapter 9
Introduction to Cost Accounting

Introduction

Management have to make decisions about what products to manufacture, their selling price, the number to be sold and the profits required to ensure that the firm earns a reasonable return on its capital employed. Cost and Management Accounting techniques provide management with information about the costs and the estimated profits at different levels of output, enabling them to make decisions.

Differences Between Financial and Cost Accounting

Companies are required by law to keep accurate records of their financial affairs which show their sales, purchases, expenses, assets and liabilities. Once a year the firm must have its accounts audited and prepare a profit and loss account and balance sheet. The Companies Act 1985 requires all companies to keep a system of financial accounting which will give a "true and fair view" of the business. It is from these accounts that the Inland Revenue will be able to calculate the amount of tax owed, and shareholders and lenders of funds to the business will be able to monitor its performance.

Financial accounting is concerned with the past and present. While this information is important, the main problem with it is that it tends to be out of date by the time it has been produced. As a result, management only know their costs and profits after they have been incurred. Cost accounting uses the information recorded by the financial accounting system to produce forecast financial statements. These will show the estimated cost of making or providing a service and, from this, a budgeted profit and loss account and balance sheet can be prepared. Management can then compare actual results with those budgeted and take corrective action immediately, instead of having to wait until the end of the financial year or quarter.

Benefits of Operating A Cost Accounting System

Unlike financial accounting, there is no legal requirement to produce cost accounts but, if they are kept, the benefits from producing them must exceed their costs. If a business has an efficient and accurate cost accounting system, costs can be ascertained before they are incurred. This information can then be used for planning and control purposes. Unless this information is available, management will not know whether they are selling the product for a profit or at a loss. The main benefit of operating a cost accounting system is that it is immediately apparent which products contribute most to the business's profit and which products or services have the highest costs in relation to their selling price.

What is Meant by the Term Cost?

In accounting the word cost means any money spent on producing a product or providing a service. This is referred to as a cost unit and the place where it is produced or provided as a cost centre. These two terms are fundamental to cost accounting. Management need to know the cost of making a product before determining its selling price. The cost price will be made up of the direct costs of production, such as direct materials and direct labour, together with its apportioned share of overheads, such as factory rent and rates. The aim is to charge all costs to the product or service, thereby providing management with accurate information before setting prices and determing output levels. If this is not done, prices may be set too low or at too high a level, damaging the future profitability of the business.

Direct Costs

These are costs which are incurred as the product is made. They include the cost of the materials used in production, plus the wages of the workers directly involved in manufacturing, together with any other direct costs of production. Collectively these costs are referred to as the prime cost.

Indirect Costs

Direct costs are not the only ones involved in making a product. Other costs, such as indirect materials, indirect labour, rent, factory insurance and cleaning, will also be incurred and these must be accounted for. Any cost which is not directly related to production is referred to as an indirect cost. Examples are indirect materials, indirect labour, rent, factory insurance and factory cleaning. These costs are not charged directly to the product or cost unit but are shared amongst them by, firstly, apportioning the overheads to cost centres, and then by absorbing them into the cost units.

The cost will be made up of all the direct costs plus any indirect costs which are incurred in producing the good or service.

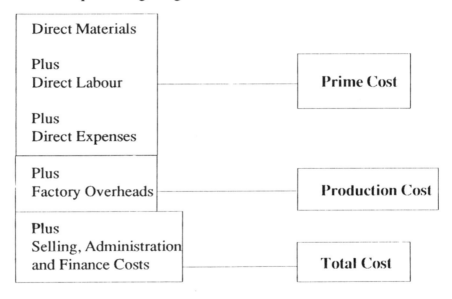

Figure 19: Costs of Making a Product

Costing Overheads

In order to establish and maintain a costing system, management must be able to allocate overheads to cost centres. The costs must be allocated or apportioned to the cost centre depending on how traceable they are to that area of the firm. Costs, such as a supervisor's wages in a production department, relate directly to that area of the firm and are therefore easy to allocate to cost centres, while factory insurance is harder to allocate because the insurance policy is likely to cover the whole factory instead of individual departments. In this case, the cost must be apportioned to the various cost centres by using a method which seems equitable to all participants. If this is not done, one centre may look profitable when in fact it is losing money because the overhead has been apportioned incorrectly.

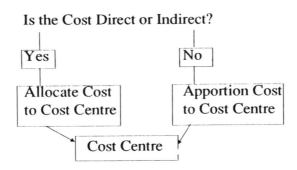

Figure 20: Allocation of Costs to Production

Methods of Cost Apportionment

Whatever system of apportionment is chosen it must be fair, practicable and cost effective to implement. In theory each cost could be worked out in minute detail and charged accordingly. Such detail would defeat the objects of setting up such a system because the costs involved would outweigh the benefits gained. The firm needs a method which is not too costly to calculate and install but which will allocate the cost to each department on a reasonable basis, according to the benefit which it receives.

There are three main methods of apportioning costs. They are according to the amount produced, the hours worked and the machine hours used, but other methods may also be appropriate, such as the quantity sold or the amount of materials used.

Whichever method is used, it is vital that the overhead cost is charged to the cost unit so that it bears both its direct costs plus its fair share of overheads. The following example shows how overhead costs can be charged to cost units:

Example

A firm knows that its overheads for a year amount to £25,000 and that it makes 10,000 handsaws a year (cost Unit). The direct costs allocated to each saw are £7, but the firm needs to know how much to charge for the overheads incurred in production. The firm can use 2,500 labour hours and 2,000 machine hours on saw production.

The firm's management must decide how to absorb the overhead cost into the cost unit. In this way they will know the actual cost of producing a saw. The three main methods used are the output, labour and machine output methods. Whichever method is chosen, the overhead absorption rate is calculated by dividing the total overhead cost by the level of activity. Examples of each method are shown below.

a) Calculation of the Overhead Absorption Rate using the Output Method.

This is calculated by the formula:

$$\frac{\text{Total Overheads for Cost Centre}}{\text{Number of Cost Units Produced}} = \frac{£25,000}{10,000} = £2.50$$

Cost of Manufacturing a Saw

Direct Costs	£7.00
Overheads	2.50
Total Cost	9.50

b) Calculation of the Overhead Absorption Rate using the Labour Hour Method

This is calculated by the formula:

$$\frac{\text{Total Overheads for Cost Centre}}{\text{Number of Labour Hours}} = \frac{£25,000}{2,500} = £10.00$$

Cost of Manufacturing a Saw

Direct Costs	£7.00
Overheads	10.00
Total Cost	17.00

c) Calculation of the Overhead Absorption Method using the Machine Hour Method

This is calculated by the formula:

$$\frac{\text{Total Overheads for Cost Centre}}{\text{Number of machine Hours}} = \frac{£25,000}{2,000} = £12.50$$

Cost of Manufacturing a Saw

Direct Costs	£7.00
Overheads	12.50
Total Cost	19.50

Choosing the Most Appropriate Method

This example shows how the cost will vary according to the method used to allocate overheads to cost units. The firm should chose a method which is appropriate and which reflects the level of activity.

Classification of Costs

Accountants classify costs according to their nature, function and behaviour. The nature defines the type of cost, such as the cost of the raw material needed to make the product, whereas functional classification describes the area of the business which has incurred the cost, such as the sales department.

Once managment know the nature and function of their costs, they need to know how they alter according to different levels of activity. Some costs will remain unchanged, while others will vary proportionately to output. This is what is meant by the term cost behaviour.

How Costs Alter According To The Level of Activity

Fixed Costs

These are costs which remain constant at a given level of activity. The cost of renting a building is an example of a fixed cost because the amount of rent paid will depend upon the space rented and not on the level of output or sales. So long as the firm does not need any additional space, this cost will remain fixed.

Examples of Fixed Costs

Management can expect the following costs to remain relatively stable regardless of the level of output within the organisation: rent, rates, road tax, depreciation, advertising and insurance payments. These do not move in sympathy with production and sales but are unavoidable and are incurred even when the business is not working.

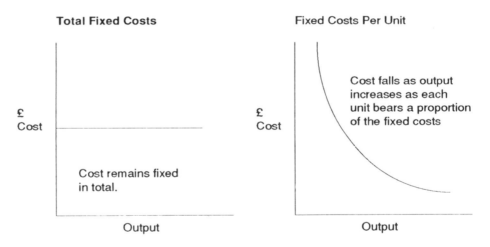

Figure 21: How Fixed Costs behave according to Activity

Variable Costs

These are costs which vary with changes in the level of output. A firm making shirts will have to purchase enough cloth to make each shirt, and the more shirts it makes the greater the cost of the material. Any cost which increases with output is a variable cost, even though the cost per unit remains the same.

The more shirts that are made, the greater the total material cost, although in accounting the material cost per shirt is assumed to remain constant. Quantity discounts are therefore ignored.

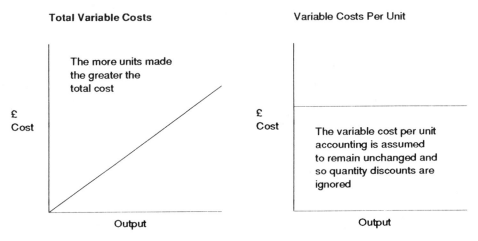

Figure 22: How Variable Costs Behave According to Activity

The Application of Fixed and Variable Costs in Management Decision Making

Example

A coach operator is planning to offer a day trip from Cardiff to London. The operator must pay for the hire of the coach and intends to give every passenger a packed lunch. These will be bought only after the customer has paid for the ticket. The coach will seat 50 people. The operator knows that it will cost £500 to hire the coach and that each packed lunch will cost £4.

In this example, the hire of the coach is a fixed cost. Once it is booked, the hirer must pay for it, even if there are no passengers. On the other hand, the packed lunches are a variable cost for they will only be provided to passengers who have booked a place. The tour operator will need £500 to cover the hire cost and will need an additional £200 to provide all travellers with a packed lunch (£4 x 50). If there are any unbooked places on the coach, the operator will save the £4 cost of the packed lunch as it is a variable cost.

The problem for the operator is to decide what price to charge for the journey. The price must be competitive with other forms of transport as well as covering costs and providing a profit.

The cost of the packed lunch is variable and so, the more people who travel, the greater the cost. As each packed lunch costs £4, the total variable cost will be the number of people requiring lunch multiplied by the price. The £500 cost of the coach, however, is fixed and so, although this cost is fixed, the cost for each passenger will fall as more people travel. This is so because the fixed cost is shared between the number of travellers. This can be seen from the table:

Cost of The Coach Trip To London

Number of Passengers	Fixed Cost Per Person	Variable Cost Per Person	Total Cost
	£	£	£
0	500	-	500
1	500	4	504
10	50	40	540
20	25	80	580
40	12.50	160	660
50	10	200	700

The table shows that, as more passengers travel on the coach, the fixed cost per passenger falls, even though the total sum required to hire the coach remains at £500. The cost of the packed lunch is variable and so, the more people travelling, the greater the cost to the operator. It is the variable cost which increases the total cost. If the total cost is divided by the number of passengers, the total cost per passenger can be calculated. The more passengers, the more competitive the operator can be on price and the greater the likelihood of selling all the seats on the coach.

The table shows that, if 40 people travel, they must each pay £12.50 to cover their fixed costs but, if 50 people travel, the fixed cost per person will fall to £10. This example shows that, although fixed costs remain fixed in total, they fall as output increases, whereas variable costs increase in proportion to output.

We have already seen that fixed costs are unaffected by changes in activity, while variable costs increase proportionately as output increases. This is important to management when considering what price to charge for a product or service, as the different costs will require different treatment. The fixed costs must be paid regardless of the level of activity, while the variable costs will only be incurred once production begins.

Consider a hotel which has been asked to quote for a firm's annual dinner. The company would like the use of a function room with a buffet reception for about 200 guests. The hotel's management must decide what the costs of providing the service are and then set a price which will cover its costs and leave a profit.

The hotel's management must charge for all the direct and indirect costs be they fixed or variable. Costs, such as the food, its preparation and service, will be direct costs and can be allocated to each person served. The indirect costs, such as supervisors' wages, hotel rent and rates, must be apportioned first to the function room (which is the cost centre) and then shared amongst each meal (which is the cost unit).

If the hotel can cover all of its direct variable costs plus any variable indirect costs, the balance which is left over can be used to pay the fixed costs. The surplus which is left after paying the variable costs is called contribution, for it will contribute to the firm's fixed costs and, ultimately, to its profits.

Accounts can then be drawn up to show the variable costs of providing a service, the contribution earned from different selling prices and the profit or loss which will be made after paying the fixed costs.

Example of an Income Statement showing the Variable and Fixed Cost of the Function Evening

	£	£
Sales		3,000
Less Variable Costs		
Food	1,200	
Direct Labour	600	
Direct Variable Overhead	200	
Prime Cost		2,000
Contribution		1,000
Less Fixed Costs		700
Profit		300

132

By using this format instead of the traditional profit and loss layout, management can see immediately the detailed break down of the costs involved in providing the product or service. Assuming that the fixed and variable overheads have been allocated and apportioned correctly, the hotel will know exactly the cost of providing the function. This greatly assists management when tendering for orders as they know their costs and required profit margins to meet their financial targets.

Chapter 10
Profit and Output Decisions

Introduction

The aim of a cost accounting system is to provide relevant cost information to management so that decisions can be made about which products should be produced, in what quantity and at what price they should be sold. By using cost accounting techniques, firms are able to make the best use of their resources, optimising the return which can be made from their capital employed.

Cost and Output Decisions

We have already seen that costs can be classified according to their behaviour. The fixed costs will remain unchanged with variations in output, while the variable costs will vary proportionately. Once the costs are known, decisions can be made on how to maximise the earnings potential of the business in relation to its costs.

The Concept of Contribution

All firms must pay their fixed costs regardless of their level of activity, but the variable costs will only be incurred as goods are produced or a service provided. If the selling price is greater than the variable cost, a surplus will be made on each sale. This surplus is called contribution because it can be used to contribute towards the fixed costs of the firm. Once these have been covered, the additional contribution from each sale will make profits for the firm.

Example
A furniture factory makes 1,200 wooden book cases. The variable cost of making each one is as follows,

Variable Cost of Production	£
Wood used in production	30
Direct Labour	15
Variable Direct Overheads	10
	55

Each book case costs the firm £55 to make, before any fixed costs are apportioned to it. If the fixed costs are £30,000 and the book cases sell for £85 each, the firm will make a £30 contribution on each book case sold.

How to Calculate Contribution

Selling Price	£85
Less Variable Costs	55
Contribution	30

On each sale the firm now receives thirty pounds which can be used to pay the fixed costs. Once these have been paid, the firm will start to make a profit.

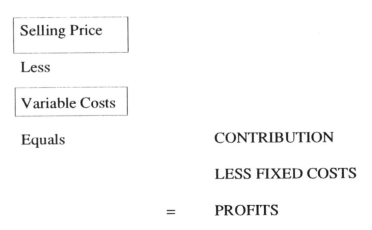

Figure 23: The Inflow & Uses of Contribution

Each £30 contributes to the fixed costs and, as soon as these have been covered, builds profits for the business.

Contribution and Profit

Contribution is not profit. This is because only the variable costs have been covered. The fixed costs have yet to be paid. Once these are covered the firm makes its profits, which is the surplus of money received over its costs.

The Break Even Concept

As long as the selling price is higher than the cost of the product or service sold, a profit will be made. While this information is important, the management need to know how many sales have to be made for the business to cover its own costs and then move into profit. There is always a danger that the profits earned are insufficient to cover all the firm's costs, leading to the business making a loss at the end of the financial year. Management need to consider both their fixed and variable costs, together with their planned level of sales, before setting realistic output and profit levels.

Break even analysis provides this information by showing the level of sales needed to cover the firm's fixed and variable costs. Once the firm has reached its break even point, any sales above this point will create profits for the firm. Sales managers then know how much stock they have to sell just to cover the business's own costs.

How to Calculate the Break Even Point

Once the selling price exceeds the variable costs, contribution will be earned which can be used to meet the fixed costs. If a firm makes £10 contribution on each sale and has fixed costs of £1,000, it will reach its break even point once one hundred units have been sold. This is so because the variable costs have already been covered and so each £10 reduces the fixed costs until they have all been covered.

If the fixed costs are divided by the contribution from each sale, the number of cost units which must be sold to break even can be calculated. This is often shown as a formula:

Number of units to break even	Fixed Costs		
	Contribution (from each sale)	=	Number of units to breakeven

Contribution = Unit Selling Price, less unit Variable Cost.

Using the same figures as in the previous example the break even point in units is

Fixed Costs	£30,000	=	1,000 book cases to break even
Contribution	30		

Another way of calculating the break even point is to work out the level of sales which must be made in order to break even. The formula is:

Level of Sales to break even	=	Total Sales Value x Fixed Costs	
		Total Contribution	= Sales to break even

Contribution = Total Sales, less total Variable Costs

Using the same figures the break even point in terms of sales is

$$\frac{\text{Total Sales Value x Fixed Costs}}{\text{Total Contribution}} = \frac{£102,000 \times £30,000}{£36,000}$$

The firm must have sales of £85,000 if it is to breakeven.

Graphical Presentation of This Information

It is also possible to calculate the break even point by plotting costs and sales on a graph. The fixed costs will be shown as a straight line because, at that level of activity, these costs will remain unchanged. The variable costs will increase the total costs as output increases and so these should be plotted above the fixed cost line, which will show the total cost line. The break even point occurs where the sales line crosses the total cost line.

The break even chart allows the relationship between costs, profits and volume to be shown as a graph. By using this method of presentation, it is immediately apparent what level of sales must be achieved if the firm is to break even.

Example of A Break Even Chart

Using the same figures as in the previous example, the break even point can now be shown graphically. It is a good idea to work out the break even point arithmetically before plotting the information as it will assist in calculating the best scale to use for the graph.

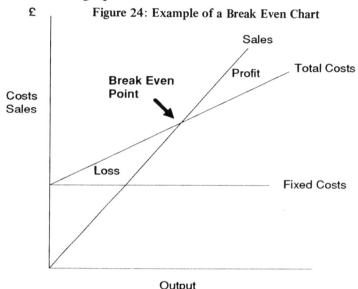

Figure 24: Example of a Break Even Chart

The chart shows that at the break even point contribution equals the firm's total costs. The difference between sales achieved and the sales needed to break even is called the margin of safety and, by multiplying the margin of safety by the contribution per sale, the firm's profit can be calculated.Once this is known it is possible to calculate the profit at any level of sales and the percentage contribution earned from each sale generated. This can be seen from the following example:

Consider the following Income Statement

	£	Percentage
Sales	100	100
Less Variable Costs	60	60
Contribution	40	40
Less Fixed Costs	20	
Profit	20	

138

In this example the contribution percentage of sales is £40 or 40% and it is possible to present this information by drawing a profit to volume graph. Consider the following example:

The Food and Beverages Company has three main product divisions. During the last six months total sales were £300,000 and variable costs were £190,000. The fixed costs were £65,000. The company would like to know its profit to volume ratio and has supplied a detailed breakdown of the sales and variable costs for each division.

	Sales Turnover £	Variable Costs £
Division One	140,000	40,000
Division Two	100,000	70,000
Division Three	60,000	80,000

The profit to volume ratio is calculated by the following formula:

$$\frac{\text{Sales - Variable Costs}}{\text{Sales}} \times 100 = \frac{£300,000 - £190,000}{£300,000} \times 100 = 36.7\%$$

This ratio shows the relationship between contribution and sales. The contribution first covers the fixed costs of £65,000 and then goes on to yield a profit of £45,000. This information can be presented as a graph by first calculating the profit to volume ratio for each division and then plotting the information on graph paper. The individual contributions are:

Division	Sales	Variables Costs	Contribution	P/V Ratio
One	£140,000	£40,000	£100,000	71%
Two	100,000	70,000	30,000	30.0%
Three	60,000	80,000	(20,000)	(33.3%)
	300,000	190,000	110,000	37%
Fixed Overheads			65,000	
Profit			45,000	

The individual and total contributions can now be plotted. The steepness of the curve will show the total contribution.

139

Profit to Volume Graph for the Food and Beverage Company

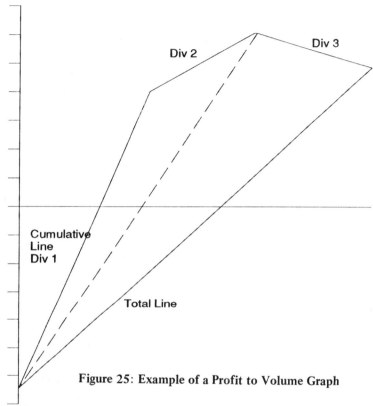

£000's

Div 2

Div 3

Cumulative
Line
Div 1

Total Line

Figure 25: Example of a Profit to Volume Graph

Explanation of the Profit to Volume Graph

The profit to volume graph shows the contribution to fixed costs from each product and the total contribution for all three divisions. The horizontal line is the fixed cost line and the first sale yields contribution which will go towards the fixed costs. As sales increase, so does the amount of contribution, until it crosses the fixed cost line and goes on to show the profit from a given level of sales.

In our example the chart shows that division three fails to make a contribution as it does not even cover its variable costs. In such a case, management must consider whether or not the price could be increased or the variable costs reduced. Unless the product assists in selling the other two products, the firm should consider launching a new product or rationalising the business so that the costs of the third division can be eliminated. This may prove to be a difficult task if the three divisions are inter-related, because the costs cannot be isolated. In such a case, it would be a better strategy to launch a new product which can earn a contribution towards the firm's fixed costs.

If management need to make a certain amount of profit, this should be added to the fixed costs before calculating the break even point. By dividing the contribution per cost unit sold into the total figure for fixed costs and profits, the required level of sales can be calculated. The formula is:

Fixed cost + Level of Profit Required
Contribution

Example

The Hillside Garden Centre specalises in selling rare orchids. Its fixed costs are £8,000 and the variable cost of each plant and its associated cost are £8. The plants sell for £20 each and the firm would like to make a £10,000 profit. The owners would like to know how many plants must be sold to achieve this level of profit?

Calculation

	£
Selling Price	20.00
Less Variable Cost	8.00
Contribution	12.00

$$\frac{\text{Fixed Costs} + \text{Profit}}{\text{Contribution}} = \text{Number of plants which must be sold to cover costs and achieve the desired profit.}$$

	£
Fixed Costs	8,000
Profit	10,000
Total	18,000

$$\frac{\text{Fixed Costs} + \text{Profit} = £18,000}{\text{Contribution} \qquad £12} = \text{1,500 plants must be sold if the garden centre is to cover its costs and reach its profit target.}$$

Limitations of Break Even Analysis

While it is important for management to know the level of sales needed to break even, the calculations are based on a number of assumptions and, if these change, different break even points will occur. The assumptions can be categorised into two main areas — those relating to costs and those relating to sales and output.

The first assumption refers to the firm's costs. It is always assumed that both fixed and variable costs increase in a straight line as output increases. This will not happen, for many firms' costs are not linear with volume. If this is the case the firm will move in and out of break even, even though its sales are increasing.

Assumptions are also made about the firm's costs because, in break even analysis, they are always neatly separated into their fixed and variable elements. In practice this may not be as easy because some costs are in fact semi-variable, having both a fixed and variable element. An example of such a cost is electricity which has a fixed standing charge plus a charge for each unit used, which is variable. It may be difficult for a business to separate its semi-variable costs. Break even analysis further assumes that fixed costs will remain constant at that level of output whereas, in practice, they might increase as might variable costs.

The second set of assumptions refer to the level of sales and the product mix of the firm, which is expected not to change. In practice the selling price may well be altered to gain additional sales and the product mix may be altered as new products are launched and old ones withdrawn.

Lastly, it is taken for granted that sales and production will always be in balance, although this may not be the case. The old business joke that sales departments can sell the stock which the firm has not yet got but can't sell the ones it has is very poignant when considering break even for it will adversely affect the calculation.

In spite of these limitations, break even is still a useful concept for it helps management determine output levels and selling prices. Ideally the firm should seek products which have a high contribution to sales ratio and which have a low break even point. Unfortunately, this last fact is often determined by the industry in which the firm operates. For example, hotels and transport operators tend to have high fixed costs and low variable costs and the nature of the business means that this cannot be altered. Nevertheless break even is still useful in helping management set prices which will maximise the contribution earned from each journey or each hotel bedroom occupied. In this way the firm may be able to reduce its losses even if it can't make a profit for, if no one travels on a train or stays at an hotel, that sale can never be regained — so any contribution which can be earned by altering the price will help to pay the fixed costs.

Chapter 11
Absorption and Marginal Costing

Introduction

Any business must cover both its fixed and variable costs if it is to make a profit. Absorption costing charges both the fixed and variable costs involved in making a product or providing a service. Marginal costing separates the fixed costs and only calculates the variable cost. Once the variable or marginal cost has been determined, this is subtracted from the selling price to find the contribution. The fixed costs are then subtracted from the contribution, thereby showing the firm's profit.

Marginal costing is, therefore, not a costing method but a costing technique for it does not calculate all of the costs in making or providing a service. Its real importance lies in the way it can be used to assist decision making, by showing the contribution which can be earned in different circumstances, which can then be used to pay the firm's fixed costs.

Figure 26: Comparison of Absorption & Marginal Costing

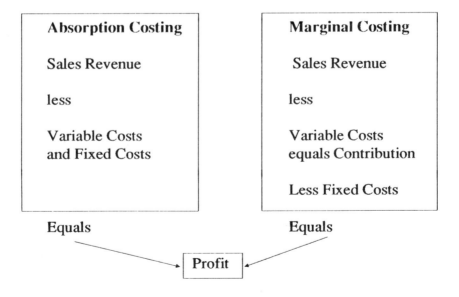

144

The different treatment of costs by the two methods can be seen by preparing a statement showing the absorption and marginal cost of making a pullover.

Cost of Manufacturing A Woollen Pullover

	Absorption Costing		Marginal Costing	
	£	£	£	£
Selling Price		50.00		50.00
Direct Materials	6.00		6.00	
Direct Labour	8.00		8.00	
Direct expenses	2.00		2.00	
Prime Cost	16.00		16.00	
Variable Overhead	2.00		2.00	
Fixed Overhead	10.00		-	
Total Cost		28.00	Marginal Cost	18.00
Profit		22.00	Contribution	32.00

How Are The Costs Calculated?

The prime cost is calculated by adding together the material, labour and direct costs. If accurate records are kept for materials ordered, delivered stored and issued, the business will know the material cost content of each product. Similarly, labour costs will be shown by clock cards, time sheets or job cards and route cards. Once again the more accurate the firm's paperwork, the better it will be able to produce accurate labour costs for different departments and products. The factory overheads are determined by estimating the following:

1 Estimated Total Factory Overheads

2 Estimated Level of Activity

By dividing 1 by 2, the firm's recovery or absorption rate can be calculated. In this example the figures were:

<u>Estimated Factory Overheads</u>	<u>£60,000</u>
Estimated Labour Hours	10,000

Absorption Rate = $\dfrac{£60,000}{10,000}$ = £6.00 per Direct Labour Hour

If it takes two hours to manufacture the pullover, the indirect factory overheads are £12. The accuracy of this figure is therefore determined by the accuracy of our estimates of cost and activity and by the suitability of our choice of activity. Other bases of activity are:

Direct Labour Cost
Machine Hours
Prime Cost
Direct material Cost
Number of Units

It is important to remember that the marginal or variable costs do not depend on the estimation of overheads and activity. They move in sympathy with production and sales. In this example the cost of producing one extra pullover is £18.00 and so ten extra pullovers would cost the firm another £180.

The difference between the selling price and the variable cost is known as contribution. Each time a pullover is sold, £32 of contribution is earned to meet the firm's fixed costs. Each sale will build a fund of contribution which can be used to pay fixed costs and which hopefully will be sufficient to yield profits for the business.

Marginal Costing

As stated earlier, marginal costing is not a cost accounting method for it only considers the variable costs involved in making a product or providing a service. The fixed costs are considered at a later stage in the calculation whereas, in absorption or full costing, they are considered alongside the variable costs. By separating the fixed and variable costs into their separate elements, management can make decisions about pricing strategies, output levels and predicted profit levels.

How Marginal Costs Behave With Changes In Output

Marginal or variable costs do not depend on the estimation of overheads and activity because they move in sympathy with production and sales. As long as a firm operates within its current operating capacity, its total variable costs will increase in proportion to output, while the fixed costs per unit will fall as the total fixed costs are spread over an increasing number of units. If management consider both the fixed and variable costs, the firm's profitability will fluctuate with changes in output because increases in output will reduce the cost per unit. This makes it difficult for management to know the costs involved before setting selling prices. There is always a danger that, if output falls, the firm may sell its products at a loss, because of the increase in fixed cost per unit produced as output levels fall. This can be seen from the following example:

The High Output Company

The managers at the High Output Company always try to produce as many units as possible so that they can be keep the fixed costs per unit as low as possible. Unfortunately the firm's sales are seasonal, and so the firm suffers from having an erratic demand for its products. During the first quarter its output and costs have been as follows.

	January	February	March
Output (units)	500	1,000	2,000
Variable Cost £2 per unit	£ 1,000	£ 2,000	£ 4,000
Fixed Costs	4,000	4,000	4,000
Total Cost	5,000	6,000	8,000
Cost Per Unit	£ 10.00	£ 6.00	£ 4.00
Selling Price	8.00	8.00	8.00
Profit/Loss (Profit per unit x output)	£(1,000)	£2,000	£8,000

This example shows how the cost of the product varies according to output. This makes it difficult to set selling prices and predict profit levels, even though the managers know all of the firm's costs. When output falls to 500 units, the firm makes a loss of £2.00 on each one sold, but once output increases to 2,000, an £8,000 profit is achieved.

Marginal costing techniques assume that the variable costs of production will remain unaltered regardless of the level of activity. It is this assumption which makes it a useful technique for appraising pricing strategies and determining output levels. The marginal or variable cost can then be subtracted from the selling price so that the contribution from each sale can be calculated. This can be seen by preparing the High Output Company's costs in marginal costing format.

	January	February	March
Output (units)	500	1,000	2,000
Selling Price	£	£	£
Per Unit	8	8	8
Less Variable Cost			
Per Unit	2	2	2
Contribution Per Unit	6	6	6
Total Contribution	3,000	6,000	12,000
Less Fixed Costs	4,000	4,000	4,000
Profit/(Loss)	(1,000)	2,000	8,000

Note: Total contribution equals contribution per unit times output.

By preparing the information in this way, management can see the contribution earned from each sale. Contribution is not profit, because the fixed costs have not yet been covered, but it can be used to pay the fixed costs and any surplus after paying them will give rise to profits. Any change in selling price will, therefore, affect the amount of contribution earned per unit, but the variable cost per unit of production will be unaffected by the level of activity. The total contribution is calculated by multiplying the output by the contribution per unit. The aim is to increase the total contribution by selling at a price which maximises sales. In this way the fixed costs will be covered and any surplus will be profits.

148

The Separation of Costs Into Their Fixed And Variable Elements

In the last three examples the management have known the costs involved because accurate cost records have been kept. These costs may not always be available and must be calculated. This can be seen in the following example:

Muddling Through Limited

The managers at Muddling Through Limited do not keep accurate cost records but they do keep records of output levels, prime costs and overheads. For the last three months the costs have been as follows:

	January	February	March
Output	7,000	11,000	16,000
Costs	£	£	£
Prime Cost	30,450	47,850	69,600
Production Overhead	43,440	51,120	60,720

Before separating the costs, it is important to remember how different costs behave according to different levels of activity.

Variable Costs: These remain fixed per unit, but the total variable cost will increase with activity.

Fixed Costs: These remain fixed in total, but fall per unit as output is increased.

Separation of Costs Into Their Fixed And Variable Components

Prime Cost

We have already seen that the prime cost is a variable cost, but this can be proved. The figures show that the costs increase with output but, if the cost per unit remains constant when the total prime cost is divided by output, it is a variable cost.

Caluculation of Prime Cost

	January £	February £	March £
Prime Cost	30,450	47,850	69,600
Output	7,000	11,000	16,000
Cost Per Unit	£4.35	£4.35	£4.35

The prime cost is, therefore, a variable cost.

Production Overhead

A fixed cost remains the same regardless of changes in activity. In this example the production overhead cost increases with output and so the production overhead must contain a fixed and a variable element. This can be proved again by dividing the highest and lowest production overhead costs by the output figure. If the cost per unit falls, there must be a fixed cost element which is bringing down the cost per unit. It is possible that the overhead cost could be completely variable. If this is the case, the cost per unit will be the same, even though output has increased, for variable costs per unit do not change with output levels.

Calculation of the variable element of the Production Overhead

Production Overhead	Cost £	Output	Cost Per Unit
Highest Level of Activity	60,720	16,000	£3.80
Lowest Level of Activity	43,440	7,000	£6.21

This shows that the cost per unit falls as output increases and so the production overhead must be made up of fixed and variable costs. These must now be separated.

If the change in output is divided by the change in cost, the variable cost per unit can be calculated. This can best be explained by a diagram.

The diagram shows the production overhead's fixed and total costs. The difference between the two lines is the variable cost and, as output increases, the distance between the two lines increases.

150

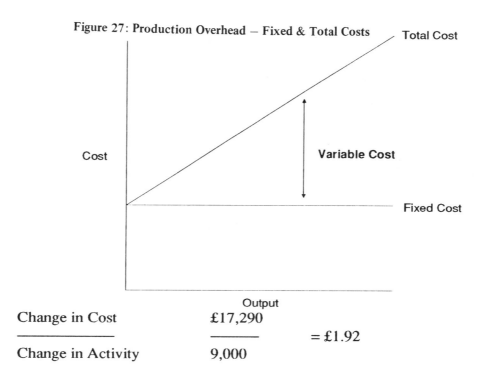

Figure 27: Production Overhead – Fixed & Total Costs

Change in Cost	£17,290
────────────	──── = £1.92
Change in Activity	9,000

Once the variable cost of the production overhead has been determined, the fixed cost can be calculated. This is done by multiplying output by the unit variable production overhead cost, thereby calculating the variable part of the overhead cost. If this is then subtracted from the total cost, the fixed costs can be determined. If there have been no additional fixed costs. they should remain unaltered in total even though output has increased.

Calculation of the fixed element of the Production Overhead

Production Overhead	January	February	March
Total Cost	43,440	51,120	60,720
Less variable cost per unit £1.92 multiplied by output	13,440	21,120	30,720
Fixed Cost	30,000	30,000	30,000

The costs have now been separated into their fixed and variable components and can be used by management to help them in their role as decision makers.

151

What Costs Are Relevant To Decision Making?

The only costs which are relevant are those that affect future cash flows as soon as the decision has been made. The following costs must be considered before any decision is taken:

Sunk Cost: Any expenditure which has already taken place in the past and which will not be affected by a particular decision under consideration can be ignored. These costs are referred to as sunk costs.

Incremental Cost: If a cost will be incurred if a particular course of action is taken, but avoided if the action is not taken, the cost is said to be incremental. Specific fixed costs appropriate to the decision may also be incremental if, as a result of not taking the action contemplated, they can be avoided. Incremental costs are sometimes called differential costs.

Opportunity cost: If the firm's resources could be put to an alternative use, then the opportunity cost is the opportunity foregone.

Financial Aspects of Decision Making

Whenever there are alternative choices of action, a decision must be made. From an accounting view point most decisions can be classified into two different categories. They are accept or reject decisons and ranking decisions. Management must make an accept or reject decision whenever there is only one opportunity available. Ranking decisons must be made whenever there is either more than one opportunity, or there is mutual exclusivity between different opportunities.

Short Term Decision Making

Whenever short term decisions are being made, the relevant costs are important for they incorporate the concept of "contribution" or "marginal costing". In the short term, the only relevant costs are the variable costs and so management must consider what will happen to profits if the sales level changes.

How Marginal Costing Techniques Assist Managerial Decision

This is best explained by studying the following examples:

Assessing Profitability

The General Manufacturing Company make and sell three products codenamed the ZX1, ZX2 and the ZX3. The relevant information is:

Product	Sales (units)	Selling Price £	Marginal Cost £	Contribution £
ZX1	1,000	15.00	10.00	5.00 per unit
ZX2	500	20.00	12.00	8.00 per unit
ZX3	100	30.00	10.00	20.00 per unit

	£
Total Contribution for Product ZX1 (Contribution per unit x output)	5,000
Total contribution for ZX2	4,000
Total contribution for ZX3	2,000
Total Contribution	11,000
Less Fixed Costs	5,000
Profit	6,000

If the firm is to maximise its profits, it must maximise its contribution. This can be achieved by making more of the three products, but the management need to know which product or products make the most profit. One way of assessing the products is to calculate the contribution to sales as a percentage. This is sometimes also called the profit to volume ratio. A ranking can then be given to each product according to the contribution earned.

Product	Contribution/Sales	Ranking
ZX1	33% (approx)	3
ZX2	40%	2
ZX3	67% (approx)	1

By ranking the products in this way, management can see that product ZX3 yields the greatest contribution. This may not be the case if there is a limiting factor. A limiting factor could be that the firm has only so many machine hours available. It will then want to earn the maximum contribution from each hour worked.

If this is the case, management need to know how long it takes to make each product. In this example the machine hours are:

Product	Machine Hours
ZX1	3 hours
ZX2	5 hours
ZX3	8 hours

The firm must make the best use of its scarce resource, which in this case is the number of machine hours. If the limiting factor is divided into the contribution, management will know how much contribution is earned from each machine hour worked.

Product	Contribution Per Limiting Factor
ZX1	£5/ 3 hours = £1.67 per machine hour
ZX2	£8/ 5 hours = £1.60 per machine hour
ZX3	£20/ 8 = £2.50 per machine hour

Once the limiting factor is taken into consideration, the firm should manaufacture and sell product ZX1 to meet the demand for ZX1, then ZX2, then ZX3, until all the available hours have been used up.

Making Decisions When There Are Limiting Factors

Example
The Radio Company manufacture two small circuit boards.The variable costs of manufacture are:

	Small £	Large £
Direct Materials	1	3
Direct Labour (3 hours)	6	3
Variable Overhead	1	1
Marginal Cost	8	7

The small circuit board sells for £14 and the large one for £11. During August the firm has only 8,000 hours of direct labour and the management need to know which product should have priority, so that the firm can maximise its profits.

Solution
In this example, labour is the limiting factor and so priority should be given to the circuit board which earns the maximum contribution from each direct labour hour.

	Small £	Large £
Selling Price	14	11
Variable Cost	8	7
Unit Contribution	6	4
Labour hours per unit	2 hours	1 hours
Contribution per labour hour (= unit of limiting factor)	£3	£4

155

Because labour is in short supply, it is more profitable to give priority to the large circuit board. Unit contribution is not the correct way to decide priorities because it takes two hours to earn £6 from the small circuit board and only one hour to earn £4 from the large circuit board.

Make or Buy Decisions

Manufacturing companies will sometimes receive quotes from suppliers for components. If the quote is below the firm's current cost for making the product, a decision must be made whether or not to buy in the component or continue making it. From a financial viewpoint the order should be accepted if the cost of the bought-in-product is less than the firm's variable cost of manufacture. This rule only applies if the idle factors of production can then be applied to more profitable work.

Example

Motor Components

Motor Components specalise in oil filters for British, European and Japanese cars. One particular filter is used extensively in British cars and the firm has received a quote from another supplier at a cost of £5 per unit. The firm's management are currently considering whether or not to accept the order. The firm's costs and production are as follows:

Production 30,000 units

	£
Variable Cost	90,000
Fixed costs	100,000
Total Costs	190,000

Cost per unit   £6.33 (total cost divided by output)

Supplier's Price £5.00 per unit.

	Manufacture £	Purchase £
Marginal Cost	90,000	-
Suppliers Price		150,000
Fixed Costs	100,000	10,000
Total Cost	190,000	260,000

It would be more expensive for the firm to purchase the components than to make them. The quote should be rejected.

Close a Department or Cost Centre

Example

The Glass Tower Hotel

The Glass Tower Hotel has three bars on the ground floor. The management are considering closing one of the bars (because it is losing money) and converting the area into a reading room for guests. The costs for the three bars are as follows:

	Caribbean Bar £	Glass Tower Bar £	Bar By The Pool £	Total £
Sales	30,000	12,000	18,000	60,000
Marginal Cost	18,000	7,000	11,000	36,000
Contribution	12,000	5,000	7,000	24,000
Fixed Costs	6,000	6,000	6,000	18,000
Profit/(loss)	6,000	(1,000)	1,000	6,000

These figures can now be used to see what would happen to the hotel's overall profitability if the Glass Tower Bar was shut or kept open.

	Close One Bar £	Keep All Bars £	Change in Sales Costs, and Profit £
Sales	48,000	60,000	12,000
Marginal Cost	29,000	36,000	7,000
Contribution	19,000	24,000	5,000
Fixed Costs	18,000	18,000	nil
Profit	1,000	6,000	5000

The hotel should not close the Glass Tower Bar, unless the area can be used to generate an additional source of revenue.

Accept Or Reject An Order

Example

The Ladies' Hand Soap Company

The Ladies' Hand Soap Company is currently only operating at 50% capacity. The firm produces boxed soap sets but has found that demand has fallen. The firm has just received an order from an overseas country for 50,000 boxed sets of soap at £3.00 a box. If the order is accepted, the firm would be able to operate at 100% capacity, but the management are worried at the low price. The firm's fixed costs are £50,000.

	Existing Orders (50% £	Overseas Order (50%) £
Selling Price (per unit)	5	3
Marginal Cost (per unit)	2	2
Fixed Costs(Absorbed fixed costs/ output)	1	0.50

	Existing Orders £	Overseas Orders £	Combined Orders £
Sales (output x selling price)	250,000	150,000	400,000
Marginal Cost	100,000	100,000	200,000
Contribution	150,000	50,000	200,000
Fixed Costs	25,000	25,000	50,000
Profit	125,000	25,000	150,000

The order should be accepted because the firm will make an extra £25,000 profit. An order should never be accepted just because the fixed cost per unit decreases. The important consideration is whether profits increase or decrease as a result of the additional business. In this case they have increased, and so the order should be accepted.

All of these examples show the relevance of marginal costing techniques in short term decision making. This is generally defined as up to six months. During this time it is unlikely that the firm's cost structure will alter and the interest lost by not receiving the money immediately will be insigificant. The aim is to maximise the firm's resources by trying to operate at optimum production levels. When seeking to do this, only the relevant costs should be considered. Many people think that the fixed costs should be ignored, but this is wrong. The fixed costs are only irrelevant if they are not affected by the decision being taken. Whatever costing system is being used, the fixed costs must, in the long term, be accounted for if the firm is to be profitable.

Chapter 12
Budgetary Control

Introduction

One of a manager's main tasks is to plan the future level of business activity. It is the establishment of a plan which is the critical phase for, once this is done, actual performance can be compared with planned. Corrective action can then be taken to ensure that future activities conform with planned results. Budgeting can assist managers in their planning role and they should regard it as a management tool, rather than just a mere accounting exercise. If this approach is adopted, accounting ceases to be just a method of recording financial information but evolves into part of the decision making process within the organisation. By establishing such a system, it will assist managers in their task of planning, controlling and co-ordinating the different functions of the firm. Each business function, such as marketing, sales, production, finance and personnel, has its own objectives, but these must interrelate with the other functions if the business is to meet its declared aims and objectives.

What is a Budget?

The Chartered Institute of Management Accountants define a budget as "a plan quantified in monetary terms, prepared and approved prior to a defined period of time, usually showing planned income to be generated and/or expenditure to be incurred during that period and the capital to be employed to attain a given objective."

This definition highlights the three essential characteristics of the budgeting process. Firstly there must be a plan. Secondly the objectives must be quantifiable. They should be set either in terms of money or activity such as the number of units to be produced or sold. Lastly the budget period must be for a certain period of time which can then be sub-divided into control periods.

How To Establish A System Of Budgetary Control

The starting point for any budgetary control system is the actual preparation of the budget, within the guidelines as defined by the firm's corporate objectives. The budgeting process cannot begin until the firm's corporate strategy and objectives have been agreed, otherwise it is impossible to formulate a budget for the business. As soon as the budget has been prepared, agreed and issued, actual results can be compared with budgeted. Management can then review and investigate the reasons for the deviations from the planned, budgeted results. This is a very important part of the budgeting process for management gain vital information about variations from the budgeted target. If the variation has been caused by inefficiency, this must be corrected and any savings which are cost effective must be made. Whenever there are likely to be permanent changes to the original plan, such as the increase in price of essential raw materials, the loss of major customers, or other uncontrollable events, the original plan and budget should be revised.

Once the corporate goals and objectives have been set, the next step is to set up a budget committee which will be responsible for overseeing the budgeting process. This committee is usually chaired by an accountant with the other members being co-opted from the different business functions. The committee's task is to advise departmental managers about the budgeting process, co-ordinate activity and ensure that the planning process is completed to its planned timetable.

Figure 28: The Stages in the Budget Process

Purpose of Drawing up Budgets

Apart from the control aspect, it is vital that each of the functional budgets is compatible with one another. For instance the sales department may estimate that they could sell 10,000 cost units of a certain product, while the production department only have the resources to manufacture 7,000. When this situation occurs, a decision must be taken either to increase capacity or to accept the limitation and lose the possible sales income. These limiting factors are referred to as either internal or external principal budget factors.

Internal Principal Budget Factor

This occurs when the limiting factor is inside the company where, for instance, the firm does not have the productive capacity to manufacture the amount which could probably be sold.

External Budget Factor

If the firm could make 3,000 units, but the sales department knows that only 2,000 could be sold, the limit on activity is from outside the business and so it is known as an external budget factor.

Whether the limiting factor is internal or external, it is important for it to be ascertained before the start of the coming financial year so that production and sales levels can be co-ordinated and controlled. If this is not done, the firm will produce stock which cannot be sold. This will inevitably lead to cash flow problems as too much working capital will be held in illiquid stock. On the other hand, if the sales department promote products which cannot be made, customers will be disappointed and orders could be lost in the future because of past supply problems.

Example of an Internal Principal Budget Factor

Budgeted Sales Product X1	7,000 units
Productive Capacity Product X1	5,000 units
Internal Limitation	2,000 units

Type of Budget	Source of Data	Responsibility
Budget Instructions and Guidelines	Corporate Objectives Corporate Plans	Directors
Sales Budget	Order Book Sales Forecasts	Marketing, Sales Directors and Staff
Production Budget	Sales Data	Production Director and Staff
Expenses		
Selling and Distribution	Sales Function	
Administration		Administration
Finance		Finance
Collation of Budgets		Finance
Preparation of cash and Master Budget (Budgeted Profit and Loss Account and Budgeted Balance Sheet)		Finance

Figure 29: Types of Budget & Sources of Data

Preparing the Budgets

The first budget to be prepared should always be the sales budget as this will affect all the other departments. The expected level of sales can be calculated by looking at past years' results and then estimating the likely level of sales by considering the firm's product mix and the level of demand in the economy. This method is particularly suitable for companies operating in the fast moving consumer goods market, where large data bases can be built up showing sales by product and region.

163

For companies operating in the non fast moving consumer goods market, such as construction and engineering, this method is not really appropriate. In such cases it is better to set targets based on market share. By knowing the size of the market, it is possible to estimate the share of that market which will be captured by the company. The sales budget can then be ascertained.

Once the sales budget has been agreed, the purchase budget can be completed. In a manufacturing company it is useful to break the products down into their component parts so that the exact quantities of each material can be budgeted for.

When these two budgets have been prepared, the manufacturing wages budget can be drawn up. The job cards will provide information about the time taken to do a job, the rates per hour, and the quantity produced so that future costs can be forecast.

Lastly, the overhead budgets must be prepared by departmental managers, such as Accounting, Marketing, Transport and Distribution and Research and Development.

If the totals of each individual group of budgets are added together, the master budget can be prepared. The master budget is really a projected profit and loss account and balance sheet which will show the business's position if its sales and costs are as budgeted.

The master budget will show the budgeted profit but, as we have already seen, profit is unlikely to be in cash. There is no point in setting a budgeted profit, if no account is taken of the firm's cash position. A budget must be prepared showing the future cash receipts and payments. This will ensure that there is always sufficient cash for the firm to meet its day to day trading obligations. A cash flow forecast will indicate the business's ability to finance its future activities. If the budget shows cumulative deficits, then there will not be sufficient funds to finance its level of trading operations and ways must be considered of either rescheduling payments, or raising additional finance to cover them.

Finally, once the budget has been prepared, actual performance must be compared with budgeted. In this way corrective action can be taken so that actual results conform to budgeted targets. If this is not done, the budget will cease to be a control document and will be of limited use to the organisation.

To illustrate the principles and explain the mechanics of budgeting we will now consider the following example:

Example

M and I Manufacturing Limited are planning their next six months business activity. The balance sheet for the last six months is as follows:

M and I Balance Sheet as at 31 December Year 5

Fixed Assets	Cost	Depreciation To Date	Net Book Value
	£	£	£
Land and Buildings	45,000	-	45,000
Plant and Machinery	30,000	3,000	27,000
	75,000	3,000	72,000

Current Assets		
Stock-Raw Materials	2,000	
Finished Goods	1,800	
Debtors	5,000	
Bank	15,000	
	23,800	

Less Current Liabilities		
Creditors	600	
Working Capital		23,200
Net Assets		95,200

Financed By		
Share Capital	60,000	
Reserves	35,200	
Shareholder's Funds		95,200

Budgeted Expenditure and Income for the next six months

a. The unit costs of production are materials- £5 per unit and direct labour- £4 per unit. Finished goods are valued on a prime cost (material + direct labour only) basis.

The sales manager anticipates the following sales volumes at a constant price of £20 per unit.

Jan	Feb	March	April	May	June
200	250	300	250	200	270

b. Production is planned at 150 units in the first two months, rising to 300 for March and April and falling back to 200 units for May and June. It is anticipated that July will also be 200 units.

c. To reduce working capital requirements, the accountant has recommended that raw material for only one month's production should be held.

d. All material is bought on one month's credit. Labour costs are incurred in line with production and paid during the month.

e. Variable overhead is £2 per unit produced from January to April, and £4 from May onwards. Fixed overheads are £700 per month. Both are payable in the month in which they are incurred. There is £750 of depreciation in the fixed overhead.

f. The directors intend to spend £10,000 on plant in March, £7,000 in May and £3,000 in June. Depreciation will not be charged on these items until the end of the year.

g. The company will take a term loan for £12,000 in February. Interest at 15% is payable every six months, the first payment being on 30 June.

h. Leasing payments cost £600 a month

i. Depreciation of plant and machinery is 5% on cost price.

j. Debtors pay their accounts two months after the sale is made. In the balance sheet the £5,000 balance is made up of £2,000 in November and £3,000 in December.

From this information it is possible to prepare the firm's functional budgets, and a budgeted profit and loss account and balance sheet.

Preparation of the Functional Budgets

In this example the functional budgets are:

1. the sales budget
2. the production budget
3. the purchases budget
4. the production cost budget
5. the cash budget

Solution

1. **The Sales Budget**

Planned sales Selling Price £20 per unit	Jan	Feb	March	April	May	June	Total
	200	250	300	250	200	270	
Value	4,000	5,000	6,000	5,000	4,000	5,400	29,400
Materials (£5)	1,000	1,250	1,500	1,250	1,000	1,350	(7,350)
Labour (£4)	800	1,000	1,200	1,000	800	1,080	(5,880)
Gross Profit							£16,170

2. **Production Budget**

From the balance sheet value of £1,800 and the detail in note (a) £1,800 /£9 (materials £5 and Labour £4) = 200 units of opening finished goods.

	Jan	Feb	March	April	May	June	
Opening stock (units)	200	150	50	50	100	100	
Production (Note b)	150	150	300	300	200	200	
Sales(note a)	200	250	300	250	200	270	
Closing Stock	150	50	50	100	100	30	Closing Stock

Note: closing stock is calculated by adding the opening stock and production and then subtracting it from the number sold. The June figure (30) will later be shown in the budgeted profit and loss account and balance sheet. The value of the closing stock will be 30 x £9 (£5 materials and £4 Labour) = £270.

3. The Purchases Budget

The opening balance sheet shows 400 units (£2,000 /£5 per unit of raw materials).

	Jan	Feb	March	April	May	June	
Opening Stock	400	250	300	300	200	200	
Production	150	150	300	300	200	200	
Purchases	-	200	300	200	200	200	
Closing Stock	250	300	300	200	200	200	Closing stock

Note

a. To reflect policy, no stocks were bought in January (note c)

b. The closing raw material stock must equate with the July planned production.

c. The closing stock is calculated by subtracting the production from the opening stock.

4. Production Cost Budget

	Jan	Feb	March	April	May	June	
Volume (note b)	150	150	300	300	200	200	
Materials	750	750	1500	1500	1000	1000	
Labour	600	600	1200	1200	800	800	
Prime Cost	1350	1350	2700	2700	1800	1800	
Variable Overhead	300	300	600	600	800	800	= 3,400

The budgeted profit and loss account can now be drawn up.

168

Budgeted profit and Loss Account
Figures in brackets () indicate source of information.

	£
Sales (i) 1,470 units @ £20	29,400
Direct material (i)	(7,350)
Direct labour (ii)	(5,880)
Gross profit	16,170

Expenses

Variable overheads (iv)	3,400	
Fixed overheads including depreciation (e)	4,200	
Lease payments (h)	3,600	
Interest (5 months)	750	
		(11,950)
Net profit		£4,220

Cash Budget

	Jan	Feb	March	April	May	June
Incoming						
Debtors (j) (i)	2000	3000	4000	5000	6000	5000
Loan		12000				
	2000	15000	4000	5000	6000	5000
Outgoings						
Material (d) (iii)	600	–	1000	1500	1000	1000
Labour (iv)	600	600	1200	1200	800	800
Variable Overhead (iv)	300	300	600	600	800	800
Fixed Overhead (e) (N B No depreciation)	575	575	575	575	575	575
Lease	600	600	600	600	600	600
Capital Equipment			10000		7000	3000
Interest (6 months)						900
	2675	2075	13975	4475	10775	7675
B/fwd (from balance sheet)	15000	14325	27250	17275	17800	13025
Movement	(675)	12925	(9975)	525	(4775)	(2675)
C/fwd	14325	27250	17275	17800	13025	10350

We can now do the budgeted balance sheet.

Budgeted Balance Sheet

Fixed assets	Cost	Depreciation	Net Book Value
Land and Buildings	£45,000	-	£45,000
Plant and Machinery	50,000	(3,750)	46,250
(e) (f)			91,250

Current Assets

Stock (iii)	Raw Materials (200 x 5)	1,000	
(iv)	Finished Goods (30 x 9)	270	
Debtors (i)		9,400	
Prepayment		150	
Bank (v)		10,350	
		21,170	

Current Liabilities

Trade Creditors (200 x 5)	(1,000)	
Net Current Assets	$\vdash\!\!\longrightarrow$	20,170
		111,420
Loan		(12,000)
Total Net Assets		£99,420

Financed by:	
Capital	£60,000
Profit brought forward	35,200
Profit from six months trading	4,220
Shareholders' funds	£99,420

The Benefits of Budgetary Control

If a system of budgetary control is to be effective, the whole organisation must be involved in the process. Budgets must be prepared by the operating divisions and it is essential that each functional area must believe in the budget which has been set. This can only be achieved if the operational areas are given guidelines as to how to prepare their budgets. In this way staff feel responsible for their budgets and are more likely to be motivated to achieve the targets. This is the major benefit from the process for it forces both management and staff to consider the future, determine planned output levels and then compare actual results with budgeted.

If the budgetary process can be presented in this way instead of as an accounting exercise, the firm will have an effective budgetary control system and will benefit from having a clear set of goals which all staff are committed to and which can be regularly reviewed throughout the year. Otherwise, the process will become a meaningless accounting exercise with unmotivated staff believing that the budgeted output, sales and profit targets are unrealistic and unfair.

Chapter 13
Standard Costing

Introduction

The Chartered Institute of Management Accountants defines a standard cost as a predetermined calculation of how much costs should be, under specified working conditions. A standard costing system assesses what the cost should be to make a product before actually making it. The actual cost can then be compared with the standard and management can investigate why a difference or variance has occurred.

How A System Of Standard Costing Supports The Budgetary Control Process

The establishment of a standard costing system allows greater control of costs within the business for the differences between actual costs and standard costs can be detected as they are incurred, allowing management to take corrective action.

Standard costing systems, therefore, support the budgetary control process but, unlike budgets, comparisons can be made with standard costs as the firm is producing the goods. If the business only has a system of budgetary control, management can only compare actual results with budgeted performance at the end of the budgeted period. This is a major limitation of budgeting for new control procedures cannot be instigated immediately. Budgets also often focus on future planned activity levels in fairly broad terms, such as production and sales rather than the costs involved of making a particular product.

The Control Process

If standards are set for the firm's direct and indirect costs, comparisons can be made with actual and planned results. Standards can be set for direct materials, both price and usage, for direct labour and for indirect fixed or variable overheads. The difference then between the goal set and the results achieved can be analysed and the reason communicated to the relevant departments. A standard costing system will only be effective in controlling costs if management analyse the reason for the variance. In itself the variance just shows that a difference has occurred. It is the analysis of the variance which will reveal the reason for the difference and it is only then that management are able to decide what action to take.

This can be seen from the following diagram

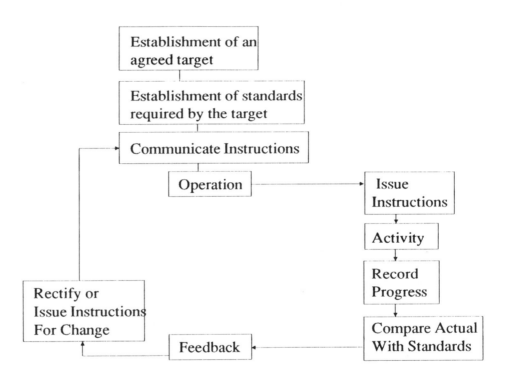

Figure 30: Cycle of Actions for a Standard Costing System

The diagram shows that corrective action is not automatic but depends upon identifying the variance. This may be adverse, meaning that the costs or usage are more than the standard envisaged, or less, in which case they are referred to as favourable. In this way standard costing monitors performance against expectation and so any variance from standard must be investigated by management.

173

The Benefits Of A Standard Costing System

It is expensive and time consuming to install a system of standard costing and if the costs involved are to be justified the firm must gain the following benefits:

1. Unit costs should be reduced because of improvements made in controlling costs.

2. Stock control procedures should be simplified because stock and work in progress can be valued at its standard cost. This makes stock control easier because stock need not be valued on a last in first out basis (LIFO) or on a first in first out basis (FIFO) or any other method such as average cost.

3. Price setting should be improved because the firm has acccurate details about its costs.

4. The system highlights variances from standards and so management are able to concentrate on that analysis. There is, therefore, no need to spend time in analysing costs which are performing to standard and so the system is often said to allow management by exception.

5. The business can benefit from establishing new working practices by reconsidering working practices before the standards are set.

Setting Standards

The Chartered Institute of Management Accountants defines four different types of standard. They are the basic, ideal, normal and the current standard. It is the firm's management who must decide which is the most appropriate for their business.

Basic standard
This is defined as "a standard established for use over a long period from which a current standard can be developed." Such a standard could remain unchanged for a long time but, if this is the case it will be useless as an effective short term attention-directing control tool. Inflation, competition and new technology have meant that management must adapt to a changing business environment if their company is to survive today's competitive pressures. While a basic standard may be of interest to see what extent prices of commodities, goods or services have

changed over a period of time, it is ineffective as a meaningful control tool, unless coupled to a costly and complicated two-tier standard costing system. Some firms set a base standard for long term comparisons while, at the same time, using a current standard for current operational control.

Ideal Standard

"A standard which can be attained under the most favourable conditions." Some managers believe that if a standard is set, assuming that all waste and inefficiency have been eliminated from the system, that the actual costs should be the same as the standard cost. No allowance is made for human error, machine breakdowns or wastage. Advocates of such a system believe that the resulting unfavourable variances will remind management of the on-going continual need for improvement in all phases of operations and that there can be no room for complacency within the organisation.

This approach contradicts many behavioural scientists' views that the setting of such variances is self destructive and dysfunctional since they actually remove motivation, for workers believe that the targets are unrealistic and unachievable.

The use of ideal standards may, however, be appropriate in new hi-tech factories where highly automated production processes controlled by computers can virtually guarantee continuous high quality output. In such cases adverse variances are likely to be reduced to levels which are almost immaterial and may be so small as to not need investigating .

Normal Standard

"A standard which can be attained if a standard unit of work is carried out efficiently, a machine properly operated or material properly used." Such a standard makes allowances for normal wastage, machine breakdown and operator failure. The standard represents future performance and objectives which are reasonably attainable and the standard is sometimes called the attainable standard. This standard has the added benefit in that it can be used for other purposes such as budgeting and inventory control. This is possible because the standard is attainable under normal circumstances and can therefore be legitimately used for other purposes.

The Current Standard

This is defined as "a standard established for use over a short period of time, related to current conditions."

Many business people use the term "current standards" for the standard currently used by the firm but this is incorrect. The current operations standards which are used during the accounting or budget period will be the attainable or normal standards; while the current standard is the one used in abnormal operating conditions, for it recognises current problems and works within present conditions.

Setting Standards

Before a standard costing system can be installed, it is necessary to build up the costs for each individual component or product. Once this has been done, standard cost cards can be produced which will establish and itemise the individual cost components of direct materials, direct or conversion labour and overheads. It will be against these standards that actual costs are compared. Each standard must provide a target for achievement, provide a yardstick which can be used to evaluate performance and, lastly, must highlight the aspects of the business not operating according to plan.

The standards can only be set by liaising with and discussing the costs with the various function heads and their staff. This is shown below.

Data Source	Information Required	Data Analysis Cost Accountant
Production Specifications	Technical	Output Levels
Financial Accountant	Overheads	Expenses
Purchasing	Material Prices	Costs
Personnel	Pay Rates	Costs

Figure 31: Information needed for a Standard Costing System

The diagram shows that the cost accountant must gather a lot of detailed information from various sources before the standards can be set. Once this has been done, further information will be required because the standards will have to be reviewed to take account of the firm's product mix, changes in material and labour costs and productivity improvements. Setting standards is an on-going process for they must reflect current costs and operating efficiencies.

We have already seen that in cost accounting there are three elements to the word cost and this is also the case when setting standard costs. The three elements are materials, labour and overheads and these can be further broken down into two parts as shown below.

Element	Materials	Labour	Overhead
Possible Variance	Price & Usage	Rate & Efficiency	Spend & Efficiency

Figure 32: The Three Elements of a Firm's Costs

Direct Materials

The price standard will be made up of prices obtained, negotiated and agreed with suppliers. This agreed price may take into account any future short term price increase. If this is the case, the final standard will be based on the mean of a range of prices likely to prevail during the time that the standard is operational.

The standard must also make an allowance for normal losses, defective material, storage, deterioration, theft and wastage in the production process. This amount should be added to the figure for planned usage.

Lastly, for many firms operating in the fast moving consumer goods market, the packaging forms an important part of the firm's promotional mix, and this added cost must be taken into consideration when setting the standard cost.

Direct Wage Costs

Most large firms set their wage costs after negotiations with the relevant trade union. With the introduction of two year agreements, this part of the standard setting process has become easier because the labour rate is already known. The main problem is to calculate the time needed to perform the task, for this will vary according to the workers' motivation and level of skill and the type of machine used.

If the firm is to control its labour costs, the time taken to complete a task should be recorded. An allowance must be built into the labour cost standard to take account of operator fatigue, together with a contingency allowance for reading diagrams and cleaning machinery. If new products are being made, the firm should also set a reject allowance to take account of problems brought about by the introduction of new manufacturing processes. When making these allowances, care must be taken that they are set at an equitable level or cost overruns will be incurred, which could add between 10 and 15 per cent to total labour costs.

Conversion Overhead

It is possible to split the conversion overhead into its fixed and variable components, although in practice this is rarely done. This is because most overheads are time related, and few vary materially with actual production or activity. As a result most businesses work only on fixed overhead controls and these will be calculated by:

1. Calculating the cost of the conversion overhead such as factory rent.

2. Selecting the base by which it is to be recovered, such as standard labour production hours, or machine produced hours, or as a percentage on standard direct materials.

3. Once the method for absorbing the overhead has been established the rate is calculated by using the following formula:

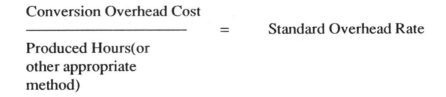

$$\frac{\text{Conversion Overhead Cost}}{\text{Produced Hours(or other appropriate method)}} = \text{Standard Overhead Rate}$$

Once all the information has been collected and staff have been consulted and involved in the process, the firm's management can compare actual costs with standard. This process is referred to as variance analysis and is explained in the next chapter.

Chapter 14
Variance Analysis

Introduction

The previous chapter explained the principles of standard costing, but the system is only effective in monitoring costs if the variances are calculated correctly and their cause analysed. A variance is the difference between planned, budgeted or standard cost and the actual costs or revenues received. When the variance is worse than the budgeted or standard cost, it is said to be adverse and it is an accounting convention that adverse variances are shown in brackets. If the costs and revenues are better than the budgeted or standard cost, the variance is deemed to be favourable. These are shown without brackets.

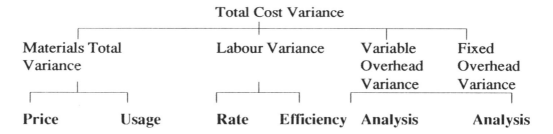

Figure 33: The Composition of Variance Analysis

The diagram shows the total cost variance (the sum of all the cost variances that can be identified). In other words it is the total standard cost less the total actual cost. The variances for materials, labour and overheads can now be computed. It is a good idea when calculating the standard cost with the actual cost to calculate the standard first. By putting the standard first, if there is an adverse variance, the answer will be negative, and is then automatically shown in brackets.

Direct Materials Price Variance

This is defined as "the difference between the standard price and the actual purchase price for the actual quantity of the material". This can be calculated at the time of delivery or at the time of usage. It is best to calculate whether or not a variance has occurred when the material is delivered. It is also good accounting practice to write off or add to profit any variance which has occurred at the earliest opportunity.

Formula For Calculating Whether Or Not A Variance Has Occurred

Actual Quantity Purchased x [Standard Price - Actual Price]

Example

A restaurant has set a standard cost of 50p per kg of sugar and a standard usage per month of 200 kgs. The Head Chef has ordered 240 kg at 60p per kg. Calculate the direct material price variance.

Formula

Actual Quantity Purchased x [Standard Price - Actual Price]

$$240 \times [50p - 60p]$$

$$= 240 \times [-10p]$$

$$= £[24] \text{ or } £24 \text{ [adverse]}$$

Note: The standard is shown first so that if the answer comes out negative, as in this example, it will always indicate an adverse variance.

Causes of Material Price Variances

In the case of materials, an adverse price variance usually means that a supplier has increased the price of the goods after the standard has been set. If prices are rising because of inflation, there is little the firm can do. Whenever the purchasing department place a large order with one supplier, an attempt should be made to fix a price for the life of the contract. This may not always be possible, sometimes the firm cannot meet the supplier's minimum order quantities and is therefore unable to take advantage of price freezes or discounts. Unfortunately this type of situation reinforces the criticism levelled at standards, that they are little more than measures of prediction rather than a measure of bargaining expertise. They are a measure of forecasting rather than a measure of operating efficiency.

The price may also be higher because a different supplier has been used or because a different quality of material has been purchased. Whatever the reason for the variance, management must analyse the cause and then decide what action to take.

Direct Material Usage Variance

This is "the difference between the standard quantity specified for the actual production, and the actual quantity used, at standard purchase price." It is calculated using the following formula:

[Standard Quantity specified for actual production - Actual Quantity used] x Standard Price.

Example
Using the same information as in the previous example, it is possible to calculate the direct material usage variance. A restaurant has set a standard cost of 50p per kg of cane based sugar and a standard usage per day of 200 kgs. The Head Chef has ordered a poorer quality beet sugar and 240 Kg are needed to provide the same degree of sweetness. Applying the formula quoted above

$$[2200-240] \quad x \cdot 50$$

$$= \quad [40] \quad x \cdot 50$$

$$= \quad £[20] \text{ or } £20 \text{ [adverse]}$$

Causes of Usage Variances

Management should be able to control usage variances because the difference will have taken place within the firm. Often the variance has been brought about by carelessness, as when materials are stored incorrectly leading to spillage or deterioration. It may also have occured because of careless usage or because the workforce is unskilled or inexperienced in using the material. Lastly, the materials used may have been of poor quality. This often brings about a high usage variance because many of the units produced fail to meet the required quality levels and have to be scrapped.

Management can combine the two variances to form the direct material total variance.

$$[200 \times 50p] \quad - [240 \times 60p]$$

$$= \quad 100 \quad - 144$$

$$= \quad 44 \text{ i.e } £44 \text{ [adverse]}$$

Note: The adverse variance is bigger than before because it includes both the increase in price and the increase in quantity.

Direct Labour Variance

This is "the difference between the standard direct labour cost and the actual direct labour cost incurred for the production achieved." By doing this, the hours worked or actually booked to the job can be compared with the actual standard hours produced at the end of the programme of work. The variance is calculated by the following formula:

[Standard direct labour hours produced x standard rate per hour]
less
[Actual direct labour hours worked x actual rate per hour]

Example

The General Building Company

The company have set a standard labour cost for building a brick wall around a business park. The firm set a standard time of 300 hours at £9 an hour. The work was completed in 270 hours at a cost of £9 an hour.

Formula

Standard direct labour hours produced x standard rate per hour =

    300 x £9 = £2,700

Less Actual direct labour hours worked x actual rate per hour =

    270 x £9 = £2430

Standard Cost	£2,700
Actual Cost	£2,430
	270 Favourable

Direct Labour Rate Variance

This is defined as "the difference between the standard and the actual direct labour rate per hour of the total hours worked/paid." The variance is calculated by the following formula:

[Standard rate per hour - Actual rate per hour] x Actual hours worked/paid.

Example

The Precision Engineering Company has set a standard for 100 direct labour hours at an hourly rate of £5.00 per hour. The work was completed in 110 hours, but the rate of pay was lower than expected at £4.50 (because of a lower than expected rate of wage inflation).

Formula

Standard rate per hour - Actual rate per hour] x Actual hours worked/paid.

            [5 - 4.50] x 110
=   0.50 x 110

=   £55 favourable

Causes of Labour Rate Variances

Labour rate variances need not arise if standards are based on the current union negotiated pay rates. Sometimes the standards are set before the pay rates have been negotiated, and so it is important for management to identify the difference between the standard rate and the agreed, settled rate. If this is not the case, other causes must be investigated. Temporary labour may also have been used and they may be paid at a different rate. Lastly, special allowances may have been paid to staff which will effectively increase the hourly rate.

Direct Labour Efficiency Variances

This is "the difference between the standard hours for the actual production achieved and the hours actually worked, valued at the standard labour rate." It is calculated by the formula:

[standard hours produced - actual hours worked] x Standard rate per hour.

Example
The Precision Engineering Company has set a standard for 100 direct labour hours at an hourly rate of £5.00 per hour. The work was completed in 110 hours, but the rate of pay was lower than expected at £4.50 (because of a lower than expected rate of wage inflation).

Formula

Standard hours produced - actual hours worked] x Standard rate per hour.

Using the data in the example

$$[100 - 110] \times 5$$

$$= \quad [-10] \times 5$$

$$= \quad £50 \text{ [adverse]}$$

Causes of Efficiency Variances

Inadequate training may be responsible for the variance. If the workers are inexperienced, they usually take longer to do the job, or there may be quality problems resulting in more rejects being produced. The cause could also be due to poor quality materials being purchased, because the usual source is temporarily out of stock. Whenever there is a variance, management must correctly identify the cause so that corrective action can be taken.

Overhead Variances

We have already seen that standards can be set for variable and fixed overheads. The variable overheads will be activity related, whereas the fixed overheads will be time related. An overhead expenditure variance is defined as "the difference between budgeted and actual overhead expenditure."

Fixed overheads are calculated by the following formula:

Fixed overhead budgeted cost - Actual conversion overhead incurred.

Variable Overheads are calculated:

[Actual units produced x Variable overhead absorption rate per unit]
            Less Actual cost.

Example

The Precision Engineering Company has just drawn up the following budget:-

Budgeted fixed overhead = £288,000 per annum over a 48 week year = £6,000 per week.

Budgeted production = 96,000 units per annum over 48 weeks = 2,000 units per week.

Variable overhead for the year was expected to be £48,000.

Actual output for the week under review was 2020 units, and the actual fixed overhead cost was £6,200.

The actual variable overhead expenditure was £1,250.

The directors would like you to calculate the two overhead expense variances.

Suggested Solution

The first task when calculating the variable overhead expense variance is to calculate the unit rate. Using the information in the question:

Budgeted Cost

Units of output [be it hours or units]

$$\frac{£48,000}{96,000} = £0.50 \text{ per unit}$$

It is now possible to calculate the individual variances, starting with the fixed overhead expenditure variance. The formula for calculating this variance is:

Fixed conversion overhead budgeted - Actual fixed conversion overhead incurred

$$6,000 - 6,200 = £200 \text{ [adverse]}$$

The variable overhead is calculated using the formula:

[Actual units produced x variable overhead absorption rate] - Actual cost.

$$(2020 \times 0.50) - 1250 = £(240) \text{ (adverse)}$$

The variable overhead expense variance is based upon actual output and recognises that the expenditure is likely to change with output. The example shows that there were 20 more units produced, which required the firm to spend an extra £10 on variable overheads.

So far we have treated variance analysis as a fairly mechanical task by calculating the different variances for materials, labour and overheads. Once these have been calculated, they need to be summarised and compared with the budgeted figure so that managerial decisions can be taken to ensure that actual costs are the same as the standard cost. The next example will show how this can be done:

Example

The Edwardian Carpet Company manufactures a range of woollen rugs. The company operates a standard costing system and has set the quarterly output level, together with the standard costs, for one of their products. The costs are shown below:

	Budgeted Output	Standard Cost £	Actual Cost £
Sales	10,000	15	9,000
Materials		8	68,000
Labour		4	41,000
Factory Overheads Fixed		2	16,000

The directors have asked you to prepare the firm's costing trading and profit and loss account and to compare the budgeted profit with the actual profit.

The first task is to prepare the firm's budgeted profit and loss account.

Edwardian Carpet's Budgeted Profit and Loss Account For The Quarter Ending Year Seven

	£	£
Sales (10,000 units at £15 per unit)		150,000
Less Variable Costs		
Materials	80,000	
Labour	40,000	
		120,000
Contribution		30,000
Less Fixed Costs		20,000
Profit		10,000

187

As there has been no alteration in the selling price, there is no need to calculate the sales variance. The actual costs for materials, labour and overheads are different from the standard cost and so the variance, be it favourable or fixed, must be calculated.

Material Price Variance

Standard price of materials
(£8 per unit x 9000 units)   72,000
Actual cost   68,000
                                    _____
                                     4,000 Favourable

Labour Rate Variance

Standard wage rate   36,000

Actual wage rate   41,000
                                    _____
                                     5,000 Adverse

Factory Overhead

Standard overhead   18,000

Actual overhead   16,000
                                    _____
                                     2,000 Favourable

Once the variances have been calculated, the costing profit and loss account can be prepared.

Edwardian Carpet's Costing Profit and Loss Account For The Quarter Ending Year Seven

	£
Budgeted Profit	10,000

Variances	Adverse £	Favourable £	
Materials		4,000	
Labour	5,000		
Fixed Overheads		2,000	
	5,000	6,000	1,000 Favourable
Actual Net Profit			11,000

The company has made a bigger profit than that estimated when the standards were set. The difference has occurred because materials and overheads were less than the standard cost, which offset the increase in wage costs. The reasons for these variances must be analysed by management and, if need be, the standards must be reset. If the standards have been set correctly, any variance shows a flaw in the system and its cause must be investigated and analysed if the business is to keep a proper check and control on its costs.

Chapter 15
Working Capital

Introduction

Working capital is the term used to describe a firm's short term use of funds. Part of the firm's capital will be locked away in fixed assets but a certain sum must be left aside to finance the day to day business expenses. Money is needed to pay the wages, purchase stock and to finance credit sales. If the firm lacks sufficient working capital to meet its short term obligations, it will be unable to continue trading and so the management of the working capital cycle is very important.

The Working Capital Cycle

Imagine a business trader who purchases stock for cash and sells it in a market for cash. The trader must ensure that s/he has sufficient cash balances to meet all the expenses of the business such as the cost of the stall and sufficient investment in stock to attract customers. If the trader finds that in one month s/he is short of cash, then addditional stock will not be purchased and gradually the cash receipts from sales will improve the business' cash position. The trader's working capital cycle is shown in the diagram below.

The effect of Credit on the Working Capital Cycle.

There are very few businesses which only buy and sell for cash. Most transactions are done on credit, which means that the buyer has a small period of time before the goods or service has to be paid for. As a result two new factors must be considered. These are time and money. The aim is to take longer to pay one's creditors and to receive payments from debtors as quickly as possible. Any delay in the cycle will mean that the firm risks not having sufficient cash deposits to meet its own liabilities. This new situation can be shown below.

The Introduction of Credit into the Working Capital Cycle.

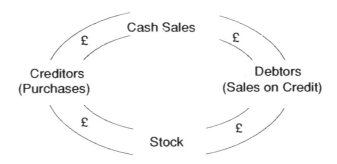

The Dangers of Using Short Term Finance

Accountants distinguish between short and long term sources of finance. The difference between the two is in the time in which the borrowed funds must be repaid. Short term finance must be repaid within the next twelve months from the balance sheet date, whereas long term finance will be repaid later than one year.

There is usually an interest rate advantage in borrowing money short term as opposed to long term because short term rates are generally cheaper. However, excessive amounts of short term debt expose the firm to greater risks. Long term debt usually has a fixed rate of interest attached to it and so temporary upward fluctuations in interest rates do not affect cash flow. Short term debt will generally be subject to a variable interest rate and so changes in rates will directly affect both costs and cash flow. Many firms later discover, to their dismay, that what they could afford at one rate of interest has suddenly become an enormous financial burden once rates rise. Often additional credit sources have to be used to finance these interest charges, such as bank overdrafts, which push businesses further into debt, thereby damaging their cash flow and liquidity.

Governments also use interest rates to regulate the level of activity within the economy. A rise in rates usually signals a slow down in economic activity, making it harder for businesses to sell their goods and services. If this happens, sales could well decrease, leading to a rise in stock levels, and the end result will be a deterioration in the business' liquidity levels.

The Management of Working Capital

Accountants define working capital as the difference between the current assets and current liabilities of a business. The manager's role is to ensure that the firm has sufficient current assets in order to meet its day to day financial obligations. The amount of money invested in current assets will depend upon the type of business which the firm is engaged in. For instance many service industries, such as hairdressing and small restaurants, need only a small amount of stock. Also most of the sales are for cash and so, in theory, they should not experience the same working capital problems as manufacturing businesses, which need to keep large investment in stocks and to sell nearly all of their products on credit. The control of working capital is important because, generally, current assets represent sixty per cent of the total assets of any business. Unlike fixed assets, current assets are continually changing. Stock is constantly being sold and bought and the investment in debtors is constantly changing as the firm sells and collects its debts. As a result most firms have the majority of their assets in a very volatile form, and so this area of the business needs constant attention.

Many small businesses find it difficult to raise long term capital to finance their capital investment programmes. As a result, the owners seek to minimise their investment in fixed assets and enter instead into hire and leasing agreements, because the assets can be acquired without having to pay for them immediately. While it can be argued that the use of assets is more important than their ownership, this form of finance often causes cash flow problems because of the high interest rates charged by the hiring or leasing company. This inevitably increases the risks of running the business and accounts for more than its fair share of business failures. It should be remembered that many firms are forced into liquidation not because they are unprofitable, but because they simply do not have sufficient working capital to meet their day to day expenses.

192

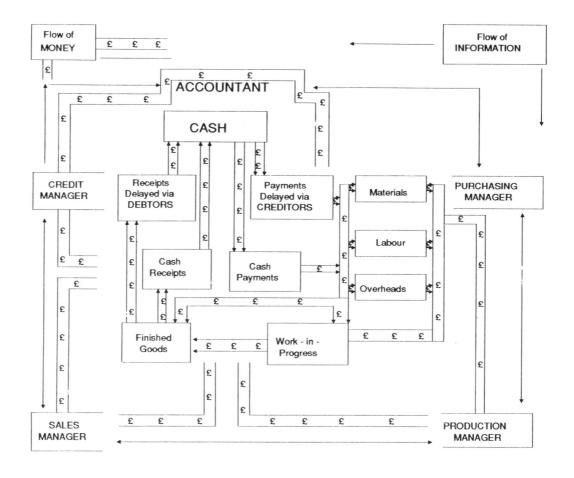

Figure 34: The Movement of Working Capital in a Manufacturing Business

The Perils of Lack of Control.

The art of managing working capital is to control two variables, time and money. As far as time is concerned, we want our money to flow from cash through stocks, and from stocks through debtors, so that it comes back again as cash as quickly as possible. We also want to delay payment to our creditors for as long as is reasonably possible so that we have the minimum amount of cash tied up in stocks and debtors and the maximum amount of funds from our creditors. In this way our creditors are providing short term interest-free finance while our own money is working hard to earn profits for the firm.

In many firms this situation does not occur. Instead of minimising the investment in stock and debtors, large amounts of cash are tied up in stock. This involves the firm in additional costs as often it has to be financed by using expensive bank loans and there is always the danger of loss from pilferage, deterioration and obsolescence. Similarly, if large amounts of money are owed to it, the firm is being denied the use of its own funds. In effect it is making an interest-free loan to other businesses and all the time that it waits for payment it runs the risk of the debtors being unable to pay and bad debts being incurred which will reduce profits and cash flow.

The Benefits of Controlling Working Capital

If the working capital cycle can be controlled effectively, there will be an increase in profits. The less cash tied up in stock and debtors, the more interest that can be earned by investing the money in short term interest bearing deposits. Similarly, if overdraft finance is required, the amount of borrowed finance can be kept to the minimum, which will minimise interest charges.

By controlling the amount of working capital, it becomes possible to support more sales with the same amount of capital. Once a firm can reduce the amount of capital it needs to generate each £ of sales, it can reduce the chances of taking on more business than it is able to support with available finances. If this situation occurs, the firm is said to be overtrading and, once this happens, there are constant cash flow problems as the firm struggles to finance its day to day running expenses.

The Need For Forecasting and Communication

In order to control the working capital cycle, forecasts must be prepared so that future investments in stock and debtors can be determined. Good forecasting always starts by looking at the projected sales as this will determine both the firm's income and stock levels. In large companies the sales director will have this information and from it a production plan can be drawn up. Once this has been done, a production schedule can be ascertained so that the purchasing department can fix the minimum, maximum and re-order levels for stocks.

Once the sales, production and buying plans have been agreed, the next step is to calculate how much cash will be required to finance this estimated level of activity. The credit controller can then assess when customers are likely to pay for the goods, thereby allowing the accountant to determine how and when to pay the creditors. The whole financial picture can then be put together into a cash flow forecast which will be discussed in the next chapter.

It is essential for all managers involved in the working capital cycle to communicate with one another. The Purchasing Department cannot fix the minimum, maximum and re-order stock levels until the production forecasts and sales budgets are determined, and purchasing needs up to date information from production so that it can constantly monitor stock levels.

Once the sales, production and buying plans have been agreed, the next task is to convert the budgeted sales and payments into forecast cash receipts and payments. The credit controller will then be able to estimate when the firm is likely to receive payments for its credit sales. It is only then that the accountant can calculate when to pay the firm's creditors by drawing up a cash flow forecast showing the estimated receipts and payments.

Good planning and communication are the key to effective control of working capital in any business. Regular meetings should be held where all the main participants can meet and discuss the current levels of activity as these will all affect the cash flows of the business. If the level of business trading deviates from the budgeted level, the firm will experience working capital problems. For example, if a firm collects all its debts in thirty days and has credit sales of £1,000 a day, at the end of a month it will be owed £30,000 from its debtors. If sales rise to £2,000 a day, its debtors will rise to £60,000 and so the business will need double the amount of money to finance its working capital requirements. This is why any deviation from the budgeted level of activity needs to be reported to management immediately, otherwise the firm may well find that its working capital requirements are insufficient. If unchecked, this could damage the financial reputation and solvency of the business.

Chapter 16
Managing Current Assets

Introduction

The current assets are of a circulating nature. Unlike fixed assets they are constantly changing and it is by using these assets effectively that profit will be made. They are recorded in the balance sheet according to how quickly they can be turned into cash. The quicker an asset can be turned into cash the more liquid it is said to be. Stock is the most illiquid and so it is shown first. Debtors are shown next, followed by bank and cash balances.

The Need for Effective Management

Current assets are very volatile assets. Stock may become obsolete or deteriorate. Debtors may not be able to pay and idle cash bank balances have an opportunity cost for they could be either earning interest or be invested in the business. The more effectively a firm can use its current assets, the greater its profitability. The amount of capital tied up in stock, debtors and cash needs to be constantly monitored, thereby ensuring that the highest return on capital can be achieved.

The Management of Stock

Most people think of stock as goods for resale. In shops they see lines of merchandise waiting to be bought. The retailer's aim is to achieve the greatest level of sales from each square metre of floor space and to ensure that the shop is fully stocked.

In a manufacturing business stock is not just the finished goods being produced. The factory will have had to purchase raw materials and, it will also have goods which are not yet completed. This work is called work in progress, and until it is finished, it cannot be sold. During the manufacturing process it is still stock but, unlike the retailer's stock, it will be impossible to sell until finished.

All stock has to be financed and until it is sold it soaks up the firm's precious cash reserves. The quicker the firm can produce and sell the goods, the quicker the cash can be released to purchase more stock, thereby allowing the business to earn more profit.

The Need For Efficient Stock Control

There is a popular joke in business that the sales department can always sell stock which the firm has not got but can't sell the goods which the firm has. While there is some truth in this statement, the aim must be to ensure that the business is fully stocked and is in a position to offer the customer a full range of merchandise. In some businesses, if you are out of stock, the sale will be lost for ever. Imagine a restaurant which has under ordered and cannot now serve certain meals. Customers can't wait until a new order has been placed and so they may well choose to eat elsewhere. Similarly, there is no point in having stock which won't sell taking up valuable shelf space. It is far better to sell it at a reduced price and invest that money in stock which will sell.

Accounting For Stock Control

A system must be designed to account for material costs and it is essential that management set up a procedure for collecting such costs as quickly and accurately as possible. This information will be needed so that costs can be determined but also to minimise the costs of holding stocks. Excessive stock holding will not only put constraints on the firm's working capital but will also involve the firm in additional costs such as storage, insurance, and the risk of loss from obsolescence, theft and wastage.

Money will also be wasted if too little stock is held. Apart from lost sales the business will experience higher stock ordering costs, and may also lose money if production has to be halted because of a lack of components or raw materials. Materials control procedures are designed to optimise a firm's investment in stock, by determining economic order quantities and by setting stock levels.

The Economic Order Quantity

This is the quantity of material that should be ordered so that the cost of ordering, together with the cost of stock-holding, is minimised. The economic order quantity can be presented as a graph or calculated by using the formula:

$$EOQ = \frac{2AC}{H}$$

where E = Economic Order Quantity.
         A = Stock usage
         C = Cost of ordering
         H = Stock holding cost per unit of stock.

Example

A gift shop knows that each month it sells 600 glass vases. The cost of placing the order is £50 and the cost of holding one vase for a year is £5. The shop's optimum order size is:

$$E = \frac{2 \times 600 \times 50}{5} = 12000$$

In order to minimise stock holding costs the shop should place orders for 12000 vases. While the model is useful, it should be remembered that the amount of stock held must take account of seasonal fluctuations. Most businesses experience seasonal demand and, if they stick rigidly to the model, they may occasionally be out of stock. The past sales records should therefore be looked at before deciding how much buffer stock should be held, to prevent lost sales from being temporarily out of stock.

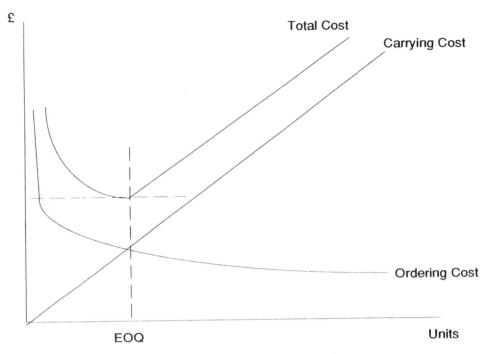

Figure 35: Graphical Presentation of Economic Order Quantity

The model shows that, while some of the costs associated with holding stock such as insurance and storing will decline as stock holdings increase, other costs such as theft, waste and obsolesence will increase as stock holdings rise. The difference in these two costs will tend to balance each other and it is therefore assumed that the total holding cost of stock is constant but that stock holding costs will increase proportionally to the rate of increase in stock held.

It is possible to ensure that stock levels are kept to their optimum for day to day trading by setting the following stock levels according to usage and the time taken to order new stocks, which is called lead time.

Re-Order Level. This is the level below which stock levels must not fall. The formula for calculating re-order level is:

Re-order level = Maximum Usage x Maximum Lead Time

Minimum Stock Level. This is the minimum amount of stock which must be held and it is an amount just below the re-order level. Once this level is reached stock must be obtained quickly if production is not to be halted by a shortage of raw materials. The formula is:

$$\text{Mimimum Stock Level} = \text{Re-Order Level} - (\text{Average Usage} \times \text{Average Lead Time})$$

Maximum Stock Level. This is the maximum level of stock which should be held. The formula is:

$$\text{Maximum Stock Level} = \text{Re-order level} - (\text{Minimum Usage} \times \text{Minimum Lead Time}) + \text{Re-order Quantity.}$$

Example

The Efficient Stock Company

The managers at the Efficient Stock Company have been assessing their stock levels. They predict the following usage:

January	300 units
February	300
March	500
April	600
May	800
June	1000
July	1000
August	1000
September	1000
October	900
November	600
December	400

The management has set the re order quantity at 2000 units and the delivery times are as follows:

Maximum Delivery Time	4 weeks
Average Delivery Time	3 weeks
Minimum Delivery Time	2 weeks

Calculate the firm's re order, maximum stock level, minimum stock level and average stock level for the next twelve months.

Re Order Level = Maximum Usage x Minimum Lead Time

$$1 \times 4 = 4000 \text{ units}$$

Maximum level = Re Order Level - (Minimum
Usage x Minimum Lead Time) + Re Order Qty.

$$4000 - (300 \times 2) + 2000$$
$$= 5400 \text{ units}$$

Minimum level = Re Order Level - (Average usage x average
Lead Time)

$$= 4000 - (700 \times 3)$$
$$= 1900 \text{ units}$$

Average Stock Level = Minimum Stock Level + ½ Re Order Quantity

$$= 1900 + \frac{1}{2} \; (ROQ \; \frac{2000}{2} = 1000$$
$$= 2900 \text{ units}$$

Management of Debtors

When goods are sold on credit, the purchasers are recorded as debtors. They are treated as short term assets because it is expected that they will pay the amount they owe soon. By selling on credit, a higher level of sales can be achieved because it gives the purchaser time to sell the goods before having to pay for them. As a result, there is always some risk that the firm will not receive payment and, while it is owed, the money it is in effect financing the other business. It is for this reason that the investment in debtors should be kept to the minimum amount, for money tied up in debtors can not be reinvested elsewhere.

Most credit controllers state that their aim is to take two months credit from their suppliers while giving only one months credit to their purchasers. If this can be achieved, the firm will have a very effective credit control policy but, in reality, it will depend on the type of business the firm is in and the size of the company. Small businesses often complain that they cannot get money out of some of their bigger customers. They know that they are helping to finance these other businesses but they are glad of the work and so they should consider charging a

201

slightly higher price to cover the extra time which they have to wait for their money.

Sometimes contracts can only be won by offering credit terms which are as good or better than competitors. This can put a large strain on the firm's working capital and this should be considered when tendering for work. Many a firm has been forced into financial problems because it could not pay its own bills because other people would not pay theirs. One way around this problem is to sell the invoices to a factoring house. The factoring house will credit the company's bank account with a certain percentage of the invoice value but the cost of this facility is high. Nevertheless, it may prove to be a successful option for small fast growing businesses who are constantly short of working capital.

The longer a debt remains unpaid, the greater the risk that it will never be paid. The company does not want to lose goodwill by constantly sending letters to the debtor but, nevertheless, an active credit control policy should be pursued. Often a personal visit is useful, and in extreme cases one might consider refusing additional credit until the account is settled. The sales force should be reminded that it is easy to sell by giving the customer credit. Unfortunately if the customer doesn't pay, you have effectively given your product away. If the sales staff aren't paid commission until the purchaser has paid, it gives them an incentive to call on their customers and chase up the debt.

Whenever interest rates rise credit controllers find it harder to collect money owed. Firms with money try to maximise their interest earnings while others, being short of cash, try to juggle their payments. As interest rates rise the firm must be ever more vigilant in its credit control policy. Long delays in payment are often the first signs that a company is in financial trouble and, if it is forced into receivership, money may well be lost as creditors with greater security seek repayment. For this reason it is always a good idea to state on the invoice that goods remain the property of the seller until paid for. If the debtor then proves to be insolvent, the stock cannot be resold to repay secured creditors.

The Management of Debtor Balances.

Although debtors represent a cost and a risk, this cost should be balanced against the extra profit made by allowing credit. Credit limits need to be reviewed regularly, and bank and trade references should always be taken up before agreeing any credit limit. Debtors' accounts should be constantly monitored and

202

appraised. It should always be remembered that the longer an account remains unpaid, the greater the probability of it not being paid.

The Management of Bank and Cash Balances

Cash is a wonderful asset. It allows the owner to make business decisions. Once a company has insufficient cash balances to cover its level of trading activity, it will be unable to trade if it cannot secure additional credit. Its directors and managers will be replaced by an administrator or a receiver and the business will probably be wound up or sold to another owner. It is for this reason that cash management is so vital.

The Payment Cycle

The amount of cash which any business needs to hold will depend upon its payment cycle. This can be illustrated by the following example. A company knows that it takes on average 15 days to turn its raw materials into finished stock and a further 40 days to receive payment from its debtors. The firm must pay its suppliers within 30 days, and so its cash conversion cycle is 55 days less 30 days = 25 days. If £5,000 of raw materials are purchased each day on 30 days credit, then the firm will have to pay for its raw materials within 30 days, while having to wait 55 days for its money. The business must be able to finance this £5,000 for 25 days and so £75,000 will be needed for working capital purposes.

Any reduction in manufacturing time or delay made in paying creditors will reduce the amount of working capital needed. Similarly, any reduction in the time taken to receive payments from debtors would also benefit the firm.

The aim is to have sufficient cash for the level of trading. Some companies are so worried about being short of cash that large cash balances are built up. When questioned, the owners say that they are waiting for the ideal investment or are considering purchasing another business, but often it is just being used as a security blanket. When this happens, the firm is not as efficient as it could be. Even assuming that the money is being invested in interest earning assets, the return is still likely to be less than could be earned by investing it in the business. If this continues over a long period of time, the business will experience lower earnings per share, which will make it vulnerable to a takeover bid if its shares are quoted on a stock exchange.

The key to having sufficient cash lies in accurate forecasting. Most businesses are seasonal. This means that they cannot rely on a steady stream of sales each month but experience peaks and troughs in sales. In these cases cash balances must be built up in the good months to carry the business through the poor months. This can be done by drawing up a cash budget. An example is shown below.

CASH BUDGET

The layout of a Cash Flow Forecast is as follows:

	January		February	
	Budget	Actual	Budget	Actual
Receipts	£	£	£	£
Cash Sales				
Debtor Payments				
Sale of Fixed Assets				
New Share Capital				
New Loans				
Total Cash In				
Payments				
Cash Payments				
Payments to Creditors				
Wages and Salaries				
Rent + Rates				
Other Business Expenses				
Interest				
Dividends				
Loan Repayments				
VAT				
Purchase of Fixed Assets				
Total Cash Out				
Surplus/Deficit				
Opening Balance				
Closing Balance				

Figure 36. Layout of a Cash Budget

Example

The Prudent Company's management know that they will incurr certain expenditure during the next six months and have projected estimated receipts and payments as follows:

	Dec	Jan	Feb	Mar	Apr	May	Jne
Sales (Units £9 per unit)	80	100	120	90	140	150	125
Raw Materials	500	600	700	550	820	905	750
Labour Costs	250	300	350	275	410	450	320
Rent	100	100	100	100	100	100	100
Overheads	180	200	230	190	260	280	235
Bank Loan				3000			
Purchase of Machinery			300			700	

The firm has an opening cash balance of £2,300. It gives one month credit on its sales and pays for its materials one month after it purchased them.

All other payments are made in the month in which they are incurred. Draw up the firm's projected cash budget for the next six months.

The cash budget seeks to show the receipts and payments of cash and so, before the budget can be prepared, management must estimate total receipts and payments for a period in advance not exceeding twelve months. Receipts and payments are only included in the month in which the money is received or paid out. Thus goods sold on one month's credit in June are not recorded as a receipt until July. Receipts are subtracted from payments and the balance is the opening balance for the next month. By drawing up a cash budget, it is possible to forecast future cash requirements so that surpluses can be lent or funds borrowed to finance a cash short fall. Non cash expenses, such as depreciation, are excluded from a cash budget.

Projected Cash Budget for The Prudent Company January to June Year Two

	January	February	March	April	May	June
	£	£	£	£	£	£
Receipts						
Sales (units x £9)	720	900	1080	810	1260	1350
Loans			3000			
Payments						
Raw Materials	500	600	700	550	820	905
Labour Costs	300	350	275	410	450	320
Rent	100	100	100	100	100	100
Overheads	200	230	190	260	280	235
Purchase of Machinery		300			700	
Opening Balance	2300	1920	1240	4055	3545	2455
Total Receipts	720	900	4080	810	1260	1350
	3020	2820	5320	4865	4805	3805
Less Payments	1100	1580	1265	1320	2350	1560
Closing Balance	1920	1240	4055	3545	2455	2245

Seven Rules For Conserving Cash

1. Keep the amount of money tied up in stock, whether it be raw materials, work in progress or finished stock, at the minimum amount consistent with maintaining production and delivery.

2. Ensure that an effective and efficient credit control policy is always maintained.

3. Always seek the best credit terms from suppliers.

4. Keep idle cash balances to the minimum for making day to day payments. Any funds not presently needed should be placed on deposit where they will earn valuable interest.

5. There may be occasions when it is better to lease or enter a hire purchase contract when acquiring fixed assets. This saves working capital since the whole sum does not have to be raised immediately.

6. Keep overheads and administrative costs to their budgeted targets.

7. Always audit the effectiveness of promotional and advertising campaigns.

If the business has insufficient funds, it will have to use overdraft finance, which means that the business is using the bank's money to pay its expenses. Naturally bankers are only prepared to lend if they believe the business can repay the money and that the managers can predict cash shortages. It is for this reason that bank managers often ask for a cash budget before they are prepared to grant an overdraft or loan facility. Bankers do not like to lend to companies who have run out of their own money and who then wish to spend theirs. In the bank's view this shows a lack of financial control which tends to make bank managers reluctant to lend, even though companies who are short of cash are a profitable source of income for the bank. Cash forecasts show that there is control and that the money is needed to finance a particular purpose rather than just to pay the business's debts. The bank then knows that profits can be earned, even thought there is an underlying risk.

If the cash budget shows that there will be a surplus of funds for a number of months, then these can be lent. Generally, the longer the money can be lent, the greater the amount of interest which can be earned. The actual payments should be recorded against the budgeted figures so that a more accurate cash position can be established and this process should be continued from one financial year to the next.

Chapter 17
Borrowing Finance

Introduction

At some time there will be a need to borrow money. The money may be needed to provide additional working capital or to finance long term fixed assets which will increase earnings in the future. The borrower's aim is to obtain the finance at the most attractive rate of interest. Before this can be done, the lender will require enough information to be reasonably certain that the money will be repaid with interest during the lifetime of the loan.

Is There A Need For Additional Finance?

If a firm is unable to finance its capital investment programmes out of its cash flow, it will be forced to raise additional capital, this is likely to involve the business in seeking some form of debt finance. Borrowing money is expensive. The loan and interest payments can only be repaid out of earnings. This will necessitate a larger return on the capital employed than the cost of borrowing. If the money is needed to provide additional working capital, it is always worth reappraising the firm's working capital control. Money tied up in stock and debtors might be able to be released, thereby reducing or even eliminating the need for costly borrowed funds. If however, the money is needed for fixed assets, then some assessment of the future profitability must be made. There is no point in investing money in additional assets if they cannot generate a return on the capital invested in them. In such a case it would be better to wait until a more attractive investment proposition occurred.

Having decided that there is a need for extra finance, the next task is to decide how the money should be borrowed. If the money is going to finance short term assets, it should be borrowed short term. Similarly, if it will be needed for a long time, such as acquiring additional fixed assets, the money should be borrowed long term. The high street clearing banks provide a range of loans to business but it is important to decide what type of finance is required before requesting a loan.

Main Sources of Finance

Short Term Borrowing

1. Bank Overdraft

This is the most popular form of business finance. It provides short term money. In theory, an overdraft is repayable on demand and so the money should only be used to finance additional current assets which can be quickly turned into cash. Overdraft finance is attractive as interest is only payable on the amount borrowed. This can reduce the cost of capital if the account can quickly be returned to a credit balance. Bankers often refer to an overdraft as a form of self liquidating finance. This means that during the life of the overdraft facility the borrower will be overdrawn for some months, and then in surplus before going back into overdraft.

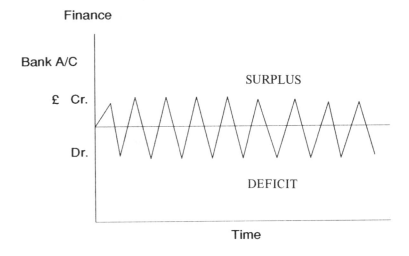

Figure 37: Using a Bank Overdraft as Self Liquidating Finance

When this happens the lender can see that the funds are being used to finance additional current assets which are later being turned into cash. If, on the other hand, this does not happen there is a danger that the overdraft is being used to pay the creditors. The business may be very short of cash and is having to borrow to pay its creditors. If there is no sign of this situation abating, banks often call in the overdraft once the firm has reached its overdraft limit and continues to write cheques to meet its liabilities. Whilst this may protect the bank's position, it will force the business into receivership.

2. Factoring Debts

This is another method of raising cash to help firms which are short of working capital. The factoring house will purchase the invoices from the company, less a given percentage, and will credit the firm's bank account immediately. The factor will then collect the debt and pay any balance owing. In effect the business is selling its debts to raise cash. This is an expensive way of raising money, but for small, fast growing firms it may still prove an attractive option as it ensures a constant flow of cash and reduces the need for internal credit control.

3. Discounting a Bill of Exchange

A customer may seek to pay for goods by accepting a bill of exchange. This is a document which allows a buyer a period of credit before the goods must be paid for. If the buyer accepts the bill, it must be signed and then sent back to the seller. Unfortunately, no money will be received until the bill matures. One way of receiving cash before the maturity date, is to sell the bill to a bank for cash. This is referred to as discounting a bill. The bank will pay a sum to the seller, less an amount to cover the interest lost by having to pay cash before receiving the proceeds of the bill.

4. Documentary Credit

This is a valuable form of credit for firms engaged in exporting. By approaching the bank for a letter of credit, the bank guarantees the payment to a foreign supplier, provided that the terms and conditions of the letter of credit are complied with. The importer can then obtain credit from the supplier.

Medium to Long Term Borrowing

5. Hire Purchase

With the advent of leasing this has proved to be a less popular form of finance. The purchaser enters into a contract to hire the asset with an option to purchase it at the end of the contract. The borrower will normally have to place a deposit and then may repay the balance over a three to five year time period. This allows time for the asset to earn funds which can be used to repay the loan.

6. Leasing

In recent years this has proved to be a very popular form of finance. The lessor (person leasing the equipment) allows the lessee to take possession of the asset if s/he agrees to make weekly or monthly repayments during the term of the lease. As with hire purchase, the borrower can make the repayments out of earnings, thereby making the asset self financing. Although the asset will be owned by the lessor during the lifetime of the agreement, it is the use of assets which is important rather than the ownership of them.

7. Sale and Lease Back

Capital can be raised by selling the firm's buildings to a financial institution, and at the same time entering into a leasing agreement. The business will gain capital for expansion and will still have the use of its premises, but it will have lost a valuable freehold asset. Rent reviews, coupled with high rates of inflation, can make this a very expensive form of finance, and should only be considered after all other sources have been investigated.

8. Term Loan

These are loans which have a fixed life. The money can be borrowed for up to twenty years, allowing it to be used to finance long term investment projects. Often the interest rate can be fixed, enabling the firm to budget its repayments and cost of capital. Term loans are attractive to small and medium sized businesses who do not have access to the capital markets and so cannot raise money by selling shares or debentures.

9. Foreign Currency Loans

Capital can be borrowed in foreign currencies. The loans may carry a lower rate of interest if interest rates are lower in other countries than in Britain, thereby making them at first instance attractive. Unless the firm is able to earn foreign currency, the borrower will be subject to exchange rate risk which could increase the size of the loan in sterling terms. This could make the loan a very expensive form of finance should sterling depreciate against a stronger foreign currency.

Lending To The Commercial Borrower

Banks and other financial institutions make their profits by lending. They are always looking for what they call a "gilt edged lending opportunity" which can best be described as one where their money is safe and will be repaid with interest over the life of the loan. This does not mean that lenders are keen to avoid risk, but they do tend to be risk averse. When they lend money, they are in effect lending other customers' deposits and so prudence demands that these balances are lent to borrowers who can repay. Before the loan is made, the lender needs to know that the borrower meets certain financial criteria which can be best summarised under the following headings.

Borrower

In some cases the lender will either not know or have only limited knowledge about the borrower. This is unfortunate, for there is obviously greater risk in lending to commercial enterprises which have no record of borrowing and repaying money from the lender. The borrower's first task is to provide information which will inform the lender about the business and the people who manage it.

If the borrower is a company, then a small report (often referred to as a business plan) should be submitted. This will contain a brief description about the business, its aims and objectives, together with a forecast outlining market opportunities. This should be presented together with the following documents.

a. Certificate of Incorporation

b. Copy of the Articles of Association

c. Copy of the Memorandum of Association

d. A recent set of audited accounts

e. Copies of past bank statements

f. A forecast cash budget

g. A report outlining the purpose of the loan

At this stage the borrower needs to provide as much information about the company as possible. Even if the borrower is known to the lender, it may still be useful for it shows that the borrower has thought about why the funds are needed and has already considered the cost and returns from the investment.

Amount

The lender will need to know how much capital will be required and for how long. It is far better to overestimate than to underestimate. Often the loan may be taken in tranches, thereby allowing a reduction in interest payments as interest will only be payable when the money is borrowed. If more money is needed at a later stage, it suggests that the initial forecasts were inaccurate and, from the lender's view, there is no guarantee that the revised estimates will prove to be any more accurate. Often the additional working capital which will be needed to operate the new investment is understated, leading to working capital problems at a later date. Ideally a break down should be given showing the amount of money needed to finance the capital investment, together with a cash flow forecast showing the working capital costs of the project.

Repayment

Whatever is borrowed must be repaid. The aim is to make the repayments as painless for the borrower as possible, thereby increasing the probability of repayment. Repayments can only be made out of earnings and so the borrower will seek time to earn money from the investment before making repayments. Large early repayments can cause working capital problems, particularly if early earnings from the investment are small. In such cases it makes sense to ask the lender if interest only payments can be made at this stage. The capital repayments can then be made when the investment starts to yield higher earnings.

The amount of money which must be repaid can be calculated by the following formula:

$$CI = \frac{PR}{1 - \frac{1}{(1+R)^n}}$$

where

CI	=	annual repayment of capital and interest
P	=	the amount of the loan
R	=	the flat rate of interest
n	=	life of the loan

Example.

A company wants to borrow £50,000 for 10 years at a fixed rate loan of 12% per annum. What will its yearly capial and interest payments be?

$$CI = \frac{PR}{1 - \frac{1}{(1+R)^n}} = \frac{£50000 \times 0.12}{1 - \left(\frac{1}{1.12}\right)^{10}}$$

$$= \frac{£6000}{(1-0.3220)} = \frac{£6000}{0.678}$$

$$= £8850 \text{ per annum}$$

Security

The lender will often require some form of security before agreeing to lend the money. This really safeguards the lender against the worst possible scenario of the borrower being unable to repay the debt. If this happens, the lender needs to be able to sell the secured asset so that the borrowed funds and accrued interest can be recovered. As far as the lender is concerned, this is a last resort and security is only taken to protect their financial position. Ideally the lender will ask for assets which are likely to remain constant in value and which can quickly be sold for cash. Land, life assurance policies, stocks and shares, and unit trusts are frequently offered as security, but guarantees from people offering to repay the loan in case of default may also prove to be acceptable. Usually the lender will only lend two thirds of the assets' market value for then, even if there is a decrease in its value, the lender's position is still secure.

A lender will generally only be prepared to lend without security if the business can repay the loan quickly. The firm must have a stable and regular cash operating cycle. There is no safe limit, but most lenders are likely to be reluctant to lend more than 50% of a firm's net assets without asking for some form of security.

Control

The lenders will want to be certain that their money is in safe hands. The management must be able to demonstrate that they have the necessary skills to run the business. They must be prepared to answer the lenders' questions and it is often a good idea to invite lenders to visit the business. Then the business can be discussed in detail and the lenders can be shown the firm's order books, its administrative facilities and the skills and expertise of the work force.

The borrower must satisfy the lender on all these points before being able to obtain the finance. The cost of the loan will be determined by the interest rate which will be made up of two parts. Firstly, there will be the cost of money, often referred to as the bank's base rate . Secondly, there will be a premium to cover the risk of lending. If the borrower can show the lender that the risk is in fact a small one, then this will be reflected in the interest charged above the bank's base rate. Often the interest payments saved by good preparation more than compensate for the cost of providing all the necessary information

Chapter 18
Gearing

Introduction

All businesses need assets so that they can trade and make profits. The money to finance these assets will have been provided either by the owners or by lenders of funds to the business. If the firm wishes to increase its level of trading, it will require additional assets and these will have to be financed. One way of paying for them is to reinvest past profits but this takes a long time and often the management want the company to expand fast to take advantage of current market opportunities. There are two ways of acquiring additional capital. One way is to raise additional money from the shareholders, who are the owners of the business, and the other is to borrow the money.

Gearing

The word gearing is used to define the capital structure of a firm. Companies can often choose how they will raise the additional capital they need. If they decide to raise more money by issuing additional shares, they are said to be increasing their equity capital while, if they chose to borrow the money, they are said to be increasing their debt capital.

The Cost of Capital

Any additional capital raised will have to be paid for and so the business must be able to generate a return from its capital employed which exceeds its cost. Shareholders will want to receive dividends from their investment and lenders will demand their interest payments. The percentage of profit paid as dividend and the rate of interest charged for the money borrowed will determine the business's cost of capital. The aim is to keep the overall cost as low as possible so that the maximum return can be made for the owners.

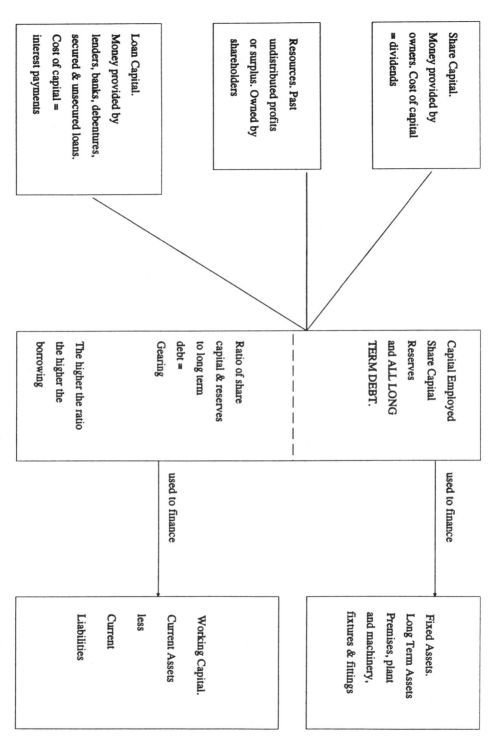

Figure 38: Sources and Uses of Capital

216

Factors To Be Considered Before Borrowing Money

Any money which has been borrowed will one day have to be repaid. While it is borrowed interest will have to be paid. The interest payments will have to be paid in cash and this will affect the cash flow. The first task must be to ensure that these payments can be met and that they will not place an intolerable burden on the business. The capital will also have to be repaid. While in some cases it is possible to repay past borrowing by additional borrowing in the future, it is more likely that money will have to be set aside to meet the final redemption of the loan or to make capital repayments during the life of the loan. These capital repayments can have a severe effect on cash flow, particularly if sales and profits fall because of a lack of demand.

The current level of interest rates must also be considered. The rate of interest which the firm has to pay will be affected by two criteria. Firstly, the general level of interest rates for borrowed money and, secondly, the risk premium which has to be paid to the lender. The greater the risk as assessed by the lender, the greater the premium required by the lender to compensate for the additional risk. The firm must assess what premium it will have to pay.

The amount of money which the firm has already borrowed will also have a bearing on whether it should increase its borrowings. Firms which have borrowed a large proportion of their capital are said to be highly geared. These firms are often unpopular with investors because of the increased risk that one day they will be unable to meet their interest payments.

Lastly, the lender will want some kind of security before granting the loan. Premises and other fixed assets offer a degree of security for the lender and the borrower must assess how much money the lender is likely to advance on the security value of the asset, and at what rate of interest.

The Advantages of Borrowing Money

The amount of profit which a firm can distribute as dividend will be determined by two main factors. Firstly, the amount of profit made and, secondly, the number of shareholders. It is not the amount of money which will be distributed as dividend which is important, but the number of shareholders who will receive a share of it. The fewer the number of shareholders, the greater the dividend per share that can be paid. One way of achieving this is to borrow money, thereby placing a limit on the number of shareholders.

Let us assume that two companies selling similar products have just published their annual results. They both have the same amount of capital employed, and have both made a net profit after tax of £15,000. If the directors decide to distribute all of this profit amongst the shareholders, then the firm which has the fewer shareholders stand to receive the larger dividend payouts. This point can be seen by looking at two companies with different capital structures but with the same long term capital base.

Example: The High Return Company and The Low Return Company.

Extract of the firms' balance sheets.

	High Return Company £	Low Return Company £
Ordinary shares £1 issued and fully paid	100,000	170,000
10% Debentures Stock	40,000	-
8% Unsecured Loan Stock	30,000	-
Total Capital	170,000	170,000
Net Profit after tax	£15,000	£15,000

Although both firms have declared the same amount of profit available for distribution, the High Return Company will be able to pay the larger dividend. This is because the dividend has only to be distributed to 100,000 ordinary shareholders, as against 170,000 of the Low Return Company

The High Return Company will also have a higher earnings per share ratio. Using the earnings per share ratio which is

$$\frac{\text{Profit after Tax and Preference Dividend}}{\text{Number of Ordinary Shares}}$$

the figures for the High Return Company are

$$\frac{£15,000}{100,000}$$

which gives earnings per share of 15p.

The profits of the Low Return Company have to be shared amongst 170,000 shareholders and so the figures show a lower earnings ratio.

$$\frac{£15,000}{170,000}$$

which results in earnings per share of approximately 9p.

Most shareholders purchase shares with the aim of maximising the return on their investment. They hope to see the share price and the size of their dividends increase over time. The amount of money which a share can earn when it is invested in one company as opposed to another is generally reflected in its share price. The higher the earnings, the more expensive the share. This should enable the investor to make a capital gain and will ensure that the shares are popular with investors, thereby making it possible one day to sell more shares to existing investors should the company need additional finance. A high share price also makes the firm less vulnerable to a hostile takeover bid as the high price of the shares may deter prospective purchasers from trying to acquire a controlling interest.

Reducing the Cost of Capital

A firm is sometimes able to reduce the overall cost of capital by borrowing. This is best explained by looking at the capital structure of the High Return and Low Return Companies.

Low Return Company's Cost of Capital

	£
170,000 Ordinary £1 shares issued and fully paid	170,000
Dividend	15,000

219

Earnings per share, as previously calculated = 9p (approx), thus, the cost of capital for the company is 9p per £1 share or 9%.

The cost of share capital is determined by the rate of dividend which the company pays to its shareholders. The shareholder will only be prepared to invest if there is the prospect of earning a reasonable return, either in the form of dividends or capital appreciation. The earnings per share ratio can therefore be used as the cost of using equity capital.

High Return Company's Cost of Capital

	£
100,000 Ordinary £1 shares issued and fully paid	100,000
£40,000 10% Debentute Stock 2020 - 2030	40,000
£30,000 8% Unsecured Loan Stock 2015 - 2020	30,000
	170,000

	£
Ordinary Shares (Dividends)	15,000
Debentures (10% Interest)	4,000
Unsecured Loan Stock (8% Interest)	2,400
Total cost of Capital	21,400

The overall cost of capital now is $\dfrac{£21,400 \times 100}{170,000}$ = 13% (approx)

The High Return Company has been able to reduce its cost of capital from 15% to 13% by raising debt capital.

Reduction in Taxation Payable

Companies pay Corporation Tax on their profits. Some expenses, such as interest payments, are tax deductible and so the tax advantage will reduce the cost of capital. If a company has borrowed £500,000 at an interest rate of 10%, then its annual interest charges will be £50,000. If the rate of Corporation tax is 50%, then the after tax cost of borrowing the money will only be £25,000. Dividend payments are not tax deductible and so no tax advantages are gained from employing additional share capital.

The Dangers of Raising Capital by Borrowing

Every time a firm borrows money it has to be able to meet the interest charges incurred. This means that a firm must always have sufficient cash to meet its interest payments. In business profits can never be guaranteed. High interest rates coupled with a downturn in demand can soon lead to reduced sales and profits. It is then that many companies (and particularly small ones) are forced into liquidation as they can no longer meet the combined pressures of high interest rates, static profits and increased overheads. Even large companies are not immune as once-famous household names such as Polly Peck, Coloroll, Sock Shop, Rush and Tompkins and British and Commonwealth have had to apply to the Companies Court for an administrator or have had to appoint a receiver.

When this happens highly geared companies become unpopular with investors. Bankers are likely to become less keen to lend and financial analysts are likey to reduce the firm's credit rating. In extreme cases the bank may call in its short term loans and creditors may also be reluctant to continue trading on the same business terms. These actions can force companies into insolvency and so highly geared companies are always considered more risky investments.

It is therefore vital that the benefits of borrowing money outweigh the risks. It is not just the amount of debt to equity capital which must be considered, but also the company's ability to repay the debt out of earnings. The higher the ratio of earnings before tax to interest charges, the smaller the risk of financial insolvency.

Companies are often forced into insolvency once they can no longer earn sufficient profits to service their debt. If the level of earnings can be increased, then the company can cope with a higher proportion of debt capital, but it is important that this ratio of debt to earnings is kept at a realistic level. One method of measuring this debt to earnings ratio is by calculating the total liquidity of the firm by the following calculation,

$$\frac{\text{Working Capital} + \text{Long Term Debt}}{\text{After Tax Earnings}}$$

This ratio shows how long it will take the firm to redeem all of its debt out of earnings. The quicker the debt can be repaid, the lower the risk, but it is for the management to decide what is an acceptable risk. This will inevitably be determined by estimated future earnings and whether or not these earnings are greatly affected by different levels of economic activity.

As a general rule firms which have stable sales can afford to borrow more money than firms with unstable sales, but ultimately it is the lenders who consider what is a safe level of debt. If the amount of debt increases too fast, they will either increase the interest charges or refuse to lend more money until the firm has increased the shareholders' stake in the business.

Before borrowing money, management must balance the benefits of increased earnings and posssible lower capital costs with the dangers of insolvency if they are ever unable to service the debt out of current earnings.

Chapter 19
Investment Appraisal

Introduction

Most business organisations seek to expand by increasing their sales and profits. In the short term this may be possible by making greater use of existing assets, but in the long term new investment will be needed to increase the productive capacity of the business. Any new investment expenditure will have to be financed. This can be done either by investing past profits back into the business, or by investing new share capital or loan capital. In either case the new investment must yield a return which will be higher than the cost of capital and consistent with the firm's present and expected return on capital employed.

Cost of Capital

The cost of capital will vary from one company to another. The cost of capital will be influenced by such factors as the company's capital structure, the cost of new sources of capital, and the amount of capital expenditure to which it is committed. The firm must also consider its opportunity cost of capital, which is the cost of investing in one project as opposed to another. Whatever a business's actual cost of capital, it is useful to consider the cost under the following headings.

Cost of Borrowing

If loan finance is required, then the minimum return from the project must be above the cost of servicing the loan. This means that the investment must make a greater return than the current or expected interest rate being charged for borrowed funds. Normally one would never invest unless this was the case but, if interest rates were very high, a company might be prepared to take a long term view knowing that the average cost of loan funds in the long term would be lower than the current interest rate.

Return on Capital Employed

Every pound that is invested in the business must make a return on its investment. The return which a business can earn on its own capital is referred to as the return on its capital employed. It can be calculated by the formula

$$\frac{\text{Profit(before interest on debt)} \times 100}{\text{Capital Employed}}$$

and this can be used as a yard stick when considering new investments.

Weighted Cost of Capital

This method seeks to average out the firm's cost of capital by adding up the amount and cost of each type of capital and then calculating the weighted return. This can be calculated as follows:

Capital	Amount	Cost	Return	Capital Structure	Cost	W'ted Av.
Shares	£40,000	12%	£4,800	20%	12%	2.4%
Reserves	£80,000	12%	£9,600	40%	12%	4.8%
6% Pref Shs	£40,000	6%	£2,400	20%	6%	1.2%
8% Loan	£40,000	8%	£3,200	20%	8%	1.6%
	£200,000		£20,000			10%

Determining the Cost of Capital

In the above example the weighted cost of capital is 10% and so, by having different sources of capital, the firm hopes to be able to reduce its overall cost. This is best illustrated by looking at how the business has calculated its cost of capital.

Shares: The example has put a cost of 12% on share capital. This figure was arrived at by looking at the rate of dividend paid to shareholders in the form of dividend payments. The higher the dividend, the higher the firm's cost of share capital.

Reserves: As we have seen earlier, reserves belong to the shareholders because they are made up of past profits which have been kept by the company to be reinvested in the business, rather than being paid out to shareholders. It therefore follows that the reserves should earn a return equal to the dividend paid on ordinary shares.

Preference Shares: These are shares which carry a fixed rate of dividend and so the cost of capital is 6%.

8% Loan: The 8% refers to the interest rate which has to be paid for borrowing the money. Interest payments are tax deductible and so, assuming a tax on profits (Corporation Tax) of 50%, the true cost of the capital to the firm would be 4%. To keep this example simple, taxation has been ignored.

Capital Investment

This is the term used to define money invested in fixed assets such as machinery and buildings. These assets will all have a limited productive life and the aim is to choose investment projects which will yield the greatest return. It is not easy to choose projects which will become the future profit earners for the business but the aim is to avoid two types of errors which are often referred to as "Drop and Go Errors". Drop Errors occur when the management decide not to proceed with an investment even though it would have been profitable. They may decide against such a project because at the time of making the investment decision they failed to see its full opportunity, or they may decide against it because in their view the initial capital costs are too high. A Go Error occurs when the firm invests in a project which fails to make the required return and which may even lose the firm money, thereby reducing its overall return on capital employed. Any investment decision involves risk, but the aim of using investment appraisal techniques is to limit that risk.

Investment Appraisal Techniques

We have already seen that cash is a scarce resource. If it is to be used to finance new investment, the firm will seek both an attractive return from its investment and will hope to recover its initial investment costs as soon as possible. The quicker the money can be recovered, the less risk is involved in the project. This is often referred to as the pay back time of the project.

The cost of the investment is not just the financial cost of using the money but the opportunity cost of foregoing one investment oportunity as opposed to another. Investment appraisal techniques provide management with information about the likely returns to be made and the level of risk from the investment. They cannot, however, select on their own the optimum investments. This can only be done by management who are able to take other factors into account, such as future market developments, before making their investment decisions. Before any investment decision is taken, it is essential to know the amount of cash which will be required to finance the new project and the amount of cash inflows which it will generate.

Cash Flow Tables

A cash flow table shows the cash inflows and outflows which are expected to occur from an investment. Cash will be needed to finance both the fixed assets and to provide the working capital which will be needed to pay for the day to day expenses. It is usually a mistake to assume that once a fixed asset has been purchased that cash inflows will immediately follow. Often additional capital is needed to pay for new stock, training and spare parts and this, if not budgeted for, can put severe constraints on a business's working capital. The purpose of drawing up a cash flow table is to be able to determine the firm's net cash flow from the new investment. This is calculated by adding up all the inflows and subtracting all of the outflows.

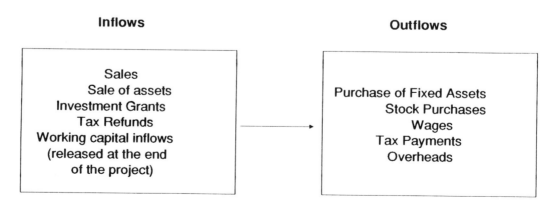

Inflows	Outflows
Sales Sale of assets Investment Grants Tax Refunds Working capital inflows (released at the end of the project)	Purchase of Fixed Assets Stock Purchases Wages Tax Payments Overheads

Figure 39: Suggested Layout for a Cash Flow Table

Year	Capital Outflow £	Sales Income £	Costs £	Profit £	Tax on Profits £	Tax saved by Allowances £	Net Cash Flow £
0							
1							
2							
3							
4							
5							

Note

It is a good idea to construct separate columns for each cash inflow & cash outflow.

227

Constructing a Cash Flow Table

The following diagram shows examples of inflows and outflows of cash.

The cash flow table only shows receipts and payments of cash and so the following expenses are never included:

a. Depreciation

b. Bad Debts

c. Accruals (money owing but which does not yet have to be paid in cash)

d. Profits or losses made on the sale of fixed assets

Example

A business which is profitable and which currently pays Corporation Tax on its profits is considering investing in a new electric saw which will cost £10,000 and which will have a life of five years. The firm has estimated that the cash inflows from the investment will be £4,400 a year and that the cost of running the machine will be £400 a year. The current rate of Corporation Tax is 40% and the investment will not enjoy any write down relief (capital allowance). The firm's accountant has estimated that the machine will have a resale value in five years' time of £1,000.

Cash Flow Table

Year	Investment	Cash Inflow	Cash Outflow	Tax	Net Cash Flow
		£	£	£	£
0	(10,000)				(10,000)
1		4,400	(400)		4,000
2		4,400	(400)	(1,600)	2,400
3		4,400	(400)	(1,600)	2,400
4		4,400	(400)	(1,600)	2,400
5	1,000	5,400	(400)	(1,600)	3,400
6				(1,600)	(1,600)

228

Points to Note

a.   Taxable income £4,400–400 = £4,000 per annum
b.   Tax payments due £4,000 x 40% = £1,600
c.   Corporation tax (tax on company profits) are always paid 9 months after the tax liability is incurred. This means that effectively the tax will be paid the following year.

Pay Back Method

Before businesses decide to invest in new machinery or other fixed assets, they need to consider how long the investment will take to pay for itself and the rate of return which will be earned on the new investment. The return must be sufficient to cover the cost of using the money. This means that a return will be needed which is consistent with the firm's present return on capital employed and which is definitely higher than the current interest rate, which is effectively the cost of borrowed capital. In addition a margin must be added to cover the cost of unsuccessful investments as not all new projects will turn out to be successful and those that are must carry those that are not.

The pay back method is concerned with how quickly the firm will be able to recoup the money invested in a new project. It is calculated by the formula

Payback   = $\dfrac{\text{Investment}}{\text{Cash Flow Per Annum}}$

The payback time is very important if the investment is likely to become obsolete because of changes in technology or market demand. In such cases the quicker the payback time, the lower the risk, although it should be remembered that business risks are not always time related.

Payback is a useful method as an initial screening process, because it eliminates the least financially viable projects when making capital investment decisions.

Example
Let us assume that a business is currently considering investing a maximum of £50,000 in new fixed assets. The firm needs to expand quickly because the market is growing fast and this expansion is placing severe constraints upon its working capital. Ideally it would like projects which require a minimum amount

229

of investment capital and which pay for themselves over a short period of time, thereby easing its cash flow problems. The management are currently considering three new projects which they expect will have a life of four years. After this time the assets will be worn out and additional investment will be required.

	Project A	Project B	Project C
Investment	£15,000	£25,000	£50,000
Life of Investment	4 Years	4 Years	4 Years
Year one Cash Inflow	£4,000	£8,000	£20,000
Year Two Cash Inflow	£6,000	£10,000	£30,000
Year Three Cash Inflow	£5,000	£12,000	£15,000
Year Four Cash Inflow	£4,000	£6,000	£9,000
Pay Back Time	3 yrs	2yrs and 7 mths	2 yrs

By adding up the inflows which are the expected level of sales and then dividing it by the initial investment, it is possible to calculate how quickly the investment will take to pay for itself. In this example, project C has the quickest pay back time which could well be a factor influencing the investment decision.

How to Calculate the Pay Back Time From An Investment

	Project A £		Project B £	Project C £	
Investment	15,000		25,000	50,000	
Cash Flow					
Year one	4,000		8,000	20,000	
Year two	6,000		10,000	30,000	50,000
Year three	5,000	15,000	12,000		2 yrs

3 yrs.   =£1,000 per month

short fall £7,000
£1,000

= 2 yrs 5 months

Advantages of the Pay Back Method

The pay back method is simple to calculate and shows how quickly the initial investment will be recovered from sales income. This probably explains why the method is so popular, for business people can see how long their investment is at risk. As a general rule the quicker the pay back time, the lower the risk. Most business people are said to be risk averse. This means that they are prepared to take the financial risk of investing capital, but would like to limit that risk by knowing that there is a reasonable probability of the investment paying for itself over a certain period of time.

Disadvantages of the Pay Back Method

The main disadvantage of the payback method is that it does not take into consideration the earnings that the investment yields after it has paid for itself. In the example, projects A and B are rejected even though they both yield greater returns than project C after the pay back period. Finally, the method assumes that all receipts and payments occur within the period under consideration. Nevertheless, it is a useful investment appraisal technique for projects which have an initial capital investment followed by a steady flow of sales income.

Accounting Rate of Return

This method is used to select the project which will yield the greatest return on investment. It is calculated by the formula:

$$R = \frac{\text{Average Net Profit (after depreciation)} \times 100}{\text{Average Capital Investment}}$$

$$\text{Where Average Net Profit} = \frac{\text{Net Profit (after depreciation)}}{\text{Life of the Investment}}$$

$$\text{And where Average Capital Investment} = \frac{\text{Capital Investment}}{2}$$

Example

A business intends to invest £20,000 in a project which will have a life of five years. The annual estimated returns are shown below:

Net Cash Inflows	£
Year One	6,000
Year Two	8,000
Year Three	6,000
Year Four	10,000
Year Five	10,000
Total Inflows	40,000

How to Calculate Accounting Rate of Return

a) Calculate Annual Depreciation

Annual depreciation is cost of the asset divided by life of the asset. Cost of assset £20,000, life 5 years. Therefore annual depreciation £4,000 a year.

b) Deduct depreciation from cash flow: £40,000 minus £20,000 = £20,0000

c) Calculate Average Annual Return: Average annual return 20,000 divided by life of investment (5 years) = £4,000. Therefore Accounting Rate of Return
$$= \frac{£4,000 \times 100}{10,000} = 40\%$$

This shows that the business will earn a return of 40% on its original investment if it proceeds with this project.

Advantages of Accounting Rate of Return
This method shows the return on the capital invested and it takes account of all profits earned throughout the project's life.

Disadvantages of Accounting Rate of Return
The main disadvantage of this method is that it does not take account of taxation payments and write down allowances which can greatly affect the net cash flows from a project.

Discounted Cash Flow

One of the main limitations of both the pay back method and the accounting rate of return is that both methods ignore the time taken to receive the cash inflows. The discounted cash flow method seeks to calculate the value of cash inflows received in the future for money received immediately is worth more than money to be received in the future. This is so because, if you invests cash in interest-earning deposits, it will increase in value because of the interest received. The interest can then be added to the capital and even more interest will accrue in the future. When money is received at a later date, the receiver has been deprived in the meantime of the use of the money and of the interest - accordingly the future cash inflow should be discounted, to ascertain its present value based on a

233

specific interest rate. In this way future cash flows can be compared with the value of money invested at the start of the project.

Year	Outflow	Discount Factor	Inflow	Net Present Value
	£	£	£	£

Figure 40: Example of Discounted Cash Flow Table Layout

Note.

1. Any additional working capital must be added to the capital cost at the beginning of the project. At the end it must be treated as an inflow and discounted.

2. Any residual value must be similarly treated as an inflow in the last year and discounted.

3. Any opportunity cost of capital should be treated as a cash outflow.

4. Any saving should be treated as a cash inflow.

How to Use Discount Tables

Figure 41: The Workings of Compounding & Discounting Tables

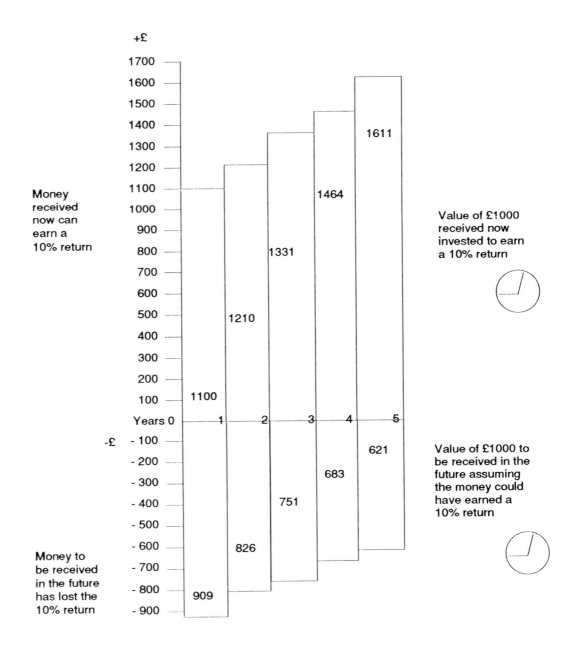

How To Use The Table

COMPOUNDING (Time makes money grow)

Year	10%	£1000 (received now + invested)	Future Value
0		£1000	£1000
1	1.100	£1000	£1100
2	1.210	£1000	£1210
3	1.331	£1000	£1331
4	1.464	£1000	£1464
5	1.611	£1000	£1611

DISCOUNTING (Time makes money less)

Year	10%	£1000 (received in the future)	Future Value
0		£1000	1000
1	0.909	£1000	909
2	0.826	£1000	826
3	0.751	£1000	751
4	0.683	£1000	683
5	0.621	£1000	621

The Time Value of Money

Even if operating in an economy with zero inflation, a business still enjoys three major benefits by receiving money immediately rather than in the future. Firstly, the money can be reinvested in the business. Secondly, the risk of the investment is negated as soon as it has paid for itself and, lastly, the money received can be used to meet the business's immediate liabilities.

Inflation gives rise to an additional problem, because it reduces the purchasing power of money and so, if the economy has a high rate of inflation, the future purchasing power of the future inflows will be eroded. This will mean that the firm's cost of capital will need to be higher to compensate for the effects of inflation and to make a return in real terms.

Example

Using the same figures as in the previous example, the management would like to know if the investment is still viable. At present the business earns a return of 15% on its capital and so any investment must yield such a return.

How to Discount Cash Inflows and Calculate An Investment's Net Present Value.

Year	Cash Outflow	Cash Inflow	Discount Factor	Net Present Value
	£	£		£
0	(20,000)	-	15%	(20,000)
1		6,000	0.870	5,220
2		8,000	0.756	6,048
3		6,000	0.658	3,948
4		10,000	0.572	5,720
5		10,000	0.497	4,970
	Total Value of Discounted Inflows			25,906
	Less Original Investment			20,000
	Net Present Value			5,906

Points To Note

a. The original investment of £20,000 is not discounted because money at the start of the project must be worth its original amount.

b. The discount figures are taken from the tables in the appendix.

c. By discounting the cash inflows, it is possible to see their value had the firm been able to receive the money immediately and earn a return of 15%.

d. By adding up the discounted returns and subtracting them from the original investment, the firm knows that the investment is financially viable. This is because all inflows have earned the required return of 15%, thereby reducing them to their present day values. In this way the money received at different future dates can be compared with the value of the original investment.

Interpreting the Net Present Value of a Project

There are only three possible outcomes when calculating the net present value of a project. These are;

a. Positive Net Present Value.

This happens when the total value of the discounted inflows is greater than the outflows. The project is therefore capable of earning a return greater than the cost of capital.

b. Negative Net Present Value.

If the total discounted outflows exceed the discounted inflows, then the project is incapable of earning a return which is greater than the cost of capital.

c. Nil Net Present Value.

In this situation the total discounted inflows exactly equal the discounted outflows. This shows that the project is capable of earning a return which equals the cost of capital and is called the internal rate of return (IRR).

Example

A firm is considering investing £20,000 and is currently evaluating the returns from three investment opportunities which it has called Project A, B and C. The cash inflows and their net present values, using a rate of return of 10%, are shown below:

Yr	DCF	Project A £		Project B £		Project C £	
0	10%	Cash Flow	NPV	Cash Flow	NPV	Cash Flow	NPV
		(20,000)	(20,000)	(20,000)	(20,000)	(20,000)	(20,000)
1	0.91	2,000	1,820	6,000	5,460	2,000	1,820
2	0.83	4,000	3,320	6,000	4,980	4,000	3,320
3	0.75	6,000	4,500	6,000	4,500	3,920	2,940
4	0.68	6,000	4,080	2,000	1,360	4,000	2,720
5	0.62	6,000	3,720	1,800	1,116	4,000	2,480
6	0.56	6,800	3,808	1,800	1,008	12,000	6,720
NPV			1,248		(1,576)		Nil

By discounting the cash inflows it can be seen that

> Project A is capable of earning a higher return than that required
> Project B is unable to earn the required rate of return
> Project C can earn the return required.

Limitations of Investment Appraisal Techniques

All methods of appraising the return from investments are based upon forecast returns and expectations about the level of inflation and interest rates. If there is a sharp increase in the rate of inflation and in the cost of money by a rise in interest rates, then the anticipated return or cost may well turn out to be very different from the estimated return. The National Westminster Bank Tower was originally forecast to cost £15 million but the final cost was £115 million. Similarly, the Thames Barrier was budgeted to cost £23 million but the final cost was £461 million, and the cost of constructing the Humber Bridge spiralled from a planned £19 million to £120 million. These examples all highlight the risks involved in investing in projects which take a long time to complete and which will yield a return only after completion.

Chapter 20
Valuation of a Business

Introduction

In accounting it is a convention that a business will trade forever. This is known as the going concern concept and it is why a balance sheet is not prepared to reflect the market value of a firm's assets. Instead, the assets are shown at their cost price or valuation, less an allowance for depreciation. Nevertheless, if the owners wish to sell the company or some other party is interested in purchasing it, a value must be placed on the business assets.

Reasons for Valuing a Company

There are three reasons why a valuation of a going concern may be sought. Firstly, if a company is quoted on a recognised stock exchange, a would-be purchaser needs to know if the market price reflects the real worth of the business. Similarly, if the directors are seeking a stock exchange listing, an offer price will have to be set for its shares which will reflect its assets and their earnings capability.

Secondly, the owners of a private company may wish to sell their shares and this will necessitate a value being placed upon them. Unlike a public company whose shares are quoted on a stock exchange, the shares in a private company have no such market value. In these cases there is no market valuation to guide a purchaser and, instead, a valuation must be calculated from the assets which the firm owns and on its ability to generate a return from them.

The last main reason for placing a value on a company's shares occurs during a takeover bid. Once a public company has its shares quoted on a stock exchange, it is possible for another outside party to try to purchase enough shares with the aim of acquiring a holding. This is how one company is able to take over another.

If the takeover bid causes the share price to rise, existing share holders may be tempted to sell, making an immediate capital gain from their investment. In an attempt to defeat the bid from the would-be predator, the directors may seek to prove that the offer price is unrealistic and that even the higher share price does not reflect the company's true worth, because of the future earnings which its assets can generate. In such a situation, it is to be hoped that the existing shareholders will not seek a short term gain at the expense of a secure long term return.

Methods of Valuing a Business

The real value of a business lies in its ability to use its assets profitably. An asset is only really worth what it can earn. Just as the market price of a fixed interest bearing bond is reflected by the current market rate of interest, a share price reflects the company's ability to earn a return on the shareholder's investment. As a general rule, the greater the earnings, the higher the share price and, similarly, if profits and earnings decrease, this will be reflected in a falling share price. The share price is, therefore, determined by the laws of supply and demand and will be influenced by investor confidence about projected returns, as well as their expectations about future political and economic events.

Ultimately a business must be worth the value of its net assets, for they could be liquidated and sold for cash. If this were done the purchaser would be guaranteed not to lose any money. Once a higher price is paid, the difference must be compensated for by expected future earnings. In accounting this difference is called goodwill.

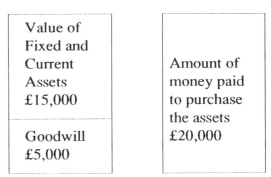

Figure 42: How Goodwill is Calculated

Goodwill is treated as an intangible fixed asset and is shown in the acquiring company's balance sheet. By valuing the difference between the market value of the assets and the amount paid for them as goodwill, the total liabilities will equal the total assets in the balance sheet.

Methods of Valuing a Firm

There are four main ways of assessing the value of a business. Ultimately it is only worth what someone will pay for it, but the would-be purchaser needs some guidance as to its true worth. The following methods are used for assessment purposes for they provide a guide to the offer price which is likely to prove acceptable to the seller.

Method One: Stock Market Valuation Method

If shares are quoted on a stock market, then the market valuation of the company will be the share price multiplied by the number of issued ordinary shares. For instance, if a company has 500,000 ordinary £1 shares with a market price of £2 a share, the company's market valuation will be £1,000,000. This does not mean that the business has assets worth a million, but it does reflect the price which investors are prepared to pay for its shares. This will be influenced by the assets, the earnings potential and investor confidence about the economy and the future earnings potential of the business. As the share price rises and falls, so does its market capitalisation. At certain times the market price may overvalue or undervalue the business and it is then useful to use other methods of valuation which can assess the market valuation. A would-be purchaser will always have to offer a higher price than the market price for, otherwise, there is no financial incentive for the owner to sell the shares. This is why the share price rises during a takeover bid and generally falls when the bid fails.

Method Two: Valuation of Assets Method

In theory a company must be worth the value of its assets. If a business can be bought for just its asset value, no premium has to be paid for its earnings potential. This is why it is always cheaper to purchase a firm which has gone into liquidation than one which is currently trading. The business which has been forced to stop trading is only worth the value of its assets, while the going concern is worth its assets plus a certain amount for its future earnings potential. This is best illustrated by looking at an example.

Example

The Golden Eagle Hotel is an established company. It is not quoted on a recognised stock market and so there is no market valuation to guide a would-be purchaser. The lowest valuation of The Golden Eagle Hotel must be the market value of its assets. Let us assume in this example that, at the time of preparing the last balance sheet, the owners declared that they no longer intended to continue running the business. As a result, the assets were revalued and so, unusually, the balance sheet reflects its market valuation.

The Golden Eagle Hotel
Balance Sheet as at 5 April Year 6

Fixed Assets	Cost Valuation £000	Depreciation £000	NBV £000
Freehold Property	450	-	450
Fixtures and Fittings	125	25	100
Motor Vehicles	50	10	40
	625	35	590

Current Assets

Stock	50		
Debtors	30		
Bank	40	120	

Less Liabilities (12 months)

Creditors	20		
Taxation	15	35	85
			675

Liabilities due after 12 months

Bank Term Loan 15% 2015		50	50
Net Assets			625

Financed By

350,000 Ordinary £1 shares issued and fully paid	350
50,000 £1 9% Preference Shares	50
Revaluation Reserve	90
Retained Profit	135
Shareholders' Funds	625

Notes to the Accounts

The Golden Eagle Hotel's earnings after tax, over the last five years have been:

Year	£'000
One	80
Two	120
Three	90
Four	110
Five	115

The average return on capital for hotels in this sector is 12% and the average earnings yield is 15%. The yield on comparable preference shares is 7%.

How to Calculate the Value of the Business?

The assets of the business are shown under the headings Fixed Assets and Current Assets. These show the long term and short term assets. If the firm had no current liabilities, the value of the fixed and current assets would be the value of the business. This is unlikely to be the case, for most businesses finance some of their assets by borrowing, allowing the firm to increase its assets and earnings potential.

By subtracting the current liabilities from the total asset figure, the net assets of the business can be calculated. If the number of ordinary shares is then divided into the net asset valuation, the asset backing per share can be calculated. In our example this is calculated as follows.

Method of Calculating the Asset Valuation of the Golden Eagle Hotel

Fixed Assets plus Current Assets = Total Assets

Current Liabilities less total assets = Net Assets

$$\frac{\text{Net Assets}}{\text{Number of ordinary shares}} = \text{Asset backing per share.}$$

Using the figures in the example this can be seen to be:

$$\frac{\text{Net Assets}}{\text{Number of ordinary share}} \qquad \frac{£625,000}{350,000} = £1.79 \text{ (approx)}$$

This is really the lowest possible valuation of the hotel for it takes no account of its future earnings potential. What is needed is a valuation which takes this into account.

Method Three: Valuation of Goodwill.

The accounts show that every year the hotel generates a profit from its assets. The profit in our example is erratic in that it goes up and down and, therefore, some way must be found of calculating the hotel's average profit. The simplest method is to calculate a simple average by adding up the total profit and then dividing it by the number of years. If the firm enjoys a steadily increasing profit, it may be more appropriate to use a weighted average.

Whichever method is used, an average profit must be calculated. We have already seen, in Chapter 7: Interpreting Financial Statements, that data is available from analysts about the average return earned by companies operating in that sector. It is now necessary to compare the return which the hotel can earn from its own capital with that earned by the rest of the industry. If the return from the hotel's capital is higher, then the purchase price will reflect this. The amount paid over the asset value is called goodwill and is really compensation to the owners in the form of a capital sum for the future earnings potential of their business.

Valuation of the Golden Eagle's Goodwill

The first task is to calculate the average profit. This can be done by calculating the mean profit, i.e. adding up the five years' profit and dividing it by the number of years.

Calculation of the Average Profit

	£				
Year One	80,000	Total Profit	£515,000		
Year Two	120,000	————	———	=	£103,000
Year Three	90,000	Years	5		Average
Year Four	110,000				Profit
Year Five	115,000				
	515,000				

Once the average profit has been calculated, any preference dividends paid and investment income earned must be deducted. This is because preference shares are regarded as being akin to debt capital as they pay a fixed rate of dividend, and so the amount is deducted from the average profit. Investment income is deducted because it does not reflect profits earned from the firm's trading assets.

Average Profit	£103,000
Less Preference Dividend (9% of £50,000)	4,500
Less Investment Income (if applicable)	-
Average maintainable profit	98,500

The last stage is to calculate whether or not the hotel can earn bigger profits than those earned by similar companies. If it can, the extra profit is called super profits. By applying a formula, the super profits can then be capitalised, thereby calculating the goodwill.

Calculation of Super Profits

	£
Average Maintainable Profit	98,500
Less Revenue which trading assets should earn (£625,000 x 12%)	75,000
Super Profits	23,500

$$\text{Goodwill} = \frac{\text{Super profits} \times 100}{\text{Average Return on capital in similar companies.}} = \frac{£23,500 \times 100}{12} = £195,833 \text{ (Goodwill)}$$

Value of the Business

	£
Net Tangible Trading Assets	625,000
Add Goodwill	195,833
Total Tangible and Intangible Assets	820,833

Value Per Share = $\dfrac{\text{Total Tangible and Intangible Assets}}{\text{Number of Ordinary Shares}}$

$$= \dfrac{£820,000}{350,000} = £2.34$$

Method Four: Valuation of Earnings

This method seeks to value the business's future earnings by capitalising the earnings yield. This is done by the formula:

$\dfrac{\text{Average Profit x 100}}{\text{Earnings Yield on Ordinary Shares in Similar Companies}}$ = $\dfrac{£98,500 \times 100}{15} = £656,667$

By dividing the capitalised value by the number of shares, a value can be placed on the firm's future earnings potential. The formula is:

$\dfrac{\text{Capitalised Earnings Value}}{\text{Number of Ordinary Shares}}$ $\dfrac{£656,667}{350,000} = £1.88$ per share

The value of a preference share is similarly based upon what it can earn. If the fixed dividend payable is higher than the industry average, the value of the share will be higher than its nominal value. If the return is lower, the value will be less. The formula is:

Value = $\dfrac{\text{Nominal Value x Dividend Payable}}{\text{Average Dividend in the Industry}}$ = $\dfrac{£1 \times 9p}{7p} = £1.29$

Evaluating a Company's Worth

The four methods which have been outlined provide a guide as to its value. The purchaser will determine its value by offering a price which is acceptable to the seller for, until this happens, no one knows the true market value of any asset. The methods of valuing a business seek to assess the true worth of the assets by placing a value on them and on their earnings potential. By doing this, the price

247

offered should be both realistic and affordable to the acquiring company. There is always a danger that if a price is paid which is in excess of the asset value and the earnings potential, the purchase may prove to be an expensive white elephant incapable of earning the anticipated return.

Financing the Purchase

There are three possible ways of financing the takeover. The most expensive method is a cash offer for the shares, for this will probably necessitate raising additional loans or will run down cash reserves. In many cases the existing owners will seek a cash bid, because they are not prepared to accept any other form of paper financial security as consideration for the purchase price.

If the purchase can be financed by offering some form of paper financial security, such as an offer of shares or some form of loan stock, the cost can be spread over several years. This will not just help the cash flow position, but will also give the firm the chance to pay for the acquisition out of earnings. This can be done in one of two ways. Firstly, the purchaser could offer an exchange of shares based on some agreed weighting. This is likely to be acceptable if the acquiring company is a household name with a high share price which is likely to increase in value in the coming years.

Another method of financing the purchase is to offer the seller some form of fixed interest security, such as a debenture, or by borrowing the finance from a bank or finance house and then paying the cash to the seller. In either case, the acquiring business will be increasing its debt capital so it must be able to service the additional debt interest payments out of future earnings.

The Dangers of Growth by Acquisition

There is always a danger that the acquiring company may pay too high a price for the assets based upon an over-optimistic valuation of asset values and future earnings. This problem is often particularly acute during a boom when people's expectations about future values exceed realistic returns. Ultimately, the boom ends, with a fall in asset, values leaving many purchasers saddled with over-valued assets, coupled with a mounting debt burden which has been used to finance the purchase. If earnings fall, the burden of servicing the debt can force an otherwise successful business into liquidation or force it to dispose of assets at unrealistic prices as it struggles to raise cash to repay debt.

The aim of these valuation methods, coupled with investment appraisal techniques, is to lessen the likelihood of overvaluing an asset. Earnings can never be guaranteed and, if the cost of the asset is high in relation to its earnings, potential investors should be cautious about investing. In the end, an asset is only worth what it can earn but, in the short term, the market value may be greater or less than its earnings potential.

Chapter 21
Foreign Exchange

Introduction

There are very few businesses which are immune from the effects of currency fluctuations, but some are more at risk than others. As soon as the value of the Pound changes relative to the currencies of our major trading partners, there will be a difference in the price of goods and services expressed in foreign currency. Any business buying and selling goods from overseas knows that its transactions are subject to an exchange risk which could make the firm extra profits or cause it to make losses as a result of these movements in the exchange rate.

What Is An Exchange Rate Risk?

Whenever one is exchanging one currency for another, there is always a danger that the rate will change. The greater the likelihood of a fluctuation in the exchange rate, the greater the risk involved. This can be seen from the following example:

The Import Export Company

The Import Export Company purchases American goods and sells them in the United Kingdom. On the first day of every month the firm buys £30,000 worth of goods from an agent in New York and settles its account in U.S. Dollars on the last day of each month. The goods are sold in the U.K. for twice their cost price. At the beginning of the month the exchange rate was £1.00 -$2.00 and so the goods cost the firm £15,000. If the exchange rate does not fluctuate, the firm stands to make a profit of £15,000. If the Pound weakens against the U.S. Dollar during the month, the goods will become more expensive and, if prices cannot be raised, profits will be reduced. When the firm comes to pay for the goods, the exchange rate has moved to £1.00 -$1.90 and so the goods now cost the firm £15,789. This will reduce the firm's profits by £789, or five per cent. Similarly, if the Pound rises against the U.S. Dollar, the goods will become cheaper and the firm will make bigger profits, provided it can sell all of the merchandise.

In this example the profit margins are large and the time periods short. This may not be the case when contracts are entered into for capital goods and the delivery time may run into months or even years. One way of avoiding the risk of currency fluctuations is to ask to be invoiced or paid in your own currency. If this is done, the exchange rate risk (be it favourable or adverse) is passed to the other party who must then decide what action to take. The extent of the risk will depend upon the strength or weakness of the particular currency. If the currency is weak, then one party stands to make losses as their currency moves lower against the stronger one. If, on the other hand, it is strong, windfall profits will be made. In certain cases the movement in the exchange rate can turn what once seemed profitable contracts into loss making ones which can damage a firm's earnings and liquidity.

How Exchange Rates are Determined

The exchange rates will be determined by the market makers according to political and economic news. Although the rates may change without any buying or selling, as when rates are set at the start of trading, the exchange rate will generally be determined by the forces of supply and demand.

During any business day some people will need to purchase foreign currency while others will want to sell it. Their transactions will determine the demand for the two currencies. When there are more buyers than sellers, the price will rise because of a shortage in supply and, if there are more sellers than buyers, the price will fall as supply exceeds demand. The exchange rates will then move upwards or downwards showing the price of one currency in terms of another.

Business transactions are not the only reason for changes in the exchange rate. Investment managers and speculators buy and sell currencies, depending on how they believe their investment portfolio will be affected by exchange rate changes. Their decisions are influenced by political and economic news, such as forecast interest and inflation rates.

If one country has higher interest rates than another, investors may be attracted to invest their money in that country, so long as a fall in the exchange rate relative to other currencies does not erode the gain made from the different interest rate.

This pool of investment funds is often referred to as "hot money" for it may suddenly be withdrawn from one country and invested in another, because of expected changes in exchange rates. A sudden withdrawal or investment will affect the exchange rate and will have a dramatic affect on the business community. Some business transactions will appear more profitable, while others could be turned into losses. It will all depend on how the exchange rate moves.

How Exchange Rates are Quoted

The exchange rate is quoted in one of two ways. Sometimes it is quoted as one unit of currency being equal to another, in which case it is referred to as an indirect quote. For example £1 is worth $1.75. It can also be shown as what is called a direct quote when a number of units of currency are equal to one or more units of another currency. For example, 100 Deutsche Marks are worth £33. The London Foreign Exchange Market uses the indirect method, whereas New York uses the direct quote.

Example of Foreign Exchange Rates Quoted on the London Market

Sterling Spot and Forward Rates

	Range	Close	1 Month	3 Month
New York	1.9135-1.9215	1.9155-1.9165	1.06-1.05pr	2.90-2.88pr
Frankfurt	2.9158-2.9268	2.9162-2.9196	1½-1pr	2⅞-2⅝pr
Tokyo	253.25-255.27	253.32-253.65	1⅛-1pr	3½-3pr
Zurich	2.5134-2.5262	2.5170-2.5202	1½-1pr	3⅛-2⅞

The table shows the exchange rates for different currencies and can be divided into two halves. The left hand side shows how the rates have moved during yesterday's trading and the final rates at the end of trading are shown under the heading Close. The right hand side shows the forward margins for people wishing to purchase or sell a currency in one or three months' time.

The exchange rate at the close of business is always shown as two figures and they are referred to as the bid and offer rate. The bid rate is the bank's buying rate and the offer its selling rate. It is easier to remember that banks always buy high and sell low on each deal so that they can make profits on each currency exchange. When they purchase currency, they buy as much as they can, so the higher rate is used. In this way the customer must part with as much currency as possible in order to gain the new one. Similarly, when the bank sells its aim is to exchange as little of its currency for the other, by using the lower rate. Once again the exchange rate works to the customer's detriment, allowing the bank to part with the smallest amount of the wanted currecy. The difference between the buying and selling rate is called the currency's spread and is really the bank's profit margin on the transaction.

Foreign currencies are always quoted to four decimal places and these are called pips. For example £1 may be quoted as £1.7542 to £1.7584 and the difference between these two rates is the currency spread.

Purchasing or Selling Foreign Currency

Different rates will be offered for buying or selling a currency, depending upon the length of time required before making the exchange. There are three different types of foreign exchange transaction and they are designed to take account of timing differences as to when the currency is wanted. They are called the spot rate, the forward rate and the swap rate.

Spot Rate

This is the current rate offered by the dealers. It will fluctuate during the day but the bank will be able to offer a rate by phoning a foreign exchange dealer, and this can then be accepted or rejected. If accepted, the currency transaction will be completed within two working days of the transaction, although it can be completed earlier if required.

The Forward Rate

A customer may need to purchase 10,000 U.S. Dollars to pay for goods in three months' time. During that time the rate may change, but it is possible to enter into a forward contract which will fix the rate, thereby guaranteeing the exchange rate regardless of the spot rate in three months' time. This is a forward contract and, by entering into such an agreement, it is possible to limit the exchange rate risk. The contract may be for a specified date or it may allow the customer to chose a date during the length of the contract, in which case it is refered to as an option forward contract. This must not be confused with an option contract which is explained later in this chapter. Once again the forward rate is calculated by applying the old maxim that banks always buy at the high rate and sell at the lower one. An example will help to illustrate this point.

Example

The Import and Export Company have agreed to purchase £20,000 worth of goods from the United States and £10,000 worth of goods from Italy. The rates are as follows:

U.S. Dollars Spot	1.7530-1.7550 three months	0.11- 0.07 cpm
Italian Lire	2220- 2380 three months	12-15lire dis

Before making the calculation, care must be taken in applying the decimal point. Most currencies such as the U.S. Dollar, Sterling and the Deutsche Mark are shown in terms of one hundred divisions of their currency unit. This means that each Amercian Cent is divided into a hundred segments and so the premium 0.07 cents means 0.0007 U.S. Dollars. Some currencies only have one unit of currency, such as the Italian Lire or the Japanese Yen, which make the calculation easier as there is no decimal calculation.

The forward rate can now be calculated by deducting the premium to the forward rate for the U.S. Dollars and adding the discount for the Italian Lire. Ocassionally a forward rate will be the same as the spot rate. In such cases it is said to be at par.

U.S. Dollars   **Bank's Buying Rate**   **Bank' Selling Rate**

1.7530-1.7550
Spot Rate	1.7550
Less Premium	007
	1.7543

Spot Rate	1.7530
Less Premium	011
	1.7519

Italian Lire   **Buying Rate**   **Selling Rate**

2220-2380
Spot Rate	2380
Add Discount	15
	2395

Spot rate	2220
Add Discount	12
	2232

When buying or selling a currency, the rate is always calculated from the bank's position. This means that, when a customer wishes to buy foreign exchange, the bank is selling it and, when the customer sells foreign currency, the bank purchases it. The premium or discount is shown the same way round as the buying and selling rate as shown for the spot price.

A Swap

A transaction is called a swap when a customer wishes to purchase or sell a currency at the spot price and then simultaneously sells or purchases it in the forward market. The swap rate is calculated by taking the difference between the premium or discount rate at the time the parties enter into the forward contract.

How Forward Rates Are Calculated

The difference in rate between the spot price and the forward rate is accounted for by the different rates of interest charged for money by different financial centres. An investor may chose to invest in the money markets or purchase paper financial securities. Financial securities pay rates of interest to the holder and are normally sold at a discount. By redeeming the securities at their face value, the holder earns interest over the life of the security. The larger the discount, the higher the rate of interest.The main sellers will be governments seeking to raise finance, but large companies may also raise finance in this way.

It is this difference in interest rates which accounts for the forward premium or discount. This is best illustrated by an example.

The International Investment Trust

The trust managers have a large cash portfolio and they wish to invest it where the funds will earn the greatest return. The fund is in German Marks, but interest rates in Germany are currently 9 per cent, as opposed to Britain's 12 per cent. The company, like other investors, seeks to invest in Britain because of the higher return and so exchanges Marks for Pounds. By doing this the investors run the risk that there will be no change in the exchange rates between the two currencies and that, if they wish to change their currency from Pounds to Marks, the exchange rate will be the same. If the exchange rates are thought by investors to be stable, the exchange can be made in the spot market.

When interest rates are higher in one centre than another, the monetary authorities are usually trying to attract an inflow of foreign currency by offering investors a higher return. This higher interest rate could be seen as a risk premium for being prepared to hold a weaker currency as opposed to a strong one. If the Pound weakened considerably against the Mark, the interest gain could disappear because of a capital loss made when the currencies were exchanged.

In such a situation investors will seek to purchase Pounds in the spot market and then immediately sell them forward for Marks. This will lead to an increase in the number of Marks being wanted and so the forward rate will rise relative to the spot rate. If the investor wishes to carry out a "swap" in Pounds against Marks, more Pounds will be needed; the foreign exchange dealer will have had to pay more Pounds to buy spot Marks than will be received for the forward resale of Marks against Pounds.

A loss will then be made in selling spot and buying forward Marks and this loss must be offset against the interest gained from moving funds from Germany to Britain. By purchasing currency forward, the investor will sacrifice part of the gain made through changes in interest rates by having to pay a premium for the currency. During normal trading conditions the premium will be at a lower rate than the percentage gain in interest. If this is not the case, there is no benefit in covering the gain forward.

As a general rule, the margin between the spot and the forward rate will be shown at a premium when the home interest rate is higher than that in the other financial centre and at a discount when the interest rates are higher in the foreign centre than they are in the home market.

The Cost Of A Forward Contract

The cost of a forward contract can be calculated as an annual percentage. The premium or discount can be calculated by using this formula:

$$\frac{\text{Premium/Discount x 360 x 100}}{\text{Forward Rate x Number of Days}}$$

Example
The Sterling US Dollar spot rate is 1.7154 and the three month forward rate is 0.85 C premium. The cost of entering into a forward contract is:

$$\frac{\text{Premium/Discount x 360 x 100}}{\text{Forward Rate x Number of Days}}$$

$$\frac{0.0085 \text{ x } 360 \text{ x} 100}{1.7154 \text{ x } 90}$$

$$= \frac{306}{154} \qquad = 1.99\%$$

What Is An Option Contract?

An option contract is similar to a forward contract but gives the person entering into it the right, but not the obligation, to buy or sell a financial instrument or futures contract at a set price on or before a specified future date. The buyer is called the option holder and has to pay a premium to the seller, who is called the option writer.

The option can be either to buy or to sell a financial instrument or futures contract. A call option gives the buyer the right to purchase the option, while a put option confers on the buyer the right to sell to the option writer. A double option gives the buyer the right to sell or buy. Once the option has been bought and the premium paid, that is the maximum loss which the buyer can incur once the decision is taken to allow it to expire.

Currency Futures Contracts

A Currency Futures Contract is an agreement to purchase or sell a standard amount of foreign exchange at an agreed price at a future date. In Britain financial futures are traded on the floor of the London International Financial Futures Exchange (Liffe) and the exchange deals in the following currencies; Sterling, Deutschmarks, Swiss Francs and Yen. All of these currencies are quoted against the US Dollar.

Before entering into a currency futures contract, buyers and sellers have to deposit a margin with the clearing house to guarantee their credit worthiness, because profits and losses will be added or subtracted on the margin on a daily basis. The margin is made up of two parts — the initial margin and the variation margin. The initial margin reflects the volatility of the future contract and ranges from 0.1% to 6% of the face value of the contract, whereas the variation margin refers to any additional money which must be paid to cover losses made on the contract.

Financial futures are highly speculative but they are nevertheless useful to business people who wish to limit their risk by transfering it to speculators who seek high risks in order to make profits.

Example of a Currencies Futures Contact:

Clothing USA
The Company specialises in importing and distributing American clothing and has just entered into a contract with an American shoe manufacturer to purchase

$45,000 worth of merchandise for delivery in 3 months' time. Payment will be made once the goods are delivered.

At the time of entering into the contract the exchange rate was £1/$1.80. The firm's treasurer believes that Sterling will weaken during the next three months and her computer forecasts predicts a future rate of £1/$1.60.

On the floor of the LIFFE Exchange a financial futures Sterling contract can be purchased at the rate of £1/$1.79. The company purchases one Sterling contract for £25,000 for delivery in three months' time.

When the company has to pay for the goods the sterling exchange spot rate is £1/$1.60 and so the treasurer's predictions were correct. The firm will have made a profit on its contract and this can be seen from the following calculations:

Calculations

Spot Rate $1.60/£1
Futures Contract (right to sell) $1.79/£1

	$
$25,000 x $1.79	44750

	£
$44,750 are worth in Sterling with a spot rate £1/$1.60	27969
Cost of futures contract	25000
Profit in Sterling	2969

This can also be calculated in Dollars	$
Future rate £25000 x $1.79	44750
Less spot rate	
£25000 x $1.60	40000
Profit in Dollars	4750

With a spot rate of £1/$1.60 $4750 = £2969.

This example shows that the firm has been able to make a profit by correctly forecasting the movement in the exchange rate. Had the firm been wrong, a loss would have been incurred. In this case the profit from the future contract will offset the extra cost of the goods bought about by the movement in the exchange rate.

Purchasing future contracts is therefore riskier than entering into forward contracts because the hedge will only be successful if the buyer is correct in both the timing and the price paid for the contract. For this reason professional advice should always be sought before entering into financial futures contracts, because of the risks involved.

How To Reduce The Risk Involved In Foreign Exchange Transactions

Forward contracts and currency options allow business people to limit their exposure to exchange risk by developing hedging strategies. Hedging involves the simultaneous purchase and sale of a currency or commodity in two different markets at the same time, together with a further sale and purchase of the same currency or commodity at a later date. By developing hedging strategies, business people are able to concentrate on managing their business, knowing that the risk of loss due to adverse exchange rate movements have been considerably reduced or eliminated. The whole principle of hedging is based on the fact that the hedger is risk averse and does not seek profits. Forward and option contracts provide a way of limiting risk exposure which is inherent in dealing in any financial security because of fluctuations in exchange rates.

By entering into a hedging position, the firm can separate the contract into two parts. These are the price of the transaction and the transaction itself. By purchasing an option contract, the buyer is able to eliminate the market risk, but is still subject to the risk of how the market price compares with the hedged position. There will always be some risk. It is never possible to predict with certainty how financial markets will behave because of the large number of variables which influence them. Nevertheless, the risk averse firm can take a position which will enable it to be certain of the financial outcome. Forward and option contracts enable a firm to benefit from foreign trade while, at the same time, limit its exposure to loss.

When exchange rates fluctuate it is generally small firms who suffer most, because the owners or managers are unaware as to how to manage the exchange risk. Many small firms try to solve the problem by adding a small percentage to their prices to cover fluctuations. Most large companies have their own treasury departments and access to foreign currency earnings which places them in a better position to manage the exchange risk. Once a firm can earn foreign currency, it can use that money to settle debts without having to exchange one currency for

259

another if the rates are unfavourable. If this is not possible, forward contracts and currency options can help the firm limit its exposure to financial losses resulting from business transactions which necessitate the use of foreign currency.

Chapter 22
The Financial Audit

Introduction

If a business is to survive it must manage its cash resources effectively while, at the same time, remaining profitable. This is an ongoing task for the firm's financial position will constantly change in accordance with its level of trading. The financial audit is concerned with analysing the firm's financial strengths and weaknesses. By doing this management can concentrate on the firm's strengths while simultaneously taking corrective action to restore liquidity and profit levels, should this prove necessary.

Unfortunately many firms fail to monitor their financial performance and only become aware of cash shortages as overdraft levels increase. By this time the firm has become totally dependent for its survival on short term debt. If this is suddenly withdrawn, the business will be forced into liquidation.

This financial check list seeks to to review all aspects of the business under five headings. They are liquidity, profitability, use of assets, cost control and financial resources. If the audit is to be effective, all the functional heads and their staff must be involved so that a complete picture of the firm's present and future level of activity can be ascertained. Only by doing this can the firm be confident of having sufficient financial resources to fund its present and future financial commitments.

Liquidity

1. Is the current cash position the same as its budgeted position?

2. Are cash balances increasing or decreasing?

3. How are cash surpluses being invested and how are cash deficits being funded?

4. Has the bank manager been informed about the firm's current short term liquidity levels?

5. Are inflation levels higher than budgeted and how is it affecting costs and cash flow?

6. How is the future economic climate likely to affect bank lending to the corporate sector?

7. Is the cash operating cycle increasing or decreasing?

8. How effectively are debtor balances being managed?

9. Are stock levels increasing or decreasing?

10. Is the creditor payment time increasing or decreasing?

Profitability

1. Are the actual sales the same as budgeted?

2. Which products are contributing most to sales and profits?

3. Are profit margins stable, increasing or decreasing?

4. How do current returns compare with forecast returns?

5. Are costs the same as budgeted?

6. Are the returns on capital employed above or below the industry average?

7. Are retained profits increasing, stable or decreasing?

8. Are dividend payments increasing, stable or decreasing?

9. What is the current price to earnings ratio? How does it compare with previous quarters?

10. Are profits and returns to investors adequate when adjusted for the affects of inflation?

Use Of Assets

1. Are stock turnover rates increasing, stable or decreasing?

2. How quickly are debtor balances being turned into cash?

3. What return is being earned from cash balances?

4. What percentage of credit sales become bad debts?

5. Are credit terms from suppliers being extended, stable or decreasing?

6. What return is being earned from investments in fixed assets?

7. Is the ratio of sales to fixed assets increasing, stable or decreasing?

8. Is the ratio of fixed to current assets increasing, stable or decreasing?

9. Which of the firm's brands or products generate the most sales and profits?

10. What are the expected returns from new investments in research and developments, new products and fixed assets?

Control of Costs

1. Are actual costs the same as budgeted costs?

2. How do actual costs compare with standard costs?

3. Should the budgets and standards be revised because of changes in activity or costs?

4. Is the actual break even point the same as the planned one?

5. Is the contribution earned from each sale increasing, stable or decreasing?

6. How are increases in labour costs affecting direct costs?

7. How do current operating levels affect fixed costs?

8. How is inflation affecting the firm's costs?

9. Is the firm able to pass increases in costs on to consumers by charging higher prices?

10. What percentage of gross profit is needed to meet the firm's overheads?

Financial Resources

1. What percentage of new investment in fixed assets is financed out of retained profits?

2. What percentage of the firm's assets are financed by the shareholders?

3. What percentage of total assets are financed by short term finance?

4. Is the firm's gearing ratio increasing, stable or decreasing?

5. Are short term interest rates likely to increase, remain stable or decrease?

6. During the coming twelve months is the business likely to have a positive or a negative cash flow?

7. What relationship does the business have with its bankers? Are they supportive or indifferent to future developments?

8. What percentage of the firm's profits are currently used to meet interest charges? How does this compare with previous quarters?

9. What is the firm's current credit rating? How does it compare with previous years?

10. How effectively does the firm communicate with investors, lenders, creditors and employees?

Glossary of Financial Terms

Absorbed Cost	Costs which have been spread over operational units, e.g. job, batch unit or contract.
Accounting	The system of recording accounting information using double entry book-keeping.
Accounting Equation	The assets of a firm are equal to its liabilities. Assets are things which the firm owns, even if it has not yet paid for them, and liabilities are claims against the firm.
Accounting Period	The amount of time covered by the financial statements of a business.
Accounting Policies	The specific accounting bases chosen and followed by a firm which the management believe are the most appropriate and which will present its results and financial position fairly.
Accounts	Receivable: A firm's credit sales to customers.
Accrual	An amount owing at the time the annual accounts are prepared. The sum owing will be shown in the balance sheet under current liabilities.
Acid Test Ratio	Current assets less stock/Current liabilities. This ratio shows the firm's ability to meet its short term liabilities out of its cash and near cash assets, such as debtors.
Accrued Expenses	Expenses which are recognised when goods received or services provided during a given accounting period have not been invoiced, or when wages have been earned but not paid by the end of that period.
Annual Accounts	The set of accounts comprising a balance sheet together with a profit and loss account and a statement of source and application of funds together with directors' report and other information as required by Companies' Act 1985. (See chapter on Company Accounts)
Appropriation Account	A financial statement which shows how the firm's net profit after taxation has been used.
Apportioned Cost	Costs which have been spread over cost centres.
Assets	Everything of value owned by a business.
Authorisd Share Capital	This is the amount of money which the company took power to raise when it was formed.

Avoidable Cost	A cost not incurred if an action is not taken, or is discontinued.
Bad Debt	A debt which has not been paid. It is an expense to the firm and the amount will be shown in the profit and loss account.
Balance Sheet	A statement showing the assets and liabilities of a business at a particular date.
Basis	The cash price less the futures price.
Basis Point	The smallest increment for measuring price.
Bear	A person who believes that a share price will fall.
Bid Price	The price a buyer will pay for a financial security or futures contract.
Bond	A financial security (certificate) showing the indebtedness of an organisation, together with the rate of interest payable and the date, if applicable, when it will be repaid.
Bonus Issue	The issuing of shares to existing shareholders by distributing a company's reserves as shares. No monetary payments are made. Sometimes called a scrip issue.
Book Value	The historical cost of an asset, less depreciation accumulated over the asset's life.
Break Even	The amount of sales needed to cover a firm's fixed and variable costs. Above the break-even point the firm makes a profit and below it makes a loss.
Bull	A person who believes share prices will rise.
Called Up Capital	This refers to shares issued by the company but not yet fully paid for by the shareholders.
Capital	The long term money which is financing a business.
Capital Employed	The long term capital which finances a firm. It includes share capital, reserves and loan capital (debentures, secured loan stock and unsecured loan stock).
Capital Expenditure	Money spent by the company on purchasing fixed assets.
Capital Loss	Losses made on the sale of fixed assets.
Capital Profit	Money made on the sale of fixed assets.

Capital Receipts	Money received by a company on the issue of shares and debentures.
Capital Reserve	Reserves which are not available for distribution as dividends, e.g., any surplus arising as a premium on the issue of shares or debentures.
Carriage Inwards	The cost of having goods delivered. It increases the cost of purchases and the amount paid is shown in the trading account.
Carriage Outwards	The cost of delivering goods to customers. The amount is treated as an expense and is shown in the profit and loss account.
Cash Budget	Budget drawn up to enable the firm to forecast future cash receipts and payments.
Cash Flow	Accounting term used to describe the cash generated and used during a given financial period.
Cash Operating Cycle	Length of time a firm has to wait before it receives cash.
Contingent Liability	Obligation which may arise in respect of past events. such as the outcome of a law case.
Convertible Loan Stock	A loan which gives the holder the right to convert to other securities, normally ordinary shares, at a pre-determined rate and time.
Corporation Tax	Tax calculated on a company's profits.
Cost Centre	A location, individual,or item of equipment for which costs may be ascertained and used for purposes of control or product costing.
Cost Unit	Item of product (usually of output or service) to which costs can be allocated or attributed.
Cumulative Preference Shares	These shares allow the owners to receive arrears of dividend before dividends are paid to the ordinary shareholders.
Current Assets	These are assets of a circulating nature which are acquired by a business in order to trade with other companies or individuals. They are shown in the balance sheet in order of liquidity, with the least liquid shown first. The order is stock, debtors,(people who owe the firm money) bank and cash balances.
Current Worth	See Net Worth.
Debenture	Normally a secured loan over the assets of a company. The debenture holders do not own the company but they are entitled to interest payments. If the interest is not paid, the debenture holders can sell the firm's assets so that they can recover their money.

267

Deferred Taxation	An amount provided to equalise the timing differences which arise between the tax charge based on the pre- tax profit in the profit and loss account and the actual tax liability, as separately computed in accordance with tax legislation. Transfers are made to a deferred taxation account, the balance on which is shown separately in the balance sheet.
Depreciation	Most assets wear out as they are used. Machinery wears out and buildings deteriorate. An allowance, called depreciation, for this fall in value must be included in the firm's accounts.
Direct Cost	A cost which can be associated wholly and specifically with a cost unit, e.g., machine, department or individual.
Discount Allowed	The cost of allowing a debtor to pay a smaller sum than the original bill if the debt is settled early. The cost is shown as an expense in the profit and loss account.
Discount Received	Money given off a bill for settling it early. It is treated as income and added to gross profit.
Discretionary Cost	A programmed cost which is subject to management discretion and control.
Dividend	A distribution to shareholders out of profits, usually in the form of cash.
Equity	The share capital of the business plus reserves.
Factoring	The technical term used to describe selling credit sales (debtors) to a factoring house or bank for cash.
Fixed Assets	Assets acquired for retention in a business for the purpose of providing goods or services. Fixed assets are not held for resale in the normal course of business. Examples are Land and Buildings, Plant and Machinery.
Fixed Cost	A cost unaffected by change of activity level in a given period of time.
Gearing	The ratio of a firm's debt to equity capital. In the U.S.A. it is called leverage.
Goodwill	Sum of money paid for the goods of a business. When a business is purchased any amount paid in excess of its net assets (Total Assets less Liabilities) represents the value placed on goodwill.
Gross Profit	The profit made on goods and services sold before expenses are deducted. The percentage profit can be calculated by the following formula:

$$\frac{\text{Profit} \times 100}{\text{Cost Price}}$$

Historical Cost	The original cost of acquiring the fixed asset.
Incremental Cost	Additional cost of one course of action over another.
Indirect Cost	A cost which cannot be directly allocated but can be apportioned to cost centres and cost units, e.g., overhead costs.
Intangible Asset	Assets which do not have a physical identity, e.g., goodwill.
Issued Share Capital	The number of shares which have been issued to shareholders and which have been fully paid for.
Leverage	See gearing
Liquid Asset	Cash and any other financial security which can be converted quickly into cash.
Listed Investment	An investment which is quoted on a recognised stock exchange, e.g., London, Tokyo, New York.
Marginal Cost	The amount of cost incurred at a given level of output by increasing the volume of output by one.
Minority Interest	Shares held in a subsidiary company by shareholders other than a holding company or its nominees.
Net Profit	The gross profit less expenses.
Net Worth	A concept denoting the excess of the book values of all assets over liabilities. In a company it represents the interests of shareholders, i.e. the paid-up share capital and reserves. If the assets are taken at current values, instead of book values, the concept is known as current worth.
Nominal Value	The face value of a share or loan stock.
Off Balance Sheet Finance	A source of finance not shown on the balance sheet because there is no corresponding asset, e.g., an operating lease.
Ordinary Shareholders	These are the owners of the company. They are entitled to a dividend, which is a share of the firm's profit.
Paid Up Capital	This refers to shares which have been issued by the company and which have been fully paid for by the shareholders.
Pay Back	The time taken for inflows from an investment to equal its cost.
Preference Shareholders	Owners of these shares enjoy preferential rights over the ordinary shareholders. Their dividend is normally at a pre-determined rate and they

receive it before the ordinary shareholders are paid. The Articles of Association sometimes make special provision for the preference shareholders by allowing them to be repaid in full before before the ordinary shareholders, in the event of the company being wound up. If there is no such provision, then all shareholders share equally the remaining assets of the company.

Prime Cost	Total of direct material, direct labour and direct expenses.
Provisions	Amounts written off or retained, by way of providing for depreciation, renewals or diminution of assets, or retained to provide for a known liability, the extent of which cannot be expressly determined, e.g., provision for bad debts.
Relevant Cost	Those costs which are pertinent to the decision being made.
Reserves	These are unappropriated profits (not distributed to shareholders as dividends) or, surplus funds made possible by the revaluation of fixed assets or, the issue of shares for more than their nominal value.
Retained Profits	These consist of undistributed profits and can be used to pay dividends, maintain the business, or absorb losses. The revenue reserve is made up of the general reserve and the profit and loss account, as shown in the balance sheet.
Returns Inwards	Sales returned to the firm by customers. The amount reduces sales and is shown in the trading account. Sometimes referred to as net sales.
Returns Outwards	Purchases returned by the firm to suppliers. The amount reduces purchases and is shown in the trading account. Sometimes referred to as net purchases.
Rights Issue	The raising of new capital by inviting existing shareholders to subscribe for shares on preferential terms. The shares can generally be bought for less than their stock market price.
Secured Creditors	Creditors whose claims are wholly or partly secured on the assets of the business.
Share Premium	This shows that the shares were once sold for more than their nominal value; the surplus is shown in the balance sheet as a capital reserve.
Sinking Fund	A fund created for the redemption of a liability. The aim is to set aside a certain sum which will, at a set date in the future, be sufficient to meet a liability.
Source and Application of Funds Statement	A financial statement which shows the external and internal sources from which funds have been obtained to finance a business during a given accounting period, and the manner in which the funds have been deployed.

Standard Cost	A predetermined cost, calculated on the basis of a desired level of operating efficiency and activity level.
Stocks	Raw materials, work in progress, finished goods and goods in transit, or on consignment, at the end of an accounting period.
Sunk Cost	Those costs invested in a project which will not be recovered, even if the project is discontinued.
Tangible Assets	Assets having a physical identity, e.g., land and buildings, plant and machinery.
Trading Account	A financial statement which shows the revenue from sales, the cost of those sales and the gross profit arising during a given accounting period.
Unappropriated Profits	Profits which the company has reinvested in the firm, instead of distributing them as dividends to the shareholders.
Unlisted Investment	An investment which is not quoted on a recognised stock exchange.
Unsecured Loan	Loan stock which carries interest, but is not secured on any of the assets of the company.
Variable Cost	Costs which vary directly with the level of activity (output), e.g., direct labour and direct materials.
Variance	A difference between the standard cost and the actual cost. The variance may be adverse, in which case the actual cost was more than the standard cost, or favourable, in which case it was less. In either case the reason for the variance must be analysed by management.
Working Capital	The difference between a firm's current assets and its current liabilities.
Work in Progress	Materials, components or products in various stages of completion during a manufacturing process. The term also applies to partly completed contracts.

The Key Accounting Ratios

RATIO   CALCULATION

Ratios Which Assess Liquidity

Current Ratio
$$\frac{\text{Current Assets}}{\text{Current Liabilities}}$$

Acid Test Ratio
$$\frac{\text{Current Assets Less Stock}}{\text{Current Liabilities}}$$

Sales to Working Capital
$$\frac{\text{Sales}}{\text{Working Capital}}$$

Sales to Capital Employed
$$\frac{\text{Sales}}{\text{Capital Employed}}$$

Net Working Capital to Sales
$$\frac{\text{Stock + Debtors - Creditors}}{\text{Sales}}$$

Ratios Which Assess Profitability

Primary Ratio or
Return on Capital Employed
$$\frac{\text{Profit} \times 100}{\text{Capital Employed}}$$

Gross Profit To Sales
$$\frac{\text{Gross Profit} \times 100}{\text{Sales}}$$

Net Profit To Sales
$$\frac{\text{Net Profit} \times 100}{\text{Sales}}$$

Ratios Which Assess How Effectively A Firm Uses Its Assets

Stock Turnover

$$\frac{\text{Cost of Goods Sold} \times 365}{\text{Average Stock}}$$

Debtors Collection Period

$$\frac{\text{Debtors} \times 365}{\text{Sales}}$$

Time Taken To Pay Creditors

$$\frac{\text{Creditors} \times 365}{\text{Purchases}}$$

Sales To Fixed Assets

$$\frac{\text{Sales}}{\text{Fixed Assets}}$$

Fixed Assets To Current Assets

$$\frac{\text{Fixed Assets}}{\text{Current Assets}}$$

Ratios Which Assess A Firm's Capital Structure

Gearing ratio

$$\frac{\text{Debt}}{\text{Equity (Share Capital)}}$$

Shareholders' Investment

$$\frac{\text{Shareholders Investment}}{\text{Total Assets}}$$

Interest Cover

$$\frac{\text{Profit Before Interest and Tax}}{\text{Interest Paid}}$$

Ratios Which Assess The Returns Paid To Investors

Earning Per Share

$$\frac{\text{Profit After Tax and Preference Share Dividend}}{\text{Number of Issued Ordinary Shares}}$$

Dividend Yield

$$\frac{\text{Ordinary Dividend Per Share} \times 100}{\text{Market Price per Share}}$$

Dividend Cover	<u>Profit After Tax less Preference Dividend</u> Gross Dividend on Ordinary Shares
Price Earnings	<u>Present Market Price Per Ordinary Share</u> Annual Earnings Per Share

Key Variances

Variance	Formula
Material Price	Expected Price of Material Used Less Actual Price of Material Used
Material Usage	(Expected Quantity of Material Used Less Actual Quantity of Material Used) Multiplied by Standard Price.
Labour Rate	Expected Cost of Hours Worked Less Actual Cost
Variable Overhead Expenditure	Expected Cost of Hours Worked Less Actual Cost
Variable Overhead Efficiency	(Expected Hours Worked Less Actual Hours Worked) Multiplied by Standard Rate
Fixed Overhead Volume	Budgeted Fixed Overheads Less Expected Fixed Overheads for the Actual Production.
Sales Price	Expected Revenue From Units Sold Less Actual Revenue
Sales Volume	(Expected Sales (units) Less Actual Sales) Multiplied by Standard Profit/Unit

RATINGS

The following two tables show the 1989 comparative ratings for corporates and banks. The rating scale can be interpreted as follows:

RATING SCALE

Long Term Ratings

AAA Obligations for which there is the lowest expectation of investment risk. Capacity for timely repayment of principal and interest is substantial such that adverse changes in business, economic, or financial conditions are unlikely to increase investment risk significantly.

AA Obligations for which there is a very low expectation of investment risk. Capacity for timely repayment of principal and interest is substantial. Adverse changes in business, economic, or financial conditions may increase investment risk albeit not very significantly.

A Obligations for which there is a low expectation of investment risk. Capacity for timely repayment of principal and interest is strong, although adverse changes in business, economic, or financial conditions may lead to increased investment risk.

BBB Obligations for which there is currently a low expectation of investment risk. Capacity for timely repayment of principal and interest is adequate, although adverse changes in business, economic, or financial conditions are more likely to lead to increased investment risk than for obligations in higher categories.

BB Obligations for which there is a possibility of investment risk developing. Capacity for timely repayment of principal and interest exists, but is susceptible over time to adverse changes in business, economic, or financial conditions.

B Obligations for which investment risk exists. Timely repayment of principal and interest is not sufficiently protected against adverse changes in business, economic, or financial conditions.

CCC Obligations for which there is a current perceived possibility of default. Timely repayment of principal and interest is dependent on favourable business, economic, or financial conditions.

CC Obligations which are highly speculative or which have a high risk of default.

C Obligations which are currently in default.

Short Term Ratings
including Commercial Paper
(Up to 12 months)

A1+ Obligations supported by the highest capacity for timely repayment.

A1 Obligations supported by a very strong capacity for timely repayment.

A2 Obligations supported by a strong capacity for timely repayment, although such capacity may be susceptible to adverse changes in business, economic, or financial conditions.

B1 Obligations supported by an adequate capacity for timely repayment. Such capacity is more susceptible to adverse changes in business, economic, or financial conditions than for obligations in higher categories.

B2 Obligations for which the capacity for timely repayment is susceptible to adverse changes in business, economic, or financial conditions.

C1 Obligations for which there is an inadequate capacity to ensure timely repayment.

D1 Obligations which have a high risk of default or which are currently in default.

* * * * * * * * * * * * * * * *

Long term ratings of BB and below are assigned where it is considered that speculative characteristics are present.

"+" or "−" may be appended to a long term rating to denote relative status within major rating categories.

Rating Watch highlights an emerging situation which may materially affect the profile of a rated corporation.

Reproduced with permission from
The Treasurer's Handbook, 1990
(Association of Corporate Treasurers).

DCF TABLES

Compound Sum of £1 (CVIF) $S = P(1 + r)^N$

Period	1%	2%	3%	4%	5%	6%	7%
1	1.010	1.020	1.030	1.040	1.050	1.060	1.070
2	1.020	1.040	1.061	1.082	1.102	1.124	1.145
3	1.030	1.061	1.093	1.125	1.158	1.191	1.225
4	1.041	1.082	1.126	1.170	1.216	1.262	1.311
5	1.051	1.104	1.159	1.217	1.276	1.338	1.403
6	1.062	1.126	1.194	1.265	1.340	1.419	1.501
7	1.072	1.149	1.230	1.316	1.407	1.504	1.606
8	1.083	1.172	1.267	1.369	1.477	1.594	1.718
9	1.094	1.195	1.305	1.423	1.551	1.689	1.838
10	1.105	1.219	1.344	1.480	1.629	1.791	1.967
11	1.116	1.243	1.384	1.539	1.710	1.898	2.105
12	1.127	1.268	1.426	1.601	1.796	2.012	2.252
13	1.138	1.294	1.469	1.665	1.886	2.133	2.410
14	1.149	1.319	1.513	1.732	1.980	2.261	2.579
15	1.161	1.346	1.558	1.801	2.079	2.397	2.759
16	1.173	1.373	1.605	1.873	2.183	2.540	2.952
17	1.184	1.400	1.653	1.948	2.292	2.693	3.159
18	1.196	1.428	1.702	2.026	2.407	2.854	3.380
19	1.208	1.457	1.754	2.107	2.527	3.026	3.617
20	1.220	1.486	1.806	2.191	2.653	3.207	3.870
25	1.282	1.641	2.094	2.666	3.386	4.292	5.427
30	1.348	1.811	2.427	3.243	4.322	5.743	7.612

Period	8%	9%	10%	12%	14%	15%	16%
1	1.080	1.090	1.100	1.120	1.140	1.150	1.160
2	1.166	1.186	1.210	1.254	1.300	1.322	1.346
3	1.260	1.295	1.331	1.405	1.482	1.521	1.561
4	1.360	1.412	1.464	1.574	1.689	1.749	1.811
5	1.469	1.539	1.611	1.762	1.925	2.011	2.100
6	1.587	1.677	1.772	1.974	2.195	2.313	2.436
7	1.714	1.828	1.949	2.211	2.502	2.660	2.826
8	1.851	1.993	2.144	2.476	2.853	3.059	3.278
9	1.999	2.172	2.358	2.773	3.252	3.518	3.803
10	2.159	2.367	2.594	3.106	3.707	4.046	4.411
11	2.332	2.580	2.853	3.479	4.226	4.652	5.117
12	2.518	2.813	3.138	3.896	4.818	5.350	5.926
13	2.720	3.066	3.452	4.363	5.492	6.153	6.886
14	2.937	3.342	3.797	4.887	6.261	7.076	7.988
15	3.172	3.642	4.177	5.474	7.138	8.137	9.266
16	3.426	3.970	4.595	6.130	8.137	9.358	10.748
17	3.700	4.328	5.054	6.866	9.276	10.761	12.468
18	3.996	4.717	5.560	7.690	10.575	12.375	14.463
19	4.316	5.142	6.116	8.613	12.056	14.232	16.777
20	4.661	5.604	6.728	9.646	13.743	16.367	19.461
25	6.848	8.623	10.835	17.000	26.462	32.919	40.874
30	10.063	13.268	17.449	29.960	50.950	66.212	85.850

Present Value of £1 (PVIF) $P = S(1 + r)^{-N}$ cont.

Period	16%	18%	20%	24%	28%	32%	36%	40%	50%	60%	70%	80%	90%
1	0.862	0.847	0.833	0.806	0.781	0.758	0.735	0.714	0.667	0.625	0.588	0.556	0.526
2	0.743	0.718	0.694	0.650	0.610	0.574	0.541	0.510	0.444	0.391	0.346	0.309	0.277
3	0.641	0.609	0.579	0.524	0.477	0.435	0.398	0.364	0.296	0.244	0.204	0.171	0.146
4	0.552	0.516	0.482	0.423	0.373	0.329	0.292	0.260	0.198	0.153	0.120	0.095	0.077
5	0.476	0.437	0.402	0.341	0.291	0.250	0.215	0.186	0.132	0.095	0.070	0.053	0.040
6	0.410	0.370	0.335	0.275	0.227	0.189	0.158	0.133	0.088	0.060	0.041	0.029	0.021
7	0.354	0.314	0.279	0.222	0.178	0.143	0.116	0.095	0.059	0.037	0.024	0.016	0.011
8	0.305	0.266	0.233	0.179	0.139	0.108	0.085	0.068	0.039	0.023	0.014	0.009	0.006
9	0.263	0.226	0.194	0.144	0.108	0.082	0.063	0.048	0.026	0.015	0.008	0.005	0.003
10	0.227	0.191	0.162	0.116	0.085	0.062	0.046	0.035	0.017	0.009	0.005	0.003	0.002
11	0.195	0.162	0.135	0.094	0.066	0.047	0.034	0.025	0.012	0.006	0.003	0.002	0.001
12	0.168	0.137	0.112	0.076	0.052	0.036	0.025	0.018	0.008	0.004	0.002	0.001	0.001
13	0.145	0.116	0.093	0.061	0.040	0.027	0.018	0.013	0.005	0.002	0.001	0.001	0.000
14	0.125	0.099	0.078	0.049	0.032	0.021	0.014	0.009	0.003	0.001	0.001	0.000	0.000
15	0.108	0.084	0.065	0.040	0.025	0.016	0.010	0.006	0.002	0.001	0.000	0.000	0.000
16	0.093	0.071	0.054	0.032	0.019	0.012	0.007	0.005	0.002	0.001	0.000	0.000	
17	0.080	0.060	0.045	0.026	0.015	0.009	0.005	0.003	0.001	0.001	0.000		
18	0.069	0.051	0.038	0.021	0.012	0.007	0.004	0.002	0.001	0.000			
19	0.060	0.043	0.031	0.017	0.009	0.005	0.003	0.002	0.000	0.000			
20	0.051	0.037	0.026	0.014	0.007	0.004	0.002	0.001	0.000	0.000			
25	0.024	0.016	0.010	0.005	0.002	0.001	0.000	0.000					
30	0.012	0.007	0.004	0.002	0.001	0.000	0.000						

Present Value of £1 (PVIF)P = $S(1 + r)^{-N}$

Period	1%	2%	3%	4%	5%	6%	7%	8%	9%	10%	12%	14%	15%
1	0.990	0.980	0.971	0.962	0.952	0.943	0.935	0.926	0.917	0.909	0.893	0.877	0.870
2	0.980	0.961	0.943	0.925	0.907	0.890	0.873	0.857	0.842	0.826	0.797	0.769	0.756
3	0.971	0.942	0.915	0.889	0.864	0.840	0.816	0.794	0.772	0.751	0.712	0.675	0.658
4	0.961	0.924	0.889	0.855	0.823	0.792	0.763	0.735	0.708	0.683	0.636	0.592	0.572
5	0.951	0.906	0.863	0.822	0.784	0.747	0.713	0.681	0.650	0.621	0.567	0.519	0.497
6	0.942	0.888	0.838	0.790	0.746	0.705	0.666	0.630	0.596	0.564	0.507	0.456	0.432
7	0.933	0.871	0.813	0.760	0.711	0.665	0.623	0.583	0.547	0.513	0.452	0.400	0.376
8	0.923	0.853	0.789	0.731	0.677	0.627	0.582	0.540	0.502	0.467	0.404	0.351	0.327
9	0.914	0.837	0.766	0.703	0.645	0.592	0.544	0.500	0.460	0.424	0.361	0.308	0.284
10	0.905	0.820	0.744	0.676	0.614	0.558	0.508	0.463	0.422	0.386	0.322	0.270	0.247
11	0.896	0.804	0.722	0.650	0.585	0.527	0.475	0.429	0.388	0.350	0.287	0.237	0.215
12	0.887	0.788	0.701	0.625	0.557	0.497	0.444	0.397	0.356	0.319	0.257	0.208	0.187
13	0.879	0.773	0.681	0.601	0.530	0.469	0.415	0.368	0.326	0.290	0.229	0.182	0.163
14	0.870	0.758	0.661	0.577	0.505	0.442	0.388	0.340	0.299	0.263	0.205	0.160	0.141
15	0.861	0.743	0.642	0.555	0.481	0.417	0.362	0.315	0.275	0.239	0.183	0.140	0.123
16	0.853	0.728	0.623	0.534	0.458	0.394	0.339	0.292	0.252	0.218	0.163	0.123	0.107
17	0.844	0.714	0.605	0.513	0.436	0.371	0.317	0.270	0.231	0.198	0.146	0.108	0.093
18	0.836	0.700	0.587	0.494	0.416	0.350	0.296	0.250	0.212	0.180	0.130	0.095	0.081
19	0.828	0.686	0.570	0.475	0.396	0.331	0.276	0.232	0.194	0.164	0.116	0.083	0.070
20	0.820	0.673	0.554	0.456	0.377	0.312	0.258	0.215	0.178	0.149	0.104	0.073	0.061
25	0.780	0.610	0.478	0.375	0.295	0.233	0.184	0.146	0.116	0.092	0.059	0.038	0.030
30	0.742	0.552	0.412	0.308	0.231	0.174	0.131	0.099	0.075	0.057	0.033	0.020	0.015

INDEX

FINANCIAL & QUANTITATIVE MANAGEMENT

Finance in organisations
Humphrey Shaw

An introduction (for not-very-numerate people) to the financial aspects of management in organisations. With diagrams, charts and clear explanations, the reader is guided through the main methods of controlling and understanding the finances of a business.
isbn 1 85450 019 8   £10.95   Paperback   Easter, 1991

A manager's guide to quantitative methods
Michael Cuming

A standard and innovative introduction to quantitative analysis which relegates algebra to appendices, tackling topical problems first and leading the manager through analysis of the real roots of the problem to workable solutions. User-friendly, the book introduces managers to the uses, misuses and potential of statistical and quantitative methods for business. "Overall this book is a comprehensive guide to quantitative methods & truly should require no previous mathematical knowledge...It is worth serious consideration for a wide range of management courses." (Seddon in *Natfhe Journal*)
isbn 0 946139 01 6   £8.90   484pp   Paperback

PEG Series — multi-media materials for business & management

PC compatible computer simulations on disk, multiple choice interactive questions & answers, case studies and tutor's manuals. Series Editor: Humphrey Shaw
Consultant programmers: Jon Carter, Brian Dakin, Wayne Griffiths

Computer simulations: Football Manager, Property Manager, Restaurant Manager
£69.99+VAT (Educ. version)
Diagnostic multiple choice questions/answers on interactive disk: Accountancy, Business Law, Hotel & Catering operations, Macro economics, Micro economics, Numeracy.
£29.99+VAT disk+manual £19.99 Hardcopy only

Case studies (books) and Tutor's Manuals
Books £5.95 Tutor's Manuals £49.00 (free with 15+ books bought direct)

Financial management
Around 50 case studies (with worked answers) on small and medium-sized businesses
isbn 1 85450 013 9 Easter, 1991. Tutor's Manual isbn 1 85450 023 6
Decision making
40 case studies in financial & quantitative management isbn 0 946139 42 3
Tutor's Manual isbn 0 946139 47 4
Entrepreneurial decision making
50 case studies on small & medium-sized businesses with crucial decisions to make.
isbn 0 946139 69 5. Tutor's Manual isbn 0 946139 74 1

CASE STUDIES IN BUSINESS & MANAGEMENT

European Business Policy: a 1992 casebook
Terry Garrison
7 highly topical and interesting pan-European case studies: Europe PLC, European Space Agency, Irish Distillers, Perestroika, Plessey PLC, The Channel Tunnel, The Berlin Wall — and a Policy Analysis Framework. isbn 1 85450 020 1 £9.95 October, 1990
Tutor's Manual of chronologies, notes and model answers isbn 1 85450 025 2 £49.00

Case studies in management: private sector, introductory level,
Second edition, editor - Sheila Ritchie
Enlarged and updated with 9 new mini-cases and 8 short to medium length studies of companies with typical contemporary problems. isbn 0 946139 02 4 £7.95
Tutor's Pack of model answers, computer programs, overhead transparencies and other materials to support the book of cases. isbn 0 946139 02 4 £49.00

Mrs Thatcher's casebook
Terry Garrison
10 topical and well-researched case studies of the Conservative Government's handling of major crises - The Falklands Crisis to De Lorean. isbn 0 946139 86 5 £12.95
Tutor's pack of notes, chronologies and other materials to support and supplement the book. isbn 0 946139 46 6 £49.00

Case studies in business law
Jeffrey Young
20 varied and topical, short case studies designed to appeal to students studying law on the first stage of a variety of business and professional courses. The book has been written for tutors of business and management who do not have a legal background. The cases may be adapted for differing levels of treatment and cover the law of Contract, Sale of Goods/ Services, Manufacturer's Liability, Employment Law, Company Law & Negligence.
isbn 0 946139 98 9 £6.95
Tutor's Manual with full analysis of each case, model answers and reference to appropriate authorities (i.e. leading cases & statutes) 0 946139 93 8 £49.00

Practical Exercises for Groups Series
Humphrey Shaw   Jon Carter   Brian Dakin   Wayne Griffiths
Multi-media series of PC compatible computer simulations for group work, case studies and tutor's manuals designed to improve managers' and trainee managers' analytical and problem solving, decision making and presentational skills. For BTEC HNC/D, BA Business Studies and other post-experience courses.
Books £5.95   Tutor's Manuals £49.00

Decision making: cases in financial & quantitative management — isbn 0 946139 42 3
Entrepreneurial decision making: case studies — isbn 0 946139 69 5
Financial management: case studies — isbn 1 85450 013 9